KT-142-129

Robert Del Grande ❦ Marcel Desaulniers ❦ Susan

Feniger & Mary Sue Milliken ❦ Ken Frank ❦ Kevin

Graham ❦ Jean Joho ❦ Emeril Lagasse ❦ Emily

Luchetti ❦ Nick Malgieri ❦ Bruce Marder ❦

Michael McCarty ❦ Alfred Portale ❦ Seppi Renggli

❦ Anne Rosenzweig ❦ Jimmy Schmidt ❦ John

Sedlar ❦ Piero Selvaggio ❦ Jackie Shen ❦ Nancy

Silverton ❦ Joachim Splichal ❦ Jacques Torres ❦

Barbara Tropp ❦ Charlie Trotter ❦ Jonathan Waxman

❦ Jasper White ❦ Barry Wine ❦ Alan Wong ❦

GREAT DESSERTS FROM THE GREAT CHEFS

Robert Del Grande ❧ Marcel Desaulniers ❧ Susan

Feniger & Mary Sue Milliken ❧ Ken Frank ❧ Kevin

Graham ❧ Jean Joho ❧ Emeril Lagasse ❧ Emily

Luchetti ❧ Nick Malgieri ❧ Bruce Marder ❧

GREAT DESSERTS FROM THE GREAT CHEFS

Michael ❧ Alfred Portale ❧ Seppi Renggli

Anne Rosenzweig ❧ Jimmy Schmidt ❧ John

Sedlar ❧ Piero Selvaggio ❧ Jackie Shens ❧ Nancy

Silverton ❧ Joachim Splichal ❧ Jacques Torres ❧

BABA S. KHALSA & ANDREA OPALENIK

Barbara Tropp ❧ Charlie Trotter ❧ Jonathan Waxman

CHRONICLE BOOKS
SAN FRANCISCO

❧ Jasper White ❧ Barry Wine ❧ Alan Wong ❧

Copyright © 1994 by Baba S. Khalsa.

All rights reserved. No part of this book may be reproduced without written permission from
the Publisher.

Printed in the United States of America.

Book and cover design by Rebecca Chamlee.
Illustrations by Roxana Villa.

Library of Congress Cataloging-in-Publication Data:

Khalsa, Baba S.
      Great desserts from the great chefs/by Baba S. Khalsa and Andrea Opalenik
          p.   cm.
      Includes index.
      ISBN 0-8118-0281-7
      1. Desserts.   2. Cooks.   I. Opalenik, Andrea.   II. Title.
TX773.K47 1994   93-43466
641.8'6—dc20   CIP

Distributed in Canada by Raincoast Books,
112 East 3rd Avenue, Vancouver, B.C. V5T 1C8

10 9 8 7 6 5 4 3 2 1

Chronicle Books
275 Fifth St.
San Francisco, CA 94103

DEDICATION

To our children, Nadine and Cory, the sweetest things in our lives.

TABLE OF CONTENTS

Recipes

BASICS 1

FRUIT DESSERTS 9

Apple Dumplings with Cinnamon-Rum Sauce / *Tom Douglas* 10

Bananas Foster / *Seppi Renggli* 12

Big Mike's Special Gratins / *Michael McCarty* 13

Butterscotch Apples in Puff Pastry, A La Mode / *John Downey* 15

Caramelized Apples and Mascarpone in Filo with Red Wine-
Black Pepper Sorbet / *Charlie Trotter* 17

Chocolate Banana Napoleons / *Jackie Shen* 20

Chocolate-Banana Soup / *Jacques Torres* 22

Crêpes with Sautéed Apples / *Jean Joho* 24

Pear Gratin / *Michael McCarty* 26

Rhubarb and Strawberry Gratin / *Joachim Splichal* 27

Strawberry Napoleons with Strawberry Sorbet / *Joachim Splichal* 28

Summer Berry Fool / *Bruce Naftaly* 30

Tropical Ratatouille Fruit Gyoza with Passion Fruit Cream and
Macadamia Praline / *Roy Yamaguchi* 31

Warm Huckleberry Compote / *Nancy Silverton* 33

Alfred Portale's Warm Pear and Fig Strudel with Pistachios and
Port Sauce / *Alfred Portale* 34

White Chocolate Raspberry Mille-Feuilles / *John Downey* 36

Winter-Fruit Dumplings / *Emily Luchetti* 38

Chilled Apple Soup with Apple Granita / *Gray Kunz* 39

Figs, Bananas, and Blueberries in Citrus Broth / *Hubert Keller* 41

Fresh Berries in Champagne and Pastis / *Kevin Graham* 42

Strawberry-Champagne Soup / *Kevin Graham* 43

Warm Peaches and Mangos with a Tamarind Glaze / *Barry Wine* 44

PIES AND CRISPS 45

Banana Caramel Cream Pie / *Jonathan Waxman (created with Toni Chiappetta)* 46

Banana Cream Pie with Banana Crust and Caramel Drizzles / *Emeril Lagasse* 48

Black Bottom Pie with Rye Whiskey Sauce / *Stephan Pyles* 50

Brêton Aux Pommes / *Nick Malgieri* 52

Lemon Crust / *Vincent Guerithault* 54

Lime-Coconut Pie / *Susan Feniger and Mary Sue Milliken* 55

Pumpkin-Pecan Pie with Nutmeg and Cinnamon / *Jimmy Schmidt* 56

Sweet Potato–Pecan Pie / *Jonathan Waxman (created with Toni Chiappetta)* 58

Berry-Pecan Buckle with Cinnamon Ice Cream / *Stephan Pyles* 60

Blueberry-Apple Crumble / *Jean Joho* 61

Rhubarb and Tapioca Crisp / *Barry Wine* 62

TARTS 65

Raspberry Crème Brûlée Tart / *Kevin Taylor* 66

Banana–Macadamia Nut Filo Tart / *Mark Militello* 68

Alfred Portale's Black Plum Tarts with Almond Cream / *Alfred Portale* 70

Blueberry Tart / *Kim Peoples* 72

Butter Pastries with Sweet Squash Filling / *Steven Howard* 73

Cranberry Streusel Tart / *Jasper White* 75

Cranberry-Walnut Tart / *Nick Malgieri* 78

SORBETS, ICE CREAMS, AND FROZEN DESSERTS 113

Sorbets 114

Ice Creams 126

Frozen Desserts 145

CUSTARDS, PUDDINGS, AND SOUFFLÉS 157

CANDIES 223

CAKES 233

PROFILES 297

FOREWORD

W HEN I WAS TWENTY-ONE YEARS OLD, I learned to make
my first professional dessert, Perla Meyers's Strawberries Imperiale. I
was working, without pay, at a small restaurant in Larkspur, California, called
464 Magnolia, which specialized in new Continental cuisine. Strawberries
Imperiale was basically a pale custard, layered with pureed and sliced fresh strawberries, and served in a fat goblet. I thought I was preparing something fancy
(it had a French name, didn't it?). And in some ways, I was right. The vanilla
pudding that I'd grown up on came from a box mix, gussied up with mushy
frozen fruit, while Strawberries Imperiale used fresh vanilla beans, Grand
Marnier, and the most perfect fresh berries we could buy that day. The lesson
was that desserts don't have to look elaborate or be complicated to make; they
just have to taste good. And that fresh, top-quality ingredients can transform a
dish from the ordinary into the memorable.

In other words, don't be intimidated by the fact that this book is a collection of recipes from professional chefs. The beauty in *Great Desserts from the Great
Chefs* is that there's a wide range of recipes from which to choose. Though these
desserts require varying levels of technique, preparation times, and different
types of kitchen equipment; you'll be proud to serve any of them.

Jimmy Schmidt's summer peach shortcake, Jasper White's cranberry-black
walnut pound cake, and Michael McCarty's big Mike's special gratin are so easy
to prepare that even the cooking-impaired can tackle them. If there seems to be
a dizzying amount of components in Ken Frank's La Toque's praline cheesecake, think of it as a sophisticated take on the classic cheesecake and reassure
yourself that each step is relatively easy.

Cooking is, after all, a matter of perspective. When I was taught this by
Bobby Miller (one of the first chefs I worked under), it was a clarifying moment
in my career. What he always maintained was that if someone knew how to
make a fantastic meat loaf, they could graduate quickly to a well-made pâté.
Bobby knew that mastering these two dishes, one simple, the other seemingly

difficult, involved the exact same skills: being able to judge the moistness, texture, and taste of the mixture. As Bobby Miller was mine, this book can be your mentor in helping you graduate from making the desserts you feel comfortable with to those that, in some cases, are more complicated. It's all a matter of perspective.

These chefs' desserts aren't just a reflection of their vast exposure to ingredients and flavor combinations. The recipes also introduce contrasts in texture, temperature, and tastes, such as the crunch in Hubert Keller's frozen nougat with candied fruits and pureed mint, or the creamy texture of Kevin Graham's chocolate truffles. And the hot and cold in Jimmy Schmidt's sweet cherry sundae, and the sweet and spicy in Vincent Guerithault's honey and jalapeño orange chutney tarts.

Among the chefs that Baba and Andrea have wisely chosen to include are those that aren't traditionally thought of as dessert chefs. So their desserts often are an extension of the type of savory food they make. Charlie Trotter's crispy quinoa pudding and Stephan Pyles's gingered couscous crème brûlée are desserts based on grains that are normally used in main courses or side dishes.

A chef may also create desserts that don't have recognizable, familiar names such as peach melba or hazelnut dacquoises. That's because one of the distinctions of contemporary desserts is that their titles may include descriptions of their sometimes nontraditional dessert ingredients. Tamarind paste, for example, is most commonly used in Asian and African cooking, as an ingredient in a sweet-sour marinade that enhances meat and fish dishes. But in Barry Wine's introduction to his warm peaches and mangos in a tamarind glaze, you'll find that he's using the exotic pods to cut the sweetness of the ripe fruit.

It's this kind of experimentation with ingredients that makes this book unique. For the first time, the home cook gets a chance to prepare desserts full of ingenuity and unusual flavors, developed by some of America's most accomplished chefs. *Great Desserts from the Great Chefs* is the first book of its kind to give insights (from both the recipes and the profiles) into how the best professional chefs create memorable desserts and how you can re-create them at home.

As a professional chef and mother of three, I know what is possible in the home kitchen. You can make every one of the well-explained recipes in this book, which I know will find a permanent place on the cookbook shelf of anyone who enjoys preparing and serving wonderful desserts at home.

—Nancy Silverton

ACKNOWLEDGMENTS

ℰℬ

WE GRATEFULLY ACKNOWLEDGE THE HELP of Keith Mathewson and Mark Stark, chef of the Bellevue Athletic Club, who tested the majority of the recipes for this book. And we thank the club for making its facilities available. We also appreciate the generosity of Karen Malody of Larry's Markets, who provided the ingredients for most of the recipes. Also at Larry's, we wish to thank Tom Micklin, Peggy Castagnola, and Nora Connor for helping us test recipes.

Many of our friends and people who just heard about the book also came forward to help with recipe-testing: Betty Paul, Beverly Wylie, Kartar Khalsa, and our mothers Rosalind Lasser and Johanna Opalenik, who engendered our love of desserts many years ago.

Susan Grode, the best and sweetest lawyer in the Milky Way, made this work possible. And Nion McEvoy and Charlotte Stone of Chronicle Books brought it to fruition.

Carolyn Miller's sharp eye and sharper blue pencil guided us in editing the book to make it more readable and usable. Janet Jefferson typed the manuscript ably and with nary a mistake.

As husband and wife, Andrea and I found this a wonderful project to share, and thoroughly enjoyed sifting recipes and flour, breaking eggs, licking spoons, and slaving together over both hot stove and word processor.

Andrea took hundreds of recipes submitted by professional chefs, written for use in a professional kitchen, and either tested them herself or had them tested. She then edited and rewrote them for the home kitchen. Without her tremendous contribution, this work would have been only a short book of chef's profiles.

INTRODUCTION

I CAN STILL SMELL MY MOTHER'S APPLE DUMPLINGS, still feel the indentations in the beater blades under my tongue as I licked the made-from-scratch frosting, still taste her bright, sharp lemon-meringue pie, her nutty, dense banana bread, and her simple boiled rhubarb. More than anything else from my childhood, I remember the love, care, and skill my mother put into her desserts. As with all her cooking, she made everything from scratch. In the fifties and sixties, there was time. Time to shop, time to sift, time to create something special, something memorable, although it seemed perfectly ordinary then.

I'm sorry that my children, brought up in the home of two working parents, won't have my memories of coming home from school to a kitchen that held some sweet surprise seemingly every day. One day it might have been fresh oatmeal-raisin or Toll House cookies. Or would it be brownies? What smell would greet me? Cinnamon? Butter? Chocolate? One sad by-product of our busy world is the dwindling amount of time available to make treats for our children.

But not all that has transpired in the last thirty-five years has been bad. Today, cooking is recognized as a respected line of work. There are many dedicated men and women in the cooking profession who have been well taught and who have now dedicated themselves to elevating cooking in America to the level of a profession, if not an art form.

Who benefits from this dedication? All of us, every time we eat in a restaurant. And not just a fine restaurant. The "trickle-down" theory may not have worked in our economy, but as surely as ice cream trickles down a cone, advances in cooking technique and presentation and improvements in the materials chefs cook with find their way into what we eat, even in fast-food outlets.

We may have less time for homemade pies, cakes, and cookies in the twenty-first century, but the level of professional dessert and pastry-making in this country gets better every year. When we order dessert in a fine restaurant, we taste the creation of a person who trained for years at a culinary academy and/or a series of kitchens and had to compete with other well-trained chefs for the job. And if the public doesn't enjoy the chef's desserts, his job on the line may be on the line. There are many waiting in the wings to take his job.

In writing *Great Desserts from the Great Chefs*, Andrea and I traveled around the country tasting the desserts of over two hundred chefs before narrowing our choices down to those represented here. There were other recipes we wanted to include, but scheduling problems prevented a few worthy chefs from having the time to participate. The recipes included here exemplify the increased consciousness about the importance of great desserts, and not just something sweet, in our lives. They include desserts our mothers never dreamed of, as well as those they could do in their sleep.

We wrote this book to help you make wonderful sweet-smelling desserts at home for special treats, entertaining, family dinners, and holidays. *Great Desserts* will demystify the process of making a fine finish to a meal and take you step-by-step through the greatest dessert recipes in America.

I hope you'll enjoy reading about the chefs: where they trained, how they feel about their art. But the heart and soul of this book is in the dessert recipes. Some of the recipes may be time-consuming, but they are always worth the investment. If you're in a rush, the ones with the smallest number of ingredients and shortest method usually take the least amount of time, of course. And if you're worried about how you might be able to render a recipe created by a professional chef with years of experience, don't be intimidated. They all put their chef's jackets on one arm at a time.

But most important, we hope these recipes, clearly explained and using ingredients you can generally find in supermarkets anywhere in the country, will make your kitchen fragrant with sweet smells, and bring smiles to the faces of those you love.

—Baba S. Khalsa

Robert Del Grande ❦ Marcel Desaulniers ❦ Susan

Feniger & Mary Sue Milliken ❦ Ken Frank ❦ Kevin

Graham ❦ Jean Joho ❦ Emeril Lagasse ❦ Emily

Luchetti ❦ Nick Malgieri ❦ Bruce Marder ❦

Michael McCarty ❦ Alfred Portale ❦ Seppi Renggli

❦ Anne Rosenzweig ❦ Jimmy Schmidt ❦ John

Sedlar ❦ Piero Selvaggio ❦ Jackie Shen ❦ Nancy

Silverton ❦ Joachim Splichal ❦ Jacques Torres ❦

Barbara Tropp ❦ Charlie Trotter ❦ Jonathan Waxman

❦ Jasper White ❦ Barry Wine ❦ Alan Wong ❦

Robert Del Grande ❦ Marcel Desaulniers ❦ Susan

Feniger & Mary Sue Milliken ❦ Ken Frank ❦ Kevin

Graham ❦ Jean Joho BASICS Emeril Lagasse ❦ Emily

Luchetti ❦ Nick Bruce Marder ❦

Michael McCarty le ❦ Seppi Renggli

❦ Anne Rosenzweig ❦ Jimmy Schmidt ❦ John

Sedlar ❦ Piero Selvaggio ❦ Jackie Shen ❦ Nancy

Silverton ❦ Joachim Splichal ❦ Jacques Torres ❦

Barbara Tropp ❦ Charlie Trotter ❦ Jonathan Waxman

❦ Jasper White ❦ Barry Wine ❦ Alan Wong ❦

CRÈME ANGLAISE

Keith Mathewson

Makes 1 to 1½ cups

1 cup heavy (whipping) cream

½ vanilla bean, cut in half lengthwise

3 egg yolks

¼ cup sugar

IN A HEAVY, MEDIUM SAUCEPAN, bring the cream and vanilla bean to a boil, stirring constantly. Meanwhile, in the bowl of an electric mixer or with a whisk beat the egg yolks and sugar until pale in color. Pour one fourth of the hot cream into the yolk mixture, stirring constantly. Pour the yolk mixture back into the remaining cream and cook over medium heat, stirring constantly, until the mixture thickens enough to coat a spoon, about 1 minute. Strain into a bowl and place this bowl in a bowl of ice. Stir until cool. Cover and store for up to 1 week in the refrigerator.

QUICK PUFF PASTRY

Makes 1½ pounds of puff pastry

1½ cups (3 sticks) unsalted butter at room temperature,
    cut into 1-inch slices

1 cup unbleached all-purpose flour

6 tablespoons pastry flour

½ tablespoon salt

½ cup plus 2 tablespoons ice water

*I*N A FOOD PROCESSOR, process the butter, flours, and salt. Blend on low speed until the butter starts to break up; quickly add the water and stop mixing while the mixture is still crumbly in texture or cut the butter into the dry ingredients with a pastry blender or 2 knives. Stir in the water with a fork and form the dough into a ball.

Turn the pastry out onto a lightly floured board or marble slab. Pat the dough together into a rectangular shape. Fold into thirds, like a letter; turn it and roll it out again. Repeat these steps twice. Wrap the dough tightly in plastic wrap and refrigerate for at least 2 hours before using.

Puff pastry will keep frozen for a month or two. Cut off whatever size piece you need, rewrap, and continue to store in the freezer.

TO TOAST AND SKIN NUTS

Preheat the oven to 350°F. Spread the nuts in a single layer on a baking sheet and toast them, stirring once or twice, until their skins darken and crack, about 7 to 10 minutes. Let cool to room temperature, then rub them between a towel or your hands to remove the skins.

TO TOAST NUTS

Preheat the oven to 350°F. Spread the nuts in a single layer on a baking sheet and toast them, stirring once or twice, for 7 to 10 minutes, or until light golden in color. Do not overcook.

TO TOAST COCONUT

Preheat the oven to 325°F. Spread the coconut on a baking sheet in a thin layer and bake, stirring once or twice, for about 10 minutes or until light golden in color.

TO CLARIFY BUTTER

In a saucepan, melt butter over low heat. With a spoon, skim the froth from the top, then carefully pour off the clear liquid into a bowl, stopping before any of the milky solids on the bottom leave the pan. Use the solids in soups or sauces.

CHOCOLATE GANACHE

Makes 1 cup

4 tablespoons heavy (whipping) cream

4 ounces semisweet chocolate, chopped

2 tablespoons unsalted butter

$\mathcal{I}$N A SMALL SAUCEPAN, bring the heavy cream to a boil and add the chocolate and butter. Remove from heat and stir with a whisk until the chocolate is completely melted.

BASIC PASTRY

1¾ cups unbleached all-purpose flour

½ teaspoon salt

½ cup (1 stick) plus 1 tablespoon cold unsalted butter, cut into bits

3 tablespoons cold vegetable shortening cut into bits

3 to 5 tablespoons ice water

*I*N A LARGE BOWL, blend the flour and salt. Cut in the butter and shortening with 2 knives or a pastry cutter until the mixture resembles fine meal. Sprinkle the mixture with 3 tablespoons of the water and toss the mixture to incorporate, adding additional water as necessary to just hold the ingredients together. Form the dough into a ball, dust with flour, wrap in plastic wrap, and chill for 1 hour.

PASTRY CREAM

Steven Howard

Makes 1 to 1¼ cups

¾ cup half-and-half	¼ cup sugar
½ vanilla bean, cut in half lengthwise	1 tablespoon unbleached all-purpose flour
1 egg	½ tablespoon cornstarch
1 egg yolk	½ tablespoon unsalted butter

IN A HEAVY, MEDIUM SAUCEPAN, bring the half-and-half and vanilla bean to a boil, stirring constantly. Meanwhile, in the bowl of an electric mixer or with a whisk, beat the egg and egg yolk, sugar, flour, and cornstarch until lemon-colored and smooth. Pour one fourth of the hot cream into the egg mixture, stirring constantly. Pour the egg mixture back into the remaining cream and cook over medium heat, stirring constantly, until the mixture boils and becomes smooth and thick enough to coat a spoon, about 1 minute. Whisk in the butter. Cover the surface with plastic wrap. Let cool completely before use.

CRÈME FRAÎCHE

Makes 1 cup

1 cup heavy cream
1 teaspoon buttermilk

IN A NONALUMINUM SAUCEPAN, heat the cream to 85° to 95°F. Stir in the buttermilk. Pour the mixture into a clean dry glass container. Cover and let stand in a warm place, between 70° and 85°F for about 24 hours or until thickened. Keeps in the refrigerator for about 10 days.

Robert Del Grande ❧ Marcel Desaulniers ❧ Susan

Feniger & Mary Sue Milliken ❧ Ken Frank ❧ Kevin

FRUIT DESSERTS

Graham ❧ Jean Joho ❧ Emeril Lagasse ❧ Emily

Luchetti ❧ Nick ❧ Bruce Marder ❧

Michael McCarty ❧ le ❧ Seppi Renggli

❧ Anne Rosenzweig ❧ Jimmy Schmidt ❧ John

Sedlar ❧ Piero Selvaggio ❧ Jackie Shen ❧ Nancy

Silverton ❧ Joachim Splichal ❧ Jacques Torres ❧

Barbara Tropp ❧ Charlie Trotter ❧ Jonathan Waxman

❧ Jasper White ❧ Barry Wine ❧ Alan Wong ❧

APPLE DUMPLINGS WITH CINNAMON-RUM SAUCE

Tom Douglas

Makes 8 dumplings

My mother's apple dumplings are my fondest dessert memory from childhood. These are as good as hers.

DATE BUTTER

10 Medjool dates, pitted and finely chopped*

½ cup (1 stick) unsalted butter at room temperature

¼ cup packed brown sugar

1 teaspoon ground cinnamon

DUMPLINGS

4 small apples (Granny Smith or Gala), peeled, halved, and cored

Juice of ½ lemon

Basic Pastry *(recipe on page 6)*

Date Butter *(left)*

1 egg yolk

1 tablespoon heavy (whipping) cream

½ cup sugar

1 tablespoon ground cinnamon

Cinnamon-Rum Sauce *(recipe follows)*

Vanilla ice cream for garnish

To MAKE THE DATE BUTTER: In the bowl of an electric mixer, beat all of the ingredients together until blended; set aside at room temperature.

TO MAKE THE DUMPLINGS: Preheat the oven to 400°F. Place the apple halves in a bowl of cold water with the lemon juice. Divide the pie crust dough in half. On a lightly floured surface, roll out one dough half to a little more than ⅛ thick. Trim the dough with a knife to make a 12-inch square. Save the dough trimmings. Cut the large square into quarters. Slash the corners of each small square like a pinwheel from each corner tip halfway to the center of the square. Repeat with the second dough half.

Drain the apples and pat dry with a towel. Fill the core of each apple half with 1 tablespoon of date butter and place the apple, core-side down, on the center of a dough square. Place 1 tablespoon of date butter on top of each apple half. Fold the corners of the dough up over each apple in an alternating pinwheel fashion. Seal the dough with a pastry brush dipped in water.

Place the dumplings on a baking sheet. Reroll the trimmings and cut out 8 decorative leaf shapes. Place 1 leaf on top of each dumpling. In a small bowl, mix the egg yolk with the cream; brush on each dumpling. In a small bowl mix the sugar with the cinnamon; sprinkle on each dumpling.

Bake in the preheated oven for 20 to 25 minutes, or until the pastry is golden and the apple is tender when pierced with a knife. Serve warm with warm cinnamon-rum sauce and a scoop of vanilla ice cream.

Cinnamon Rum Sauce

1 cup packed brown sugar	2 cinnamon sticks
1 tablespoon cornstarch	1 tablespoon unsalted butter
Pinch of salt	1 tablespoon rum
1 cup boiling water	

In a medium saucepan over high heat, bring the brown sugar, cornstarch, salt, water, and cinnamon sticks to a boil. Lower heat and simmer for 5 minutes. Remove from heat and stir in the butter and rum. Remove the cinnamon sticks. Serve warm.

Mejdool dates are a large meaty date found in health food stores and Middle Eastern markets.

BANANAS FOSTER

Seppi Renggli

Serves 2 to 4

A dessert that originated in New Orleans is flavored here with three citrus zests and is best served with vanilla ice cream.

SAUCE	BANANAS
⅓ cup dark rum	3 tablespoons butter
2 tablespoons unsalted butter	2 ripe bananas
1 cup packed dark brown sugar	3 tablespoons packed brown sugar
1 cinnamon stick	2 tablespoons orange juice
1 teaspoon grated orange zest	1 teaspoon grated orange zest
2 teaspoons grated lemon zest	¼ cup Myers's dark rum
1 teaspoon grated lime zest	
Juice of 1 orange	Vanilla Bean Ice Cream
Juice of 1 lemon	*(recipe on page 144)*
Juice of 1 lime	Whipped cream for garnish

TO MAKE THE SAUCE: In a saucepan, bring all of the ingredients to a boil. Simmer for 20 minutes; keep warm.

TO MAKE THE BANANAS: In a medium sauté pan or skillet, heat the butter until it begins to brown and to smell nutty. Place the whole bananas in the butter and cook over low heat until lightly browned, about 4 to 5 minutes. Turn and add the brown sugar, juice, zest, and rum. Heat the liquid slightly and ignite it with a match. Shake the pan until the flames subside. Spoon the sauce over the bananas and let cook until browned on the second side, about 5 minutes. Serve with the sauce and garnish with vanilla ice cream and whipped cream.

BIG MIKE'S SPECIAL GRATINS

Michael McCarty

Makes 6 gratins

In these dessert gratins, peaches and berries are tossed with framboise liqueur, then topped with crème anglaise, cream, Grand Marnier, and praline powder before being browned under the broiler.

2 firm, ripe Freestone peaches

1½ cups each fresh raspberries, blackberries, and blueberries

¾ cup framboise liqueur

¾ cup sugar

3 cups crème anglaise *(recipe on page 2)*

3 cups heavy (whipping) cream, lightly whipped just until thickened

¾ cup Grand Marnier

¾ cup Praline Powder *(recipe follows)*

PREHEAT THE BROILER TO VERY HOT. Bring a medium saucepan of water to a boil. Add the peaches and cook for about 30 seconds, then drain well and rinse under cold running water. With a small, sharp knife, nick the skins of the peaches and carefully peel off the skins. Halve and pit the peaches, then cut them into thin slices. Arrange a fan of slices — about one fourth of a peach — in the center of each of 6 individual gratin dishes, reserving the remaining half peach for another recipe, if you like.

In a large bowl, toss the berries with the framboise and ¼ cup of the sugar. Arrange about ¾ cup of the berries around the peach slices in each gratin dish. In a large bowl, stir together the crème anglaise and cream. With a whisk, briefly blend in the Grand Marnier. Pour this mixture over the fruit.

Sprinkle each serving with the praline powder and the remaining ½ cup sugar. Place the gratin dishes under the broiler until the surface of the cream is browned and bubbly, 20 to 30 seconds. Place each gratin dish on a serving plate and serve immediately.

Praline Powder

2 tablespoons water

½ cup sugar

¾ cup (4 ounces) hazelnuts,
   toasted and skinned *(see page 4)*

In a medium saucepan, bring the water and sugar to a boil, then continue boiling until mixture reaches a light caramel color and becomes thick and opaque, about 8 to 10 minutes. Immediately pour in the hazelnuts and take the pan from the heat. Stir constantly with a wooden spoon until the sugar crystallizes, about 1 minute. Return the pan to medium-high heat, stirring until the sugar becomes liquid again and then turns a dark caramel color, 5 to 10 minutes. Immediately pour the mixture out on a baking sheet and let cool until hardened. Break the praline into pieces and process in a food processor or blender until pulverized. Store in an airtight container. Makes about 1 cup.

BUTTERSCOTCH APPLES IN
PUFF PASTRY, À LA MODE

John Downey

Makes 8 pastries

We developed this recipe for a winemaker dinner held at Byron Vineyards. The dessert was paired with a nectarlike late-harvest Johannesburg Riesling from Firestone Vineyards.

The vanilla bean ice cream can be made ahead. It will keep for a month or more, especially if there is a lock on the freezer door. The rest of the dessert needs to be made the same day it is served, and it does require last-minute attention.

—John Downey

1 pound Quick Puff Pastry
(recipe on page 3)
1 egg yolk, lightly beaten
1 cup sugar
½ cup water
3 cups (6 sticks) unsalted butter, cut into small chunks

5 large Granny Smith apples, peeled, halved, and cores removed

1 quart Vanilla Bean Ice Cream
(recipe on page 144)
Fresh apple leaves or mint leaves for garnish

PREHEAT THE OVEN TO 450°F. Line a baking sheet with baking parchment or aluminum foil. On a lightly floured board, roll out the puff pastry to a ¼-inch thickness. Cover lightly with plastic wrap and chill for 2 hours. Cut the pastry into eight 2-by-4-inch rectangles. Place the rectangles on the prepared baking sheet. Brush the tops with the egg yolk, taking great care not to let the egg run over the sides. If the egg yolk drips, it will glue the pastry layers together and keep them from rising evenly. Bake in the preheated oven for 15 minutes. Reduce heat to 300°F and bake 15 minutes longer, or until nicely browned. Turn the oven off, but leave the pastries in the oven to dry out for 1 hour.

In a 3-quart saucepan, place the sugar and water. Cook over medium heat until the syrup starts to turn brown. Quickly and carefully add the chunks of butter and stir into the caramel. Put the apples in the caramel and cook for about 20 minutes, or until tender when tested with the point of a knife. Remove the cooked apples with a slotted spoon, and keep both the apples and sauce warm.

Just before serving, split each pastry rectangle in half and set the tops aside. Place the bottoms on individual dessert plates. Place a warm apple half on one side of the pastry layer and a scoop of vanilla bean ice cream beside it. Stir the warm sauce well, and coat both the apple and the ice cream generously with it. Lay the pastry lids on top, garnish with apple or mint leaves, and serve immediately.

CARAMELIZED APPLES AND MASCARPONE IN FILO

with Red Wine - Black Pepper Sorbet

Charlie Trotter

Makes 6 pastries

This complex dessert is time-consuming, but the happy memories of those who have eaten it will last even longer. A caramelized apple filled with Mascarpone mousse is placed on a filo dough square topped with a square of genoise cake and served with sorbet and caramel sauce.

SORBET

1 bottle Merlot or Pinot Noir wine

½ cup sugar

Freshly ground black pepper to taste

1 egg white

DRIED APPLES

1 Macintosh apple, peeled and cored

2 tablespoons sifted powdered sugar for dusting

MASCARPONE MOUSSE

1 egg white

1 tablespoon sugar

½ cup (4 ounces) Mascarpone cheese at room temperature

GENOISE

5 eggs at room temperature

½ cup sugar

¾ cup, (4 ounces) hazelnuts, toasted and skinned *(see page 4)*

½ cup unbleached all-purpose flour

1 tablespoon unsalted butter, melted and cooled to room temperature

CARAMELIZED APPLES

1 cup sugar

3 tablespoons butter

3 Granny Smith apples, peeled, halved, and cored

Three 14-by-18-inch sheets filo dough

½ cup powdered sugar, sifted

*T*O MAKE THE SORBET: In a large nonaluminum saucepan, boil the wine over high heat for about 10 minutes, or until it has reduced to 2 cups. Whisk in the sugar and add pepper to taste; let cool. Whisk in the egg white. Freeze in an ice cream maker according to the manufacturer's instructions.

TO MAKE THE DRIED APPLES: Preheat the oven to 200°F. Butter a baking sheet. Cut the apple into $1/16$-inch crosswise slices and place them $1/8$ inch apart on the prepared pan. Place in the preheated oven for 45 minutes, checking frequently, until the slices are lightly browned and dried. Remove from the pan and place the apple slices on a dry baking sheet. Preheat the broiler. Sprinkle the apple slices with powdered sugar and caramelize the sugar under the broiler about 3 inches from the heat for 1 minute.

TO MAKE THE Mascarpone mousse: In the bowl of an electric mixer, whip the egg white and sugar until stiff peaks form. Fold in the Mascarpone cheese just until smooth.

TO MAKE THE GENOISE: Preheat the oven to 350°F. Grease and flour an 6-by-9-inch cake pan. In the bowl of an electric mixer, whip the eggs with the sugar until tripled in volume. In a blender or food processor, finely grind the nuts with the flour. Fold into the eggs, then fold in the butter. Spread into the prepared pan and bake in the preheated oven for about 20 minutes, or until golden. Let cool, then cut into six $2\frac{1}{2}$-inch squares.

TO MAKE THE CARAMELIZED APPLES: In a heavy 10-inch sauté pan or skillet over high heat, stir the sugar and 2 tablespoons of the butter until the sugar melts and begins to brown. Place the apples in the caramel, lower heat to medium, and cook the apples, turning occasionally, until they are saturated with the caramel but still somewhat firm, about 10 minutes. Remove from the caramel with a slotted spoon; let cool. Reserve the caramel.

Melt the remaining 1 tablespoon of butter. On a pastry board, brush a sheet of filo dough with the butter and sprinkle with one third the powdered sugar. Press another layer on top and repeat the process with the third layer.

To assemble, preheat the oven to 400°F. Cut the filo into six 6-by-7-inch rectangles. Place an apple half in the center of each and fill the cores with the mousse. Top with a square of cake. Fold the edges of the filo over the cake, wrapping it like a package.

Place the packets on a baking sheet and bake in the preheated oven for about 10 minutes. Warm the reserved caramel sauce and ladle onto 6 warm plates. Place a packet on each pool of sauce. Top with a dried apple slice, then a scoop of sorbet. Top with another dried apple slice sticking out of the sorbet. Serve at once.

CHOCOLATE BANANA NAPOLEONS

Jackie Shen

Makes 8 napoleons

An unusual version of the napoleon, this dessert incorporates the crunchiness of filo with the creaminess of milk chocolate mousse.
—Jackie Shen

MILK CHOCOLATE MOUSSE

8 ounces milk chocolate, chopped

4 eggs, separated

¼ cup very hot water

1 cup heavy (whipping) cream

¼ cup sugar

BANANAS FOSTER SAUCE

½ cup (1 stick) butter

½ cup packed brown sugar

½ cup honey

Juice of 1 lemon

½ teaspoon ground cinnamon

½ cup banana liqueur

FILO LAYER

½ cup sugar

1 teaspoon ground cinnamon

4 tablespoons butter

Three 14-by-18-inch sheets filo dough

4 bananas

1 cup (5 ounces) unsalted macadamia nuts, toasted and chopped *(see page 4)*

To MAKE THE MILK CHOCOLATE MOUSSE: In a double boiler over barely simmering water, melt the chocolate. In a medium bowl, mix the melted chocolate, egg yolks, and hot water briskly with a wire whip until smooth. Continue mixing until the mixture cools to room temperature, then set aside.

In the bowl of an electric mixer, whip the cream until stiff peaks form. Fold into the chocolate mixture. In the bowl of an electric mixer, beat the egg whites until soft peaks form. Add the sugar and continue beating until stiff peaks form. Fold into the chocolate mixture and chill.

TO MAKE THE BANANAS FOSTER SAUCE: In a small saucepan, bring the butter, brown sugar, honey, lemon juice, and cinnamon to a boil. Add the banana liqueur; set aside and keep warm.

TO MAKE THE FILO LAYER: Preheat the oven to 350°F. Line a baking sheet with baking parchment or aluminum foil. In a small bowl, mix the sugar and cinnamon. In a small saucepan, melt the butter. Lay out 1 sheet of filo dough. Brush lightly with the melted butter. Sprinkle lightly with the cinnamon-sugar mixture. Repeat twice. Top with 1 sheet of filo, but no butter or sugar. Press the layers together. With a very sharp knife, cut into 24 rectangles. Transfer to the prepared baking sheet. Top with another sheet of baking parchment or aluminum foil and bake in the preheated oven for about 5 minutes, or until the butter and sugar melt and caramelize and the filo browns lightly.

To assemble, use 3 filo rectangles per napoleon. Fit a pastry bag with a No. 9 star or tube tip and fill with the milk chocolate mousse. Pipe the mousse onto a filo rectangle. Repeat and top with a third rectangle (do not add mousse to the top).

Cut the bananas into ¼-inch slices and toss with the warm bananas Foster sauce. Pour over the napoleon and garnish with the chopped macadamia nuts. Serve immediately.

CHOCOLATE-BANANA SOUP

Jacques Torres

Serves 4

Rum-soaked raisins and thick-sliced sautéed bananas join rich chocolate in this warm dessert soup.

¼ cup raisins	**MERINGUE**
½ cup dark rum	6 egg whites at room temperature
4 bananas, cut into ½-inch-thick	¼ teaspoon cream of tartar
crosswise slices	Pinch of salt
¼ cup sugar	¾ cup powdered sugar, sifted
2 tablespoons unsalted butter	1 teaspoon vanilla extract
5½ ounces semisweet chocolate	
(preferably Valrhona brand), chopped	
2 cups plus 2 tablespoons milk	

IN A MEDIUM BOWL, place the raisins and rum; cover and soak overnight. Add the sliced bananas and sugar and toss. In a medium sauté pan or skillet, melt the butter and sauté the bananas until soft, about 5 minutes. Spoon the banana mixture into four 6-ounce custard cups. Place the chopped chocolate in a bowl. In a medium saucepan, heat the milk until just boiling and pour over the chocolate; whisk until smooth. Pour the chocolate over the bananas until each cup is nearly full; let cool.

TO MAKE THE MERINGUE: In the clean, dry bowl of an electric mixer at medium speed, beat the egg whites until foamy. Beat in the cream of tartar and salt, increasing the speed to high. When soft peaks form, add the powdered sugar and beat until stiff peaks form. Beat in the vanilla extract.

To serve, preheat the oven to 350°F. Pipe the meringue decoratively onto the soup. Place the cups in a large baking pan filled with hot water to halfway up the sides of the cups. Test the temperature with a toothpick, and when the soup is warm, bake in the preheated oven until the meringue is lightly browned, about 15 minutes.

CRÊPES
with Sautéed Apples
Jean Joho
Serves 12

Apples and raisins sautéed with kirsch and cinnamon fill crepes sprinkled with cinnamon sugar before briefly going under the broiler.

CRÊPES	APPLE FILLING
1½ cups milk	2 tablespoons butter
3 eggs	4 baking apples (such as Granny
1¼ cups unbleached all-purpose flour	Smiths), peeled, cored, and sliced
¼ teaspoon ground cinnamon	2 tablespoons packed brown sugar
4 tablespoons butter, melted	½ cup raisins
	1 teaspoon ground cinnamon
	2 tablespoons kirsch, preferably Alsatian
	4 teaspoons ground cinnamon mixed
	with ½ teaspoon sugar for sprinkling

To MAKE THE CRÊPES: In a medium bowl, whisk together the milk, eggs, flour, and cinnamon. Whisk in 3 tablespoons of the melted butter. Cover and let sit at room temperature for 30 minutes.

Lightly brush an 8-inch nonstick skillet with a little of the remaining melted butter, heat over medium-high heat, and pour ¼ cup of batter into the pan, tilting it to spread the batter over the entire bottom of the pan. Cook for 30 to 60 seconds, or until browned, then turn and cook the crepe on the other side for 10 to 15 seconds, or until browned; transfer to a plate. Repeat until all the batter has been used. Use right away, or cover and store the crepes for 1 day. To store, place each crepe on a wire rack to dry out for 5 minutes. Stack the crepes, wrap in aluminum foil, and place in a plastic bag in the refrigerator.

TO MAKE THE APPLE FILLING: Preheat the broiler. In a medium skillet, melt the butter and sauté the apples with the brown sugar for 5 minutes, or until tender. Add the raisins, cinnamon, and kirsch. Mix well and remove from heat. Spoon ⅓ cup apple mixture into each warm crepe and roll the crepe loosely. Place 1 crepe each on individual heatproof serving plates. Sprinkle with the cinnamon and sugar mixture. Place under the broiler 4 inches from the heat for 15 to 30 seconds, or until browned. Repeat to finish all the crepes and serve at once.

PEAR GRATIN
Michael McCarty
Serves 6

This warm dessert matches ripe sliced pears and a Crème Anglaise sauce made with pear liqueur.

3 firm, ripe Bartlett or other pears

3 cups crème anglaise

(recipe on page 2)

3 cups heavy (whipping) cream, lightly whipped just until thickened

¾ cup Poire Williams or other pear liqueur, or to taste

¾ cup sugar

1 cup (4 ounces) walnuts, chopped

PREHEAT THE BROILER TO VERY HOT. Peel, halve, and core each pear. Place each pear half cut side down; with a sharp knife, cut it lengthwise into thin slices, keeping the slices together to retain the shape of the pear half. With a spatula, carefully transfer each pear half to an individual gratin dish. In a large bowl, combine the crème anglaise and the lightly whipped cream. With a whisk, blend in the pear liqueur. Pour this mixture over the pears, coming about three fourths the way up the sides of each pear.

Sprinkle the cream mixture surrounding each pear with the sugar, then the walnuts; do not sprinkle these over the pears. Place the gratin dishes under the preheated broiler until the surface of the cream is browned and bubbly, about 20 to 30 seconds. Place each gratin dish on a serving plate and serve immediately.

RHUBARB AND STRAWBERRY GRATIN

Joachim Splichal

Serves 4

In the late summer, serve this colorful gratin enriched with whipped cream.

1¾ cups strawberries, stemmed and sliced

10 ounces rhubarb (about 3 stalks)

1 tablespoon butter

6 tablespoons sugar

2 large egg yolks

2 tablespoons dry white wine

½ cup heavy (whipping) cream, whipped

PREHEAT THE BROILER. Divide 1 cup of the strawberries equally among 4 shallow heatproof soup bowls; set aside. Puree the remaining strawberries in a blender or food processor; set aside. Peel and cut the rhubarb into 1-inch pieces. In a medium skillet, melt the butter and sauté the rhubarb with 4 tablespoons of the sugar for 10 minutes, or until tender. Let cool.

In a double boiler over boiling water, whip the egg yolks, remaining 2 tablespoons sugar, strawberry puree, and white wine for about 4 to 6 minutes, or until thick enough to coat a spoon. Add the whipped cream. Cover the strawberries and rhubarb with the cream and place under the broiler about 4 inches from the heat until golden brown and bubbly, about 20 to 30 seconds.

STRAWBERRY NAPOLEONS
with Strawberry Sorbet

Joachim Splichal

Makes 6 napoleons

Napoleons made with circles of filo, topped with a fluffy pastry cream and fresh strawberries.

PASTRIES	PASTRY CREAM
10 14-by-18-inch sheets filo dough	4 egg yolks
4 tablespoons butter, melted	1 cup sugar
½ cup sugar	2 tablespoons cornstarch
	2 cups milk
	½ vanilla bean, split in half lengthwise
	¼ cup plus 1 tablespoon heavy (whipping) cream, whipped
	2 cups strawberries, stemmed and cut into small dice
	Strawberry Sorbet *(recipe on page 123)*

To make the pastries: Preheat the oven to 300°F. Brush each sheet of filo with melted butter and sprinkle with sugar, making 2 stacks of 5 sheets each. Cut nine 4-inch circles from each stack to make 18 circles. Bake in the preheated oven for 10 minutes, or until lightly golden; let cool. Preheat the broiler and place the circles under the broiler for 30 to 60 seconds, or until golden brown.

To make the pastry cream: In the bowl of an electric mixer, mix the egg yolks, ½ cup of the sugar, and cornstarch until smooth. In a large saucepan, bring to a boil the milk, the remaining ½ cup sugar, and vanilla bean. Whisk into the yolk mixture and return to the saucepan. Cook over medium heat, stirring constantly, for 5 minutes, or until the mixture coats a spoon. Place the saucepan over a bowl of ice and whip until cold; then fold in the whipped cream.

To assemble, put 2 tablespoons pastry cream on each of 6 filo circles and top with 2 tablespoons diced strawberries. Repeat twice. Serve with strawberry sorbet.

SUMMER BERRY FOOL

Bruce Naftaly

Serves 6 to 8

A simple but elegant dessert made with fresh berries and cream and scented with lavender.

2 cups (8 ounces) fresh blackberries

½ cup (4 ounces) fresh black currants

1 cup (4 ounces) fresh raspberries

1 tablespoon fresh lavender or minced fresh mint leaves

½ cup sugar, or to taste

1 cup heavy (whipping) cream, whipped

Whole berries for garnish

PLACE THE BERRIES and lavender leaves or mint in a large saucepan, cover, and cook over medium heat for about 15 minutes, or until the berries are soft and lightly cooked. Pass through a food mill or push through a sieve to remove the seeds and leaves. Add the sugar and chill the puree. Carefully fold in the whipped cream. Serve in chilled glasses or bowls and garnish with whole berries.

TROPICAL RATATOUILLE FRUIT GYOZA

with Passion Fruit Cream and Macadamia Praline

Roy Yamaguchi

Makes 16 *gyozas*; serves 4

Diced orange, banana, mango, papaya, and pineapple and dried cherries form the "ratatouille", which is combined with macadamia praline and sealed in pot-sticker dumplings cooked crispy on one side and soft on the other.

MACADAMIA PRALINE	TROPICAL FRUIT RATATOUILLE GYOZA
½ cup sugar	¼ cup diced orange
2 tablespoons water	¼ cup diced banana
¼ cup macadamia nuts, toasted and chopped *(see page 4)*	¼ cup diced mango
	¼ cup diced papaya
	¼ cup diced pineapple
	¼ cup dried cherries
PASSION FRUIT CREAM	½ tablespoon julienned fresh mint leaves
4 cups milk	¼ teaspoon ground cinnamon
1 vanilla bean, split in half lengthwise	¹⁄₁₆ teaspoon ground allspice
8 egg yolks	Macadamia Praline (above)
¾ cup plus 1 tablespoon sugar	2 tablespoons sugar
½ cup passion fruit puree*	¼ teaspoon fresh lemon juice
Juice of 1 passion fruit	1 tablespoon cornstarch
	1 tablespoon cold water
	16 *gyoza* wrappers*
	3 tablespoons vegetable oil
	2 tablespoons minced crystallized ginger

$\mathcal{T}$O MAKE THE MACADAMIA NUT PRALINE: In a small, heavy sauté pan or skillet, cook the sugar and water until the mixture turns a light caramel color and thickens, about 5 to 7 minutes. Quickly toss in the macadamia nuts to coat them thoroughly. Remove from heat and turn out onto a sheet of aluminum foil. Let cool, then chop into small pieces. Cover and set aside.

TO MAKE THE PASSION FRUIT CREAM: In a large saucepan, bring the milk and vanilla bean to a boil. Meanwhile, in the bowl of an electric mixer, whip the egg yolks and sugar until creamy. Add the boiling milk to the yolks and whip. Return to the saucepan and cook, stirring constantly with a wooden spoon, until the cream begins to thicken, about 5 minutes; do not boil. Strain immediately into a bowl set over a bowl of ice. Add the passion fruit syrup and juice. Mix and let cool.

TO MAKE THE GYOZA: In a bowl mix the fruits, mint, spices, and ½ cup of the macadamia praline. Cover and refrigerate for 1 hour. In a heavy, medium sauté pan or skillet, melt the sugar. Stir in the fruits and cook for 1 minute. Stir in the lemon juice; let cool.

In a small bowl, mix the cornstarch and cold water. Place 3 tablespoons of the fruit mixture on each *gyoza* wrapper. Moisten the edges of the wrapper with the cornstarch mixture. Fold into a half-moon shape and press the edges closed. Repeat to make 16 *gyozas*. In a large skillet with a lid, heat the oil until hot. Place all the *gyozas* in the skillet and fry all together on one side only. Add just enough water to cover the bottom of the skillet. Cover and cook until the liquid has completely evaporated, about 5 minutes; only one side of the *gyozas* will be crisp. Transfer to paper towels and pat dry.

To serve, cover each of 4 plates with about 3 tablespoons of the passion fruit cream. Place 4 warm *gyozas* on each plate, crisp side up. Garnish with the remaining macadamia praline and the crystallized ginger.

Passion fruit puree may be found at finer specialty food stores, or it can be ordered from Made in France, 2748 Clearwater Street, Los Angeles, CA 90039; Telephone (213) 663-6027. Gyoza wrappers are available in the Asian food section of most grocery stores.

WARM HUCKLEBERRY COMPOTE

Nancy Silverton

Serves 4 to 6

A light fruit dessert flavored with citrus, cinnamon, nutmeg, cloves, and a touch of black pepper. This dessert may be made ahead of time and reheated.

4 cups (1 pound) fresh huckleberries or stemmed black currants	1 cinnamon stick
1½ cups sugar	½ teaspoon freshly grated nutmeg
¾ cup fresh orange juice	¼ teaspoon finely ground black pepper
Julienned zest of ½ lemon, finely chopped	Pinch of ground cloves
	3 tablespoons plus 1 teaspoon cornstarch
	¼ cup water

IN A LARGE BOWL, toss together the berries, sugar, orange juice, lemon zest, cinnamon stick, nutmeg, black pepper, and cloves. Place in a saucepan and bring to a low boil, while stirring occasionally. Strain the berries, reserving the juice; set aside. Return the juice to the saucepan and bring to a boil. In a small bowl, mix together the cornstarch and water. Add to the boiling juice mixture and stir it constantly with a wooden spoon until thickened, about 1 minute. Pour the thickened juice over the berries and mix gently. Serve warm.

ALFRED PORTALE'S WARM PEAR AND FIG STRUDEL

with Pistachios and Port Sauce

Alfred Portale

Makes 10 pastries

A late summer - early autumn strudel featuring fruit poached in a broth flavored with vanilla, cinnamon, cloves, citrus, and rum.

POACHED FRUIT

1½ cups water

1¼ cups sugar

1 vanilla bean, split lengthwise

2 cinnamon sticks

Pinch of ground cloves

One 2-inch strip lemon zest

One 2-inch strip orange zest

6 to 7 Bosc pears, peeled, halved, and cored

12 to 14 fresh figs, or dried figs soaked for 20 minutes in warm water

2 tablespoons dark rum

RUBY PORT SAUCE

2 cups good-quality ruby port

1 tablespoon sugar

2 teaspoons cornstarch

ALMOND CREAM

1 cup milk

¼ cup unbleached all-purpose flour

4 tablespoons granulated sugar

3 egg yolks

⅛ teaspoon almond extract or to taste

1 pound 14-by-18-inch sheets filo dough

4 tablespoons butter, melted and cooled

3 tablespoons shelled unsalted pistachio nuts, toasted, peeled, and chopped *(see page 4)*

Sifted powdered sugar for dusting

Fresh mint sprigs for garnish

1 quart Vanilla Bean Ice Cream *(recipe on page 144)*

$\mathcal{T}$o make the poached fruit: In a large nonaluminum pot, stir the water, sugar, vanilla bean, cinnamon sticks, cloves, and zests. Add the pears and cover the pot. Bring the liquid to a simmer and poach until pears are tender, about 10 minutes. Remove the pears to a large bowl with half of the poaching liquid. Poach the figs in the remaining liquid for about 10 minutes, or until soft. Remove from heat, add rum, and chill.

To make the ruby port sauce: Reserve 2 tablespoons of the port. In a medium saucepan, stir the remaining port with the sugar. Bring to a boil over high heat and cook for about 15 minutes, or until reduced to about 1 cup. In a small bowl, whisk the reserved 2 tablespoons port with the cornstarch. Whisk into the boiling liquid until thickened; chill.

To make the almond cream: In a medium saucepan, heat the milk almost to a boil. In a heavy, medium saucepan, mix the flour and 2 tablespoons of the sugar. In a medium bowl, whisk together the egg yolks and remaining 2 tablespoons sugar until pale in color. Whisk the hot milk into the sugar and flour mixture and cook over medium heat, stirring constantly, until the mixture reaches a boil. Continue cooking for 4 minutes, stirring constantly.

Pour the hot mixture into the yolks, stirring constantly. Return to the saucepan and cook, stirring constantly, until the cream is thickened, about 5 minutes. Remove from heat; strain and let cool. Add the almond extract. Cover and refrigerate until ready to use.

To assemble, remove the pears and figs from the poaching liquid and cut into large dice; set aside. Cut the filo sheets lengthwise into 5 equal strips. Cover the filo with a damp kitchen towel to keep it from drying out. Stack 3 strips of filo crosswise in a 4-inch pastry ring with the sides overlapping (the ends of the strips will hang over the sides); brush with the melted butter. Stack another 3 strips crosswise from the first strips and brush with the melted butter. Fill the ring with the diced fruit and place 1 tablespoonful of almond cream on top. Sprinkle with toasted pistachios. Draw up the ends of the filo dough and pinch the sides together to form a top. Continue this process for all the remaining pastries.

Place the pastries on a greased baking sheet and bake in the preheated oven for 10 to 15 minutes, or until a light golden brown. Serve warm, dusted with powdered sugar, drizzled with port sauce, and garnished with mint. Serve with vanilla bean ice cream.

WHITE CHOCOLATE RASPBERRY MILLE-FEUILLES

John Downey

Makes one 9-inch pastry; serves 10

This rich white chocolate and raspberry dessert, developed by pastry chef Jeff Hausz, was an instant favorite at Downey's Restaurant. What makes it so distinctive is the method of baking the puff pastry circles under weights so that they stay thin but retain their flaky layers.

—John Downey

4½ cups heavy (whipping) cream

1 pound white chocolate,* chopped

⅓ recipe (8 ounces) Quick Puff Pastry

  (recipe on page 3)

3 cups (12 ounces) fresh raspberries,

  plus a few for garnish

Sifted powdered sugar for dusting

*I*N A MEDIUM SAUCEPAN, bring 1½ cups of the cream to boil and turn off the heat. Add the white chocolate and let sit until the chocolate is melted; stir until blended. Cover and refrigerate until firm and cold, at least overnight.

Preheat the oven to 350°F. Cut the puff pastry in half and roll each half out to a ⅛-inch thickness. Cut each piece of dough into an 11- or 12-inch circle. Cut 2 rectangles of baking parchment or aluminum foil to cover an 18-by-26-inch baking sheet. Line the baking sheet with one piece of paper or foil and place the 2 pastry circles about 1 inch apart on the pan. Place the second piece of paper or foil on top of the pastry and a second baking sheet on top of that. Place tiles, bricks, or heavy cookware on top to hold the sheet together; do not use cans of food, as they might explode. Bake in the preheated oven until golden brown, about 10 minutes. The pastry circles will bake up very thin, but will still produce many flaky layers. Let cool completely.

Place a 9-inch round cake pan on one circle and cut around it with a sharp paring knife to trim the circle. Repeat with the second circle; wrap each securely in plastic wrap. (The pastry also may be frozen, before trimming, for several weeks. Thaw in the refrigerator, heat in a 300°F oven for 5 minutes, and let cool completely before proceeding.)

TO ASSEMBLE: No more than 3 hours before serving (to prevent the pastry from becoming soggy), stir the remaining 3 cups of the whipping cream into the chocolate mixture until well blended. Whip until stiff peaks form. You will have about 9 cups for the filling. Transfer some of the filling to a pastry bag with a plain tip.

Pipe a single layer of the chocolate mixture on one pastry circle, leaving a ½-inch margin around the outside of the circle. In this space, pipe a 2-inch-high wall of white chocolate. Place raspberries on the outside of the wall, pressing slightly so they will adhere to the wall. Cover the wall neatly and completely. Spread the remaining berries on top of the pastry inside the wall. Cover the berries with the rest of the white chocolate mixture, smoothing the top. Place the second pastry circle on top and press down gently with a cake pan to adhere the two parts; stop when the sides bulge just slightly. Refrigerate for 2 hours before serving.

When ready to serve, dust the top generously with powdered sugar and garnish with a few additional raspberries. Cut into wedges with a serrated bread knife.

The white chocolate should be top quality, made from cocoa butter; do not use white "coating" chocolate or any product that lists palm oil.

WINTER-FRUIT DUMPLINGS

Emily Luchetti

Makes 6 dumplings

Dried apricots, raisins, sour cherries, and pears, softened in a broth of white wine before baking in a cream cheese–enriched dumpling dough.

1½ cups (12 ounces) dried apricots, cut into ¼-inch-thick strips

1 cup (8 ounces) dried pears, cut into ¼-inch-thick strips

⅔ cup (4 ounces) golden raisins

1½ cups (10 ounces) dried sour cherries, pitted

1 cup fruity white wine, such as Gewürztraminer or Riesling

1¼ cups water

1 cup (8 ounces) cream cheese at room temperature

½ cup (1 stick) butter at room temperature

2 tablespoons sugar

¼ cup heavy (whipping) cream

Pinch of salt

2½ cups unbleached all-purpose flour

1 egg, lightly beaten

1 cup whipped cream or crème anglaise *(recipe on page 2)*

IN A LARGE, HEAVY SAUCEPAN, simmer the apricots, pears, raisins, cherries, wine, and water over medium heat until the fruit is soft, about 20 minutes. Let cool and strain the fruit (reserve the liquid for another use).

Preheat the oven to 350°F. In the bowl of an electric mixer, beat the cream cheese, butter, sugar, and cream on medium speed until well blended. Add the salt and flour and mix until incorporated. On a lightly floured board, roll the dough out ¼ inch thick and cut it into six 6½-inch circles. Place about ½ cup of the dried fruit mixture in the middle of each circle. Gather the dough together at the top and press it together to seal. Brush each dumpling with the lightly beaten egg. Bake in the preheated oven for about 25 minutes, or until golden brown. Serve warm with whipped cream or crème anglaise.

CHILLED APPLE SOUP
with Apple Granita
Gray Kunz
Serves 4

The cinnamon in the granita and the vanilla bean in the soup are the surprises in this recipe that elevate it from the delicious to the sublime.

SOUP AND GRANITA	TUILE COOKIES
Winesap apples, cored and quartered	4 tablespoons butter at room temperature
2 cinnamon sticks	⅓ cup powdered sugar
4 cups water	2 egg whites
About ½ cup sugar, or to taste	6 tablespoons flour
	1 apple, cored and thinly sliced
MAPLE SYRUP	½ cup apple balls made with a small
½ cup maple syrup	melon baller
½ vanilla bean, cut in half lengthwise	
	Sifted powdered sugar for dusting
	¼ cup unsalted pistachios, chopped

To MAKE THE SOUP AND GRANITA: In a large saucepan, place the apples, cinnamon sticks, and water. Add sugar to taste and simmer for 45 minutes. Let cool and strain through a cheesecloth. Freeze one fourth of the soup in a shallow pan. Refrigerate the remaining soup.

TO MAKE THE MAPLE SYRUP: In a small saucepan, heat the maple syrup and vanilla bean over medium heat until hot. Keep warm.

TO MAKE THE TUILES: Preheat the oven to 350°F. In the bowl of an electric mixer, cream the butter and sugar until light and fluffy. Gradually beat in the egg whites and flour with a wooden spoon. Spread the batter on nonstick baking pans, making 4 strips, each 1 inch wide and long enough to bridge the serving bowls. Bake for 5 to 7 minutes, or until golden brown. Let cool slightly, then remove from pan to a wire rack to cool.

To serve, scrape the surface of the frozen apple soup with a fork to form ice crystals. Pour the soup into chilled plates. Add the apple slices and apple balls. Top each plate with a tuile cookie resting on the edges of the soup bowl. Place a scoop of granita in the center of the cookie. Dust with the powdered sugar and sprinkle with chopped pistachios. Spoon the warm maple syrup over the granita.

FIGS, BANANAS, AND BLUEBERRIES IN CITRUS BROTH

Hubert Keller

Serves 4

Ginger, honey, and rum make this fruit soup extraordinary.

1½ cups fresh orange juice	1 tablespoon rum
1 cup fresh grapefruit juice	16 to 20 ripe black figs
3 tablespoons fresh lemon juice	1 banana
½ teaspoon finely shredded peeled fresh ginger	3 tablespoons blueberries
2 tablespoons honey	8 fresh mint leaves for garnish

IN A MEDIUM NONALUMINUM SAUCEPAN, bring to a boil the citrus juices, ginger, honey, and rum. Meanwhile, prick each fig with a fork several times. Peel the banana and cut it into slices. Plunge the fruits gently into the boiling juices. Turn off heat, cover, and let cool. Refrigerate for 1 hour. Serve in shallow, rimmed soup plates and garnish with fresh mint leaves.

FRESH BERRIES IN CHAMPAGNE AND PASTIS

Kevin Graham

Serves 4

For an elegant dessert, it's hard to top this presentation of berries in champagne glasses with pastis or Pernod liqueur.

1 cup fresh raspberries

1 cup fresh blueberries

1 cup fresh strawberries, stemmed

½ cup pastis or Pernod liqueur

About 2 cups chilled champagne

RINSE AND DRY THE BERRIES. Cut the strawberries into quarters. Place equal layers of fruit in each of 4 champagne glasses, beginning with a layer of raspberries, then blueberries and finally strawberries. Cover and refrigerate for 1 hour.

Just before serving, spoon 2 tablespoons of pastis or Pernod over the fruit in each glass and fill the glasses with champagne. Serve immediately.

Note: *Any fresh fruit, except grapes, may be substituted for the berries.*

STRAWBERRY-CHAMPAGNE SOUP

Kevin Graham

Serves 4

This fruit soup features Chartreuse liqueur, honey, and fresh mint.

2 pints fresh strawberries, chilled and stemmed

½ cup fresh orange juice

¼ cup honey

¼ cup Chartreuse liqueur

½ bottle chilled dry champagne

10 fresh mint leaves, shredded

CHILL 4 SMALL GLASS BOWLS in the freezer. Place the strawberries in a blender or food processor and puree them with the orange juice. In a small saucepan over high heat, mix the honey and Chartreuse and bring to a quick boil. Immediately remove from heat and transfer to a large bowl. Fold in the strawberry puree. Cover and refrigerate.

When the mixture is thoroughly chilled, add the champagne and spoon equal portions into the 4 chilled glass bowls. Garnish with shredded mint leaves and serve immediately.

WARM PEACHES AND MANGOS

with a Tamarind Glaze

Barry Wine

Serves 6

The tartness of tamarind, which comes from the pods of a tropical tree, makes it a natural complement for the one-dimensional sweetness of ripe peaches and mangoes. The small amount of sugar in the glaze makes this dessert low calorie and low fat, while providing the palate with a blend of intense interest. The julienne of mint provides color contrast for visual interest.

—Barry Wine

6 ounces tamarind pods, peeled, or ¼ block (3 ounces) tamarind (do not substitute ready-made tamarind paste)*

1 cup water

¼ cup sugar

4 ripe peaches, peeled and thinly sliced

4 ripe mangoes, peeled and thinly sliced

Fresh mint leaves julienned for garnish

PREHEAT THE BROILER. In a medium saucepan, combine the tamarind, water, and sugar. Bring to a simmer over medium heat and cook the mixture for 4 to 5 minutes, stirring constantly to prevent scorching. Strain through a fine-meshed sieve to make a smooth paste.

Dividing the fruit among 6 ovenproof serving plates, alternate slices of peach and mango to form a circular fan. Brush the arranged fruit lightly with the glaze and place each plate under the broiler 3 to 4 inches from the heat until the glaze begins to bubble slightly and the fruit is warm, about 1 minute. Serve garnished with julienned mint.

Available at Indian, Latino, or Middle Eastern markets.

Robert Del Grande ❦ Marcel Desaulniers ❦ Susan

Feniger & Mary Sue Milliken ❦ Ken Frank ❦ Kevin

PIES AND CRISPS

Graham ❦ Jean Joho ❦ Emeril Lagasse ❦ Emily

Luchetti ❦ Nick  Bruce Marder ❦

Michael McCarty ❦ ... le ❦ Seppi Renggli

❦ Anne Rosenzweig ❦ Jimmy Schmidt ❦ John

Sedlar ❦ Piero Selvaggio ❦ Jackie Shen ❦ Nancy

Silverton ❦ Joachim Splichal ❦ Jacques Torres ❦

Barbara Tropp ❦ Charlie Trotter ❦ Jonathan Waxman

❦ Jasper White ❦ Barry Wine ❦ Alan Wong ❦

BANANA CARAMEL CREAM PIE

Jonathan Waxman (created with Toni Chiappetta)

Makes one 9-inch pie

A buttery crust topped with sliced bananas, pastry cream, and whipped cream, and served with warm caramel sauce and more sliced bananas.

CARAMEL SAUCE	PASTRY CREAM
1½ cups sugar	2 cups light cream or half-and-half
1 cup heavy (whipping) cream	½ vanilla bean, split lengthwise
	6 egg yolks
BASIC PASTRY	½ cup plus 2 tablespoons sugar
1½ cups pastry flour	1 tablespoon cornstarch
1 tablespoon sugar	1 tablespoon cake flour
½ teaspoon salt	1 tablespoon unsalted butter
½ cup (1 stick) chilled unsalted butter, cut into small pieces	3 ripe bananas
¼ cup ice water	1 cup heavy (whipping) cream, whipped to soft peaks

To MAKE THE CARAMEL SAUCE: In a medium, heavy saucepan over medium heat, melt the sugar, stirring constantly. When all the sugar has melted, continue to cook until it has reached a golden color and the sugar is just starting to smoke. Remove the saucepan from heat and stir in the heavy cream, taking care not to splash yourself with the hot syrup. Return to the heat and continue to cook until all of the sugar has remelted; let cool.

To MAKE THE BASIC PASTRY: In a mixing bowl, combine the flour, sugar, and salt. Cut in the butter until it resembles coarse meal. Add the cold water and mix until all of the dry ingredients are wet and the dough just comes together. Turn the dough out onto a lightly floured surface and work lightly with the heel of your hand until the dough forms a ball. Wrap in plastic wrap and chill for a minimum of 30 minutes.

Roll the dough out on a lightly floured surface to a 12-inch circle. Brush off any excess flour and place in a 9-inch pie pan. Gently push the dough into the bottom of the pan and up the sides. Leave 1 inch of the dough hanging over the side and roll it up to form an even top edge. Chill the crust for a minimum of 1 hour.

Preheat the oven to 350°F. Place a piece of aluminum foil shiny side down over the crust and fill with 1 inch of rice or dried beans. Bake in the lower third of the preheated oven for 10 to 15 minutes. Remove the weights and foil when the edges are starting to brown and continue to bake for 5 minutes, or until the bottom is dry and golden brown. Spread ¼ cup of the caramel sauce evenly over the bottom of the pie shell and bake for 5 more minutes. The caramel will begin to bubble around the edges. Remove from the oven and chill until set.

TO MAKE THE PASTRY CREAM: In a medium, heavy pan, scald the cream and vanilla bean. In the bowl of an electric mixer, beat the egg yolks and sugar until a ribbon is formed on the surface of the batter when the beaters are lifted. Into a small bowl, sift the cornstarch and flour; mix into the egg yolk mixture. Whisk ½ cup of the hot cream into the egg mixture. Pour this mixture back into the remaining cream and cook over medium heat, whisking constantly. Bring the mixture to a full boil and cook for 1 minute. Strain the mixture into a medium bowl and whisk in the butter. Put a piece of plastic wrap directly on top of the cream and chill.

To assemble, thinly slice 1 banana and place the slices in a layer on the bottom of the prebaked crust. Cover with a layer of pastry cream about 1½ inches thick. Spread with a layer of whipped cream, cover with plastic wrap, and chill for a minimum of 3 hours. To serve, cut the remaining bananas into slices and warm the remaining caramel sauce. Pool warm caramel sauce on each serving plate and place a slice of pie in the center of the plate. Garnish with slices of banana on the top of the pie and next to it.

BANANA CREAM PIE
with Banana Crust and Caramel Drizzles

Emeril Lagasse

Makes one 9-inch pie

As I planned the opening of Emeril's, I wanted to create a signature dessert that would represent the flavors of my childhood in Massachusetts as well as those of my adopted home, New Orleans. I had thought of and discarded many ideas and was about to go bananas before finally hitting on the fruit of the same name. In fact, the word banana is said to have roots in the Portuguese language, and Portuguese navigators were responsible for transplanting the fruit from Africa to the Canary Islands. More importantly —to me —I have fond childhood memories of creamy-soft banana pies served on special occasions. As for New Orleans, one of the most popular desserts of the area is a concoction called Bananas Foster, and so I get my crosscultural dish, which is my version of banana cream pie. There are three secrets to this pie: the bananas in the crust, the old-fashioned pastry cream, and the whole vanilla bean.

—Emeril Lagasse

BANANA PIE CRUST

½ cup (1 stick) unsalted butter at room temperature

¼ cup packed light brown sugar

2 cups graham cracker crumbs (about 7 graham crackers)

1 very ripe banana, mashed

FILLING

3 cups heavy (whipping) cream

1 vanilla bean, split lengthwise

1 tablespoon unsalted butter

¾ cup cornstarch

2½ cups sugar

½ teaspoon salt

5 egg yolks

4 ripe bananas, sliced ¼ inch thick

Caramel Drizzle Sauce *(recipe follows)*

Whipped cream and shaved chocolate for garnish

*T*O MAKE THE PIE CRUST: Preheat the oven to 375°F. In the bowl of an electric mixer, cream the butter and the sugar. Add the graham cracker crumbs and mashed banana, and mix until evenly combined; press into a 9-inch pie pan. Bake in the preheated oven until brown, about 14 minutes. Let cool before filling.

TO MAKE THE FILLING: In a large saucepan, heat 2 cups of the cream. Scrape the vanilla bean and stir in the pulp with the butter; bring to a simmer. Meanwhile, combine the remaining 1 cup cream with the cornstarch and stir until thoroughly blended and smooth. When the mixture in the saucepan begins to simmer, stream in the cream-cornstarch mixture, whisking constantly.

In a small bowl, mix the sugar and salt, then whisk vigorously into the cream mixture until the mixture is thick. Whisk in the egg yolks one at a time. Remove from heat and whisk until smooth and creamy.

Spread about one third of the filling in the pie crust and cover with half the banana slices. Spread another one third of the filling and arrange the remaining banana slices over that. Cover with the remaining filling and smooth out the top. Cover and refrigerate at least 2 hours, or until firm. To serve, cut into wedges and top with the drizzle sauce, whipped cream, and shaved chocolate.

Caramel Drizzle Sauce

1 cup sugar
¼ cup water
1 cup heavy (whipping) cream

In a small, heavy saucepan, combine the sugar and water. Bring to a boil over medium heat, stirring often, until the syrup becomes a deep nutty-brown and reaches the consistency of thin syrup, about 13 minutes; remove from heat. Stir in the cream. Return to heat and bring to a boil; remove from heat.

BLACK BOTTOM PIE
with Rye Whiskey Sauce
Stephan Pyles
Makes one 9-inch pie

Stephan Pyles reinterprets a Southern classic with his original rye whiskey caramel sauce.

1 recipe Basic Pastry, chilled *(recipe on page 6)*	1 cup plus 2 tablespoons packed light brown sugar
1 ounce bittersweet chocolate, chopped	1 cup light corn syrup
5 teaspoons heavy (whipping) cream	2 teaspoons vanilla extract
1 teaspoon sugar	5 teaspoons bourbon
½ cup (1 stick) plus 1 tablespoon unsalted butter	5 eggs
	1 cup (4 ounces) pecan halves
	Rye Whiskey Sauce *(recipe follows)*

On a lightly floured board, roll the dough out ⅛ inch thick and 10 inches in diameter. Fit the dough into the pan, and trim and crimp the edges; chill.

Preheat the oven to 350°F. In a double boiler over barely simmering water, melt the chocolate. In a small, heavy saucepan, heat the cream, add the sugar, and stir until the sugar is dissolved. Whisk in the melted chocolate and continue whisking until thoroughly blended. Pour the chocolate mixture over the bottom of the chilled pie shell, spreading the mixture evenly. Place the pie shell in the freezer to set the chocolate.

Melt the butter and set aside. In the bowl of an electric mixer, beat the brown sugar, corn syrup, vanilla, and bourbon until smooth. Add the eggs one at a time, blending thoroughly after each addition. Add the melted butter and beat until smooth. Remove the pie shell from the freezer. Spread the pecan halves evenly over bottom of pie shell. Pour the filling over the pecans. Bake in the preheated oven until the center of the pie is set, about 45 minutes. Serve with rye whiskey sauce.

Rye Whiskey Sauce

½ cup (1 stick) unsalted butter
⅔ cup sugar
2 eggs
1 tablespoon very hot water
½ cup heavy (whipping) cream
½ cup rye whiskey

In a double boiler over barely simmering water, melt the butter. In the bowl of an electric mixer, beat the sugar and eggs; stir into the butter. Add the hot water and cook over medium heat, stirring constantly, until the mixture has thickened enough to coat the spoon, about 7 minutes. Let cool to room temperature. Stir in the cream and whiskey.

BRÊTON AUX POMMES

Nick Malgieri

Makes one 9- or 10-inch pie

This apple "pie" from Brittany is as easy to prepare as it is delightful to serve and eat.

—Nick Malgieri

PASTRY DOUGH	FILLING
1 cup (2 sticks) butter at room temperature	2 pounds Golden Delicious apples
1 cup sugar	½ cup sugar
1 tablespoon dark rum	3 tablespoons butter
1 teaspoon vanilla extract	2 tablespoons fresh lemon juice
4 egg yolks	2 tablespoons dark rum
2¾ cups unbleached all-purpose flour	1 egg yolk, beaten

TO MAKE THE PASTRY DOUGH: In the bowl of an electric mixer, beat the butter until smooth. Beat in the sugar in a stream. Continue beating until the mixture is light and fluffy. Beat in the rum and vanilla, then the yolks one at a time, beating until the mixture is very smooth and light. Beat in the flour until it is absorbed, without overmixing.

TO MAKE THE FILLING: Peel, core, and slice the apples. Place in a large saucepan with the sugar, butter, lemon juice, and rum. Cook the apples, covered, until they exude their juices, about 5 minutes. Uncover the apples, lower the heat, and cook until the juices have evaporated; let cool.

To bake, preheat the oven to 350°F. Butter a 9- or 10-inch springform pan and line the bottom with baking parchment or waxed paper. Butter the paper. Place half the dough in the pan and press with your fingertips evenly over the bottom of the pan and about 1 inch up the sides. Spread the cooled apple filling over the dough.

Flour the remaining dough and press it into a 9- or 10-inch disk on a cardboard circle or a tart pan bottom. Slide the dough over the apple filling and press it into place, making sure that the sides are straight and even. Brush the top of the *brêton* with the beaten egg yolk and trace a lattice pattern on it with the tines of a fork. Bake in the preheated oven for 40 to 45 minutes, or until crust is golden.

LEMON CRUST

Vincent Guerithault

Makes one 8-inch square pie; serves 4 to 6

*This lemon pie is easier to prepare than the traditional lemon meringue—
and just as good.*

½ cup (1 stick) butter at room temperature

1¼ cups sugar

1¼ cups unbleached all-purpose flour

4 eggs

Grated zest of 1 lemon

Juice of 1 lemon

1 tablespoon baking powder

PREHEAT THE OVEN TO 350°F. Butter and flour an 8-inch square baking pan. In the bowl of an electric mixer, cream the butter with ¼ cup of the sugar. Add ¼ cup of the flour and blend well. Pat the dough into the prepared pan and bake in the preheated oven for 10 to 15 minutes, or until golden brown.

Meanwhile, in the bowl of an electric mixer, mix the eggs with the lemon zest, lemon juice, and baking powder. Mix in the remaining sugar and flour. When the crust is ready, pour the egg mixture over it and bake for 15 more minutes, or until set.

LIME-COCONUT PIE

Susan Feniger and Mary Sue Milliken

Makes one 10-inch pie; serves 8

This tart, Mexican-inspired pie topped with toasted coconut is a favorite at the Border Grill.

1 cup sugar cookie crumbs	Pinch of salt
2½ cups loosely packed dried,	1½ cups sugar
unsweetened coconut flakes	8 large egg yolks
3 tablespoons butter	5 egg whites
1 cup fresh lime juice	¼ teaspoon cream of tartar
3 level tablespoons cornmeal	Grated zest of 1 lime

PREHEAT THE OVEN TO 300°F. In a large bowl, mix the sugar cookie crumbs and coconut. Line a 10-inch glass pie plate with two thirds of this mixture. Reserve the remaining mixture for the topping.

In a double boiler, place the butter, lime juice, cornmeal, salt, and 1 cup of the sugar. Cook over medium heat, stirring frequently, for 15 minutes, or until the curd is thickened. In the bowl of an electric mixer, beat the egg yolks until thick. Add to the curd and cook an additional 5 minutes, stirring; let cool.

In a clean, dry bowl of an electric mixer, whip the 8 egg whites with the cream of tartar until soft peaks form. Add the remaining ½ cup sugar and lime zest. Gently fold into the curd and pour into the coconut pie shell. Top with the reserved coconut mix. Bake in the preheated oven for 30 minutes, or until the pie rises and the coconut is toasted. Chill thoroughly before serving.

PUMPKIN-PECAN PIE
with Nutmeg and Cinnamon

Jimmy Schmidt

Makes one 10-inch pie

A traditional pumpkin pie with just the right amount of spice and topped with pecans.

Sweet Pie Pastry *(recipe follows)*	⅓ cup packed brown sugar
⅓ cup granulated sugar	1 teaspoon freshly ground nutmeg
1 cup water	1 teaspoon ground cinnamon
Juice of ½ lemon	¾ cup pumpkin puree
1 cup light corn syrup	1½ cups (6 ounces) pecans
¼ cup light rum	
4 tablespoons unsalted butter	4 fresh mint springs for garnish
3 eggs	Vanilla Bean Ice Cream
	(recipe on page 144)

PREHEAT THE OVEN TO 350°F. Roll out the pastry dough to a ⅛-inch thickness and press into a 10-inch pie pan. Trim and crimp the edges. In a medium, heavy saucepan, mix the granulated sugar, water, and lemon juice. Cook over high heat to a dark caramel, about 350°F on a candy thermometer. Add the corn syrup, mixing well. Add the rum and butter, and cook for 2 minutes; remove from heat.

In a large bowl, mix the eggs, brown sugar, nutmeg, and cinnamon. Slowly add the syrup mixture while constantly whisking. Mix in the pumpkin puree, stirring until blended. Pour the filling into the pie pan. Arrange the pecans evenly over the top. Bake in the middle rack of the preheated oven until the filling is set and the pie is golden, about 45 minutes. Remove to a wire rack and let cool until solid, about 4 hours. Cut into wedges, garnish with mint, and serve with vanilla ice cream.

Sweet Pie Pastry

2 cups unbleached all-purpose flour, sifted

½ cup sugar

1 cup (2 sticks) cold butter, cut into marble-sized pieces

2 egg yolks

¼ cup half-and-half

Line a baking sheet with baking parchment or grease it. In a bowl, mix the flour and sugar. Cut in the butter until the mixture is a coarse meal. In a small bowl, whip together the yolks and half-and-half until smooth. Slowly add the egg mixture to the flour mixture. Stir until the mixture comes together in a ball. Remove the pastry to the prepared pan and flatten the dough into a rectangle. Cover with plastic wrap and refrigerate for at least 2 hours.

SWEET POTATO-PECAN PIE

Jonathan Waxman (created with Toni Chiappetta)

Makes one 9-inch pie

A many-splendored pie composed of a buttery crust, sweet potato puree, whole pecans, and a maple syrup topping.

1 recipe Basic Pastry *(recipe on page 6)*

SWEET POTATO FILLING	MAPLE SYRUP TOPPING
1½ pounds sweet potatoes	4 eggs
¼ cup packed brown sugar	⅔ cup granulated sugar
2 tablespoons maple syrup	⅔ cup maple syrup
1 egg	½ cup corn syrup
1 tablespoon heavy (whipping) cream	6 tablespoons butter, melted
1 tablespoon unsalted butter at room temperature	
1 tablespoon vanilla extract	1½ cups (6 ounces) pecans, toasted *(see page 4)*
¼ teaspoon salt	Softly whipped cream or crème
¼ teaspoon ground cinnamon	fraîche for garnish *(recipe on page 8)*
⅛ teaspoon ground allspice	
⅛ teaspoon ground nutmeg	

To make the pastry shell: Preheat the oven to 350°F. On a lightly floured board, roll the dough out ⅛ inch thick and 10 inches in diameter. Fit the dough into a 9-inch pie pan and trim and crimp the edges. Bake in the preheated oven until very light golden, about 10 to 15 minutes.

To make the sweet potato filling: Preheat the oven to 425°F. Wash the sweet potatoes and prick with a fork. Bake in the preheated oven for 40 minutes to 1 hour, or until the centers are soft when pierced with a knife. Let cool, then peel and mash. In the bowl of an electric mixer, beat all the filling ingredients together until smooth; do not overbeat.

To make the maple syrup topping: In a medium bowl, lightly whisk the eggs, sugar, maple syrup, and corn syrup until smooth. Whisk in the melted butter.

Preheat the oven to 350°F. Spoon the sweet potato filling into the prebaked crust. Place the pecans on top and gently ladle the maple syrup topping over the nuts. Bake in the preheated oven for about 50 minutes, or until the nut layer is set and puffy; be careful not to let it crack. Let cool to room temperature. Serve with whipped cream or crème fraîche.

BERRY-PECAN BUCKLE
with Cinnamon Ice Cream
Stephan Pyles
Serves 6 to 8

Anyone's resolve would buckle when presented with this old-fashioned berry treat served with a complementary cinnamon ice cream.

1 cup (2 sticks) butter at room temperature	**CRUMBLY TOPPING**
	½ cup granulated sugar
⅓ cup granulated sugar	½ cup packed dark brown sugar
1 egg, beaten	1 cup unbleached all-purpose flour
2 cups unbleached all-purpose flour	½ teaspoon ground nutmeg
2 teaspoons baking powder	½ cup (1 stick) butter at room temperature
1 teaspoon buttermilk	⅓ cup pecans, toasted and chopped
4 cups assorted fresh berries	*(see page 4)*
	Cinnamon Ice Cream *(recipe on page 131)*

PREHEAT THE OVEN TO 350°F. Butter and flour an 8-inch square baking dish. In the bowl of an electric mixer, beat the butter and sugar together until light and fluffy. Add the beaten egg and mix. In a medium bowl, sift the flour and baking powder together. Alternately add the flour mixture and the buttermilk to the sugar-butter mixture and beat until blended. Pour the batter into the prepared dish and cover with the berries.

In a medium bowl, blend all the ingredients for the crumbly topping together with your fingertips or a pastry blender; sprinkle over the berries. Bake in the preheated oven for 1 hour, or until golden. Let cool slightly and serve with cinnamon ice cream.

BLUEBERRY-APPLE CRUMBLE

Jean Joho

Serves 12

Serve this in the fall when fresh blueberries and new-crop apples are both available.

FILLING | TOPPING

FILLING	TOPPING
2½ cups fresh blueberries	1 cup rolled oats
3 pounds (about 10) Granny Smith apples, peeled, cored, and diced (7 cups)	⅓ cup unbleached all-purpose flour
2 teaspoons grated lemon zest	¾ cup packed light brown sugar
1 tablespoon fresh lemon juice	Pinch of salt
½ cup unbleached all-purpose flour	3 tablespoons vegetable oil
¾ cup granulated sugar	2 tablespoons cold butter, cut into small bits
⅓ cup packed light brown sugar	
1¼ teaspoons ground cinnamon	

To MAKE THE FILLING: Preheat the oven to 400°F. Lightly oil two 8-by-11-inch ceramic baking dishes; set aside. In a large bowl, combine the berries, apples, lemon zest, and lemon juice. In a small bowl, stir together the flour, sugars, and cinnamon. Stir into the fruit mixture. Divide evenly into the prepared baking dishes. Bake in the preheated oven for 20 minutes, or until the filling bubbles around the edges. Stir and set aside.

To MAKE THE TOPPING: In a medium bowl, combine the oats, flour, brown sugar, and salt. Sprinkle the oil over the mixture and then cut in the butter until the mixture resembles coarse meal. Sprinkle the topping evenly over the fruit. Bake for 30 minutes, or until the top is browned. Let sit for 15 minutes before serving.

RHUBARB AND TAPIOCA CRISP

Barry Wine

Serves 6

Two favorite flavors from my childhood are paired in this crisp topped with nutty oatmeal streusel.

TAPIOCA CREAM

1½ cups milk

3 tablespoons granulated sugar

1½ tablespoons quick-cooking tapioca

1 egg yolk

1 teaspoon vanilla extract

Grated zest of 1 medium orange

Pinch of salt

2 to 3 teaspoons orange flower water

1 cup heavy (whipping) cream, whipped to stiff peaks

OATMEAL STREUSEL

1 cup packed light brown sugar

¾ cup unbleached all-purpose flour

¼ teaspoon salt

½ cup (1 stick) chilled unsalted butter, cut into small chunks

¾ cup rolled oats

RHUBARB-TAPIOCA FILLING

2 pounds rhubarb, cut into ¼-inch pieces

1 cup granulated sugar

3 tablespoons quick-cooking tapioca

1 teaspoon vanilla extract

Grated zest of 1 medium orange

2 tablespoons unsalted butter

TO MAKE THE TAPIOCA CREAM: In a medium, heavy saucepan, mix the milk, sugar, tapioca, egg yolk, vanilla, orange zest, and salt. Let stand for 5 minutes. Place the pan over medium heat and cook until the mixture just comes to a boil. Stir frequently to avoid scalding the tapioca. Pour into a bowl and place a piece of plastic wrap over the surface of the tapioca to prevent a skin from forming. Refrigerate for about 20 minutes, or until cool. Fold the orange flower water and the whipped cream into the tapioca; chill.

To make the oatmeal streusel: In a medium bowl, combine the sugar, flour, and salt. Cut in the butter until the mixture is the texture of coarse cornmeal. Stir in the oats. Toss to blend; set aside.

To make the rhubarb-tapioca filling: In a large bowl, mix all the ingredients. Let stand for 15 minutes.

Preheat the oven to 325°F. Spoon the rhubarb mixture into a 6-by-8-inch pan. Press the streusel mixture evenly over the top. Bake for about 25 to 30 minutes, or until the streusel is a deep golden brown and the rhubarb is tender when a knife is inserted. Serve warm with the tapioca cream.

Robert Del Grande ❦ Marcel Desaulniers ❦ Susan

Feniger & Mary Sue Milliken ❦ Ken Frank ❦ Kevin

Graham ❦ Jean Joho ❦ Emeril Lagasse ❦ Emily

Luchetti ❦ Nick Malgieri ❦ Bruce Marder ❦

Michael McCarty ❦ Alfred Portale ❦ Seppi Renggli

❦ Anne Rosenzweig ❦ Jimmy Schmidt ❦ John

Sedlar ❦ Piero Selvaggio ❦ Jackie Shen ❦ Nancy

Silverton ❦ Joachim Splichal ❦ Jacques Torres ❦

Barbara Tropp ❦ Charlie Trotter ❦ Jonathan Waxman

❦ Jasper White ❦ Barry Wine ❦ Alan Wong ❦

Robert Del Grande 🍎 Marcel Desaulniers 🍎 Susan

Feniger & Mary Sue Milliken 🍎 Ken Frank 🍎 Kevin

Graham 🍎 Jean John  Emeril Lagasse 🍎 Emily

Luchetti 🍎 Nick Bruce Marder 🍎

Michael McCarty le 🍎 Seppi Renggli

🍎 Anne Rosenzweig 🍎 Jimmy Schmidt 🍎 John

Sedlar 🍎 Piero Selvaggio 🍎 Jackie Shen 🍎 Nancy

Silverton 🍎 Joachim Splichal 🍎 Jacques Torres 🍎

Barbara Tropp 🍎 Charlie Trotter 🍎 Jonathan Waxman

🍎 Jasper White 🍎 Barry Wine 🍎 Alan Wong 🍎

RASPBERRY CRÈME BRÛLÉE TART

Kevin Taylor

Makes four 4-inch tarts

Whole fresh raspberries are incorporated into these custards served over a pastry crust.

SWEET PASTRY	CRÈME BRÛLÉE
⅔ cup sugar	3 cups heavy (whipping) cream
1 egg	1 vanilla bean, split in half lengthwise
¾ cup (1½ sticks) butter	8 tablespoons sugar
1¼ cups unbleached all-purpose flour	7 egg yolks
Pinch of salt	2 cups fresh raspberries

To MAKE THE SWEET PASTRY: Preheat the oven to 350°F. In the bowl of an electric mixer, beat the sugar and egg together. In a medium bowl, rub the butter into the flour and salt until it has the appearance of bread crumbs. Add the egg-sugar mixture and mix to make a paste; do not overmix. Cover and chill in the refrigerator for at least 30 minutes.

Divide the pastry into 4 even balls. On a lightly floured board, roll out each to a ⅛-inch thickness. Fit the pastry into four 4-inch tart tins; trim the edges. Place a piece of parchment paper or aluminum foil shiny side down over the crust and fill with a 1-inch layer of uncooked rice or dried beans. Bake in the preheated oven until evenly browned, about 10 minutes.

TO MAKE THE CRÈME BRÛLÉE: In a small saucepan, bring the cream and vanilla bean to a boil and simmer until it is reduced by half. Strain. In a double boiler over barely simmering water, whisk and cook the sugar and egg yolks until they thicken, about 3 minutes. Remove from heat. Slowly whisk the cream into the yolks and cook over barely simmering water for 10 to 20 minutes, stirring frequently; the custard will thicken slightly. Let cool.

Distribute the fresh raspberries evenly among the 4 tart shells and cover with the custard; chill. To serve, preheat the broiler. Sprinkle 2 tablespoons of the granulated sugar on top of each tart and caramelize under the broiler 3 inches from the heat for 1 minute, or until golden brown.

BANANA-MACADAMIA NUT FILO TART

Mark Militello

Makes one 10-inch tart; serves 8

The crust is made one layer at a time with filo or strudel dough, then topped with a filling featuring whole macadamias and sliced banana.

CRUST	FILLING
½ cup (1 stick) unsalted butter	6 tablespoons unsalted butter
8 sheets filo dough or strudel dough	4 large eggs
3 to 4 tablespoons powered sugar, sifted	¾ cup light corn syrup
	1 cup firmly packed brown sugar
	2 teaspoons vanilla extract
	½ teaspoon salt
	1 cup (5 ounces) whole unsalted macadamia nuts
	1 ripe banana
	2 to 3 tablespoons powdered sugar, sifted
	1 cup heavy (whipping) cream, whipped to stiff peaks

To MAKE THE CRUST: In a small saucepan, melt the butter; let cool. Lightly butter a 10-inch springform pan and line it with 1 sheet of the filo dough. Gently ease the dough into the bottom and sides of the pan so as not to tear it. The dough will hang down over the sides of the pan. Brush with melted butter and sprinkle with a little powdered sugar.

Place a second sheet of filo on top of the first layer, perpendicular to the first. Brush with butter and sprinkle with powdered sugar. Continue assembling the crust in this fashion, until all the filo is used up and the dough hangs down all the way around the edge of the pan; set aside.

TO MAKE THE FILLING: Preheat the oven to 325°F. In a small saucepan, melt the butter and let cool. In a large bowl, combine the eggs, corn syrup, brown sugar, vanilla, and salt, and whisk until mixed. Whisk in the cooled butter. Arrange the macadamia nuts over the bottom of the crust. Peel the banana and cut it into ¼-inch-thick slices. Arrange these slices on top of the macadamia nuts. Pour the filling over the nuts and bananas. Gently fold the filo dough over the filling. Brush the top with the remaining butter and sprinkle with powdered sugar.

Bake the tart in the preheated oven for 1 hour, or until the filling is set but still soft. Let cool to room temperature and remove the side of the pan. To serve, lightly dust the top of the tart with powdered sugar. Cut the tart into wedges. Serve each piece with a ruff of unsweetened whipped cream.

ALFRED PORTALE'S BLACK PLUM TARTS

with Almond Cream

Alfred Portale

Serves 6

A late-summer treat filled with almond-flavored pastry cream.

ALMOND CREAM	
1½ cups (12 ounces) blanched almonds	1 recipe (1 pound) fresh or thawed frozen Quick Puff Pastry *(recipe on page 3)*
½ cup (1 stick) unsalted butter at room temperature	6 to 8 ripe black plums, cut into ¼-inch slices
Grated zest of 2 lemons	3 tablespoons melted butter
Grated zest of 1 orange	3 tablespoons sugar
¼ cup sugar	
2 eggs	Cinnamon Ice Cream
1 tablespoon brandy	*(recipe on page 131)*
2 teaspoons almond extract	6 fresh mint sprigs

To MAKE THE ALMOND CREAM: Grind the almonds to a fine meal in a food processor or with a nut grinder. In the bowl of an electric mixer, cream the butter, then add the zests and sugar. Mix in the eggs, brandy, and almond extract. Stir in the almond meal; cover and refrigerate until used.

Preheat the oven to 425°F. On a lightly floured board, roll the puff pastry to a thickness of ⅛ inch. Cut six 6-inch circles; prick them all over with a fork. Place the pastry on a baking sheet and chill for at least 20 minutes. Spread a thin layer of almond cream on each pastry. Arrange the plum slices in a circle over the almond cream, leaving a ⅛-inch border of pastry. Brush with the melted butter and sprinkle with the sugar.

Bake in the preheated oven for 10 to 15 minutes, or until the pastry is golden. Serve warm with cinnamon ice cream and mint sprigs.

BLUEBERRY TART

Kim Peoples

Makes one 10-inch tart

Ground almonds enrich this traditional summer tart.

1 Basic Pastry *(recipe on page 6)*

1½ cups (15 ounces) blanched almonds

2 cups sugar

9 eggs, separated

4 cups blueberries

To PREPARE THE TART SHELL: Preheat the oven to 350°F. On a lightly floured board, roll the dough out ⅛ inch thick and 12 inches in diameter. Fit the dough into the pan, and trim and crimp the edges. Bake in the preheated oven until very light golden, about 10 to 15 minutes.

Preheat the oven to 375°F. In a food processor or with a nut grinder, grind the almonds to a fine meal. In the bowl of an electric mixer, beat 1 cup of the sugar and the egg yolks until a ribbon forms on the surface of the batter when the beaters are lifted. Stir in the ground almonds and gently fold in the blueberries. In the clean, dry bowl of an electric mixer, whip the egg whites to soft peaks. Add the remaining 1 cup of sugar and whip to stiff peaks. Fold the whites into the yolk mixture. Pour into the prebaked tart shell and bake in the preheated oven for 30 minutes, or until golden brown.

BUTTER PASTRIES
with Sweet Squash Filling

Steven Howard

Makes 10 pastries

Think of this dessert as a variation of pumpkin pie, served with a passion fruit-pistachio sauce.

BUTTER PASTRY

2 tablespoons butter, melted

3 sheets 14-by-18-inch filo dough

2 tablespoons superfine sugar

2 tablespoons nuts, ground

SWEET SQUASH FILLING

1 pound butternut squash

½ cup Pastry Cream

(recipe on page 7)

1 pound Mascarpone cheese at room temperature

2 teaspoons ground cinnamon

ITALIAN MERINGUE

6 egg whites

⅛ teaspoon cream of tartar

1¾ cups sugar

½ cup water

PASSION FRUIT-PISTACHIO SAUCE

2⅓ cups sugar

2 cups water

Passion fruit puree to taste*

1 cup crème anglaise *(recipe on page 2)*

¼ teaspoon pistachio extract

Salt to taste

To make the butter pastry: Preheat the oven to 350°F. Butter each layer of filo and sprinkle with the sugar and ground nuts. Cut into 4-inch squares and place on a baking sheet layered with baking parchment or aluminum foil. Place another piece of parchment or foil on top of the filo squares, then set another baking sheet on top. Bake in the preheated oven for 10 minutes, until the filo is uniformly golden brown.

TO MAKE THE SWEET SQUASH FILLING: Peel and seed the squash. Cut into 2-inch pieces and steam for 10 minutes, or until soft; let cool. In the bowl of an electric mixer, mix the squash, pastry cream, Mascarpone, and cinnamon until smooth.

TO MAKE THE ITALIAN MERINGUE: In the clean, dry bowl of an electric mixer, beat the egg whites and cream of tartar to soft peaks. Add 1 cup of the sugar and beat to stiff peaks. In a saucepan, heat the remaining ¾ cup sugar with the water. Simmer until the syrup reaches the soft ball stage (about 242°F on a candy thermometer) or when a small quantity of syrup when dropped into ice water forms a ball that flattens when removed from the water. Pour the hot syrup in a thin stream into the egg whites while beating at high speed.

TO MAKE THE PASSION FRUIT-PISTACHIO SAUCE: In a large, heavy saucepan, boil the sugar and the water for about 10 minutes, or until it reaches the hard ball stage (when a small amount is dropped into ice water it will form a firm, but pliable, ball). Add the passion fruit puree, crème anglaise, and pistachio extract. Season with salt to take off the sweet edge of the caramel.

To assemble, fold the Italian meringue into the squash mixture. Pipe onto the pastry squares. Serve at room temperature with the passion fruit-pistachio sauce.

Passion fruit puree is available at finer specialty food stores, or it can be ordered from Made in France, 2748 Clearwater Street, Los Angeles, CA 90039; Telephone (213) 663-6027.

CRANBERRY STREUSEL TART

Jasper White

Makes one 10-inch tart

This dessert combines the flavor of New England cranberries with an Old World streusel topping. It is a fine example of how New England cooks combine their worldly cooking experience with the familiar flavors they love. This dessert was created by Killian Weigand, pastry chef at the Bostonian Hotel and one of the best in all of New England. We worked together for more than five years, and he remains a dear friend and professional associate. I advise you to make the streusel topping well in advance; it will keep indefinitely.

—Jasper White

Sugar Crust *(recipe follows)*

CRANBERRY FILLING

Two 12-ounce bags (6 cups) fresh cranberries

¾ cup sugar

1 cinnamon stick

Grated zest and juice of 1 orange

ALMOND STREUSEL TOPPING

¾ cup (1½ sticks) unsalted butter at room temperature

⅓ cup (2 ounces) almond paste, cut into pieces

1 cup sugar

1⅓ cups unbleached all-purpose flour

2 tablespoons fresh lemon juice

2 teaspoons ground cinnamon

Vanilla Bean Ice Cream *(recipe on page 144)*

$\mathcal{P}$REPARE THE SUGAR CRUST. TO MAKE THE CRANBERRY FILLING: In a large saucepan, stir the cranberries, sugar, cinnamon stick, and orange zest and juice. Simmer slowly for 20 minutes, or until the cranberry mixture becomes thick and heavy. Remove the cinnamon stick and let the filling cool.

TO MAKE THE ALMOND STREUSEL TOPPING: In a small pan, melt half of the butter (6 tablespoons); set aside to cool. In the bowl of an electric mixer, mix the almond paste and sugar until thoroughly combined. The mixture will resemble coarse cornmeal. Add the remaining 6 tablespoons butter and continue mixing until creamy. Add the flour, melted butter, lemon juice, and cinnamon; mix until smooth. Refrigerate until completely chilled and hard, about 30 minutes.

Preheat the oven to 375°F. Fill the tart shell with the cranberry filling just to within ¼ inch of the top of the crust, to prevent it from bubbling over. Using the large holes of a grater, grate the streusel topping over the cranberry mixture. Try to distribute it evenly over the entire top. The streusel layer should be about ½ inch thick and will come up above the edge of the pan. Place in the lower third of the preheated oven and bake for about 50 minutes, or until the top is a rich golden brown. Let cool on a rack for at least 30 minutes before serving. Serve warm or at room temperature with vanilla ice cream.

Sugar Crust

1½ cups unbleached all-purpose flour

¼ teaspoon salt

3 tablespoons sugar

¾ cup (1½ sticks) cold unsalted butter, cut into bits

About 2 tablespoons cold milk

In a large bowl, mix the flour, salt, and sugar. Add the butter and, using a pastry cutter or your fingers, mix in the butter until it is broken up into small pieces and the mixture resembles coarse bread crumbs. Slowly add the milk, using just enough to make the dough stick together.

Knead the dough on a lightly floured surface until it is fairly smooth; do not overwork the dough or it will be tough. Wrap in waxed paper or plastic wrap and refrigerate for at least 30 minutes.

On a lightly floured board, roll the dough into a 12-inch circle. Fit the pastry into the pan, trim the edges, and chill.

CRANBERRY-WALNUT TART

Nick Malgieri

Makes one 10-inch tart; serves 8 to 10

This pungent tart appeals to those who like desserts that are not too sweet. A perfect finale to a rich holiday meal, it is both light and easy to prepare in advance.

—Nick Malgieri

One 12-ounce bag (3 cups) cranberries, picked over	4 tablespoons butter
½ cup packed light brown sugar	¼ teaspoon ground cinnamon
½ cup granulated sugar	¼ teaspoon ground ginger
1 tablespoon grated orange zest	¾ cup (3 ounces) walnut pieces
⅓ cup fresh orange juice	Basic Pastry *(recipe on page 6)*

PREHEAT THE OVEN TO 350°F. In a medium saucepan, place the cranberries, sugars, orange zest, and juice. Bring to a boil over medium heat. Lower heat and simmer for about 5 minutes, or until thickened, stirring occasionally. Remove from heat and stir in the butter, ground cinnamon, and ginger. Let cool to room temperature, then stir in the walnuts.

On a lightly floured board, roll the dough out into a 12-inch circle ⅛ inch thick. Fit the dough into the pan and trim and crimp the edges. Pour the cooled filling into the pastry shell and smooth the top. Bake the tart in the preheated oven on the lowest rack for about 30 to 40 minutes, or until the pastry is baked through and golden and the filling just begins to bubble at the edges. (Take care not to overbake the tart or the filling may boil over.) Let cool. Unmold and serve at room temperature.

CROSTATA FRUIT

Lisa Doumani

Serves 4

Stone fruits like peach, nectarine, plum or apricot are perfect for this midsummer tart.

ALMOND CREAM

¼ cup blanched almonds

¼ cup (1 stick) unsalted butter at room temperature

¼ cup powdered sugar, sifted

Zest of ¼ lemon, cut into julienne and minced

1 egg

⅛ teaspoon vanilla extract

⅛ teaspoon almond extract

¾ recipe (12 ounces) fresh or thawed frozen Quick Puff Pastry *(recipe on page 3)*

3 peaches, or other ripe fruit about the same size such as plums or pears, peeled, halved, and cut into ⅛-inch-thick slices

3 tablespoons sugar

Vanilla Bean Ice Cream *(recipe on page 144)* or sweetened crème fraîche *(recipe on page 8)*

To MAKE THE ALMOND CREAM: In a food processor or nut grinder, grind the almonds to a fine meal. In the bowl of an electric mixer, cream the butter and sugar. Mix in the lemon zest, egg, and vanilla and almond extracts. Add the almond meal and mix thoroughly. Cover and refrigerate for up to 4 days.

Preheat the oven to 325°F. Roll out the puff pastry into four 5-inch circles. Spread each pastry round with 2 tablespoons of the almond cream to within ½ inch of the edge of the puff pastry. Lay the fruit on the cream in a circular form, overlapping the slices to make a flowerlike pattern. Sprinkle the edges of the dough with the sugar. Bake in the preheated oven for 20 to 30 minutes, or until the pastry is golden and the underside of the pastry is fully cooked. Serve warm with vanilla ice cream or sweetened crème fraîche.

DOUBLE-CHOCOLATE WALNUT TART

Marcel Desaulniers

Makes one 10-inch tart; serves 8

This densely chocolate dessert can be prepared 2 to 3 days in advance of serving. If making the tart ahead, let it cool thoroughly, cover with plastic wrap, and refrigerate until 30 to 60 minutes before serving.
—Marcel Desaulniers

TART SHELL	TART FILLING
1½ cups unbleached all-purpose flour	1½ cups (6 ounces) walnut halves
1 tablespoon sugar	6 ounces semisweet chocolate, chopped
Pinch of salt	2 ounces unsweetened chocolate, chopped
6 tablespoons cold unsalted butter	½ cup (1 stick) unsalted butter
¼ cup ice water	8 egg yolks
	¼ cup sugar

To MAKE THE TART SHELL: Preheat the oven to 350°F. In a medium bowl, mix 1¼ cups of the flour, sugar, and salt. Cut in the butter until the mixture develops a mealy texture. Add the ice water and continue to mix until the dough just comes together. Form the dough into a smooth round ball, wrap in plastic wrap and refrigerate for at least 4 hours.

On a lightly floured board, roll the dough (using the remaining ¼ cup of flour as necessary to prevent the dough from sticking) into a circle about 13 inches in diameter and ⅛ to ¼ inch thick. Line a 10-by-¾-inch false-bottomed tart pan with the dough, gently pressing the dough around the bottom and sides.

Cut away the excess dough, leaving a ¾-inch border. Crimp the border around the top edge of the pan. Refrigerate for 30 minutes.

Line the dough with an 18-by-18-inch piece of aluminum foil (use 2 pieces of foil if necessary). Weigh down the foil with rice, dried beans, or pie weights. Bake in the center of the preheated oven for 20 minutes, then rotate the tart shell 180° and bake another 10 minutes, or until very light golden. Remove the foil and weights. Let cool to room temperature.

TO MAKE THE TART FILLING: Preheat the oven to 300°F. Set aside 36 walnut halves. Crush the remaining walnuts with the bottom of a sauté pan. In a double boiler over barely simmering water, melt the chocolates and butter. Stir the mixture until smooth and set aside at room temperature until needed.

In the bowl of an electric mixer, beat the egg yolks and sugar on high speed for 2 minutes. Scrape down the sides of the bowl, then beat on high speed for 3 to 4 minutes, or until slightly thickened and pale in color. Add the melted chocolate and mix on low for 20 seconds. Stir in the crushed walnuts. Use a rubber spatula to thoroughly combine the filling, scraping down the sides, then transfer it to the cooled prebaked tart shell, spreading the filling evenly.

Arrange the 36 reserved walnut halves on top of the filling. Bake the tart in a preheated oven for 30 minutes, or until the crust is golden and the filling is set. Remove the tart from the oven and let cool for 1 hour at room temperature before removing from the pan.

HAZELNUT TARTS
with Chocolate Sauce

Barry Wine
Serves 8

Chocolate and hazelnut: a flavor combination greater than the sum of the individual parts.

TART DOUGH

3 tablespoons unsalted butter at room temperature

¼ cup sugar

¾ cup unbleached all-purpose flour

Pinch of salt

2 egg yolks

HAZELNUT FILLING

1 cup (5 ounces) hazelnuts, toasted and skinned *(see page 4)*

½ cup (1 stick) plus 1 tablespoon unsalted butter at room temperature

¾ cup sugar

2 large eggs

2 teaspoons vanilla extract

3 tablespoons dark rum

¼ teaspoon salt

CHOCOLATE SAUCE

3 ounces bittersweet chocolate, chopped

1¼ cups water

½ cup unsweetened cocoa powder

2 tablespoons sugar

1 teaspoon vanilla extract

2 tablespoons dark rum

4 cups fresh raspberries

To MAKE THE TART DOUGH: In the bowl of an electric mixer, cream the butter and sugar until light. Add the flour and salt. Add the yolks and mix until just combined. Wrap in plastic wrap and chill for 15 to 20 minutes. On a lightly floured board, roll the dough out to a ⅟₁₆-inch thickness and cut into eight 5-inch circles. Line eight 4-by-1 inch tart pans with the dough. Trim the edges, prick the bottoms with a fork, and place in the freezer while preparing the filling.

To make the filling: Preheat the oven to 325°F. In a food processor or with a nut grinder, coarsely grind the hazelnuts. In the bowl of an electric mixer, cream the butter and sugar until light. Add the ground hazelnuts, then beat in the eggs one at a time. Add the vanilla, rum, and salt; beat until incorporated. Pipe the hazelnut mixture into the prepared tart shells, filling them only halfway.

Bake the tarts in the preheated oven until the hazelnut filling is an even, golden brown, about 25 to 30 minutes. Let cool before removing from the tins.

To make the chocolate sauce: In a double boiler over barely simmering water, melt the chocolate; stir until smooth and set aside. In a small saucepan, bring the water to a boil, then whisk in the cocoa powder and sugar. When the mixture is smooth, stir in the melted chocolate, vanilla, and dark rum. Pour a pool of chocolate sauce on each of 8 dessert plates and top with a tart. Garnish each tart with a sprinkling of raspberries.

HONEY, JALAPEÑO, AND ORANGE CHUTNEY TARTS

Vincent Guerithault

Makes ten 4-inch tarts

Vincent Guerithault's surprising and successful marriage of French technique and Southwest flavors will leave your mouth tingling.

PASTRY

1 cup unbleached all-purpose flour

1 teaspoon sugar

¾ cup (1½ sticks) unsalted butter, cut into bits

1 tablespoon water

HONEY, JALAPEÑO, AND ORANGE CHUTNEY

2 jalapeño chilies

10 oranges

2 teaspoons minced fresh ginger

1 tablespoon grated orange zest

1 cup sugar

1 cup water

6 tablespoons honey

1 unpeeled orange, cut into thin crosswise slices for garnish

To MAKE THE PASTRY: In a medium bowl, combine the flour and sugar. Cut the butter into the dry ingredients with a pastry cutter or 2 knives until the mixture resembles coarse meal. Stir in the water with a fork until the mixture forms a dough, being careful not to overmix. Form into a ball, wrap in plastic wrap, and chill in refrigerator for about 2 hours.

Preheat the oven to 350°F. On a lightly floured board, roll the dough out and cut it into ten 6-inch circles. Fit the pastry into the shells, trim, and crimp the edges; refrigerate for 30 minutes. Line each tart with aluminum foil. Weigh down the foil with rice, beans, or pie weights. Bake in the preheated oven for about 15 minutes, or until golden; let cool.

To make the chutney: Place the chilies on a tray under the broiler about 3 or 4 inches from the heat. Broil for 1 to 3 minutes on each side. Remove from the broiler; place in a paper bag and close the bag. When cool enough to handle, wearing rubber gloves, peel off the skins, remove the seeds, and mince the jalapeños.

Grate the zest of 6 of the oranges, then juice the zested oranges. Cut the remaining 4 unpeeled oranges into thin crosswise slices. In a large, heavy skillet, combine the jalapeños, ginger, orange zest and juice, sugar, and water. Cook slowly until the sugar is dissolved. Add the honey and the 4 sliced oranges. Simmer for about 15 minutes, or until the oranges are translucent. Keeping the orange slices intact, drain the ingredients through a strainer, reserving the liquid. Set the orange slices aside, return the liquid to the skillet, and reduce the liquid over low heat until thickened, about 10 minutes. Fold in the cooked orange slices and let cool. To serve, spoon the chutney into the pastry shells and arrange the uncooked orange slices on top.

HOT CHOCOLATE TARTS

Steven Howard

Makes eight 4-inch tarts

Chocolate mousse and chocolate chunks top shortbread flavored with cocoa.

CHOCOLATE SHORTBREAD

1¼ cups unbleached all-purpose flour

¼ cup unsweetened cocoa powder

1¼ cups powdered sugar, sifted

1 cup (2 sticks) unsalted butter, cut
 into pieces, at room temperature

CHOCOLATE MOUSSE

24 ounces semisweet chocolate,
 chopped

1 cup (2 sticks) unsalted butter at
 room temperature

1 cup plus 2 tablespoons sugar

6 eggs, separated

1 tablespoon pure vanilla extract

8 ounces semisweet chocolate, cut
 into large chunks

To MAKE THE CHOCOLATE SHORTBREAD: Preheat the oven to 350°F. Grease eight 4-inch English muffin rings and place them on a greased baking sheet. In a bowl sift together the flour, cocoa, and sugar. Cut in the butter with a pastry cutter or two knives until the ingredients resemble coarse meal. Fill each of the prepared muffin rings with an equal portion of the dough and press down to evenly coat the bottom and sides of the ring. Bake in the preheated oven for 10 minutes, or until golden; let cool.

TO MAKE THE CHOCOLATE MOUSSE: In a double boiler over barely simmering water, stir the chocolate until melted. Set aside to cool slightly. In the bowl of an electric mixer, cream the butter and sugar until light and fluffy. Whip in the egg yolks and vanilla at low speed until well combined. Fold in the melted chocolate and continue mixing at medium speed; set aside. In the dry, clean bowl of an electric mixer, whip the egg whites until stiff peaks form. Fold into the chocolate mixture.

To serve, divide the chocolate chunks evenly among the shortbreads and cover with the mousse mixture.

HOT NECTARINE TATIN

Steven Howard

Makes six 3-inch tarts

At the peak of summer, choose firm, perfectly ripe nectarines to star in this variation of tarte tatin.

1 recipe Basic Pastry *(recipe on page 6)*

7 tablespoons unsalted butter

½ cup plus 2 tablespoons sugar

¼ cup heavy (whipping) cream

11 ripe small nectarines

1 cup Pastry Cream *(recipe on page 7)*

2½ cups blackberries

To make the tart shells: Roll the pastry into a ⅛-inch-thick rectangle. Using a 5-inch round pastry cutter, cut 6 circles. Fit the circles into 3-inch tart pans and trim and crimp the edges. Bake in the preheated oven for 10 to 15 minutes, or until light golden.

In a small, heavy saucepan over medium heat, melt the butter. Stir in the sugar and cook until it turns amber in color; immediately stir in the heavy cream. (The cream will separate.) Stir well. Pour into six 3-inch soufflé dishes and let cool.

Preheat the oven to 375°F. Peel, halve, and pit the nectarines. Place 3 halves on end on top of the caramel, in each soufflé dish, resting against the sides of the pots. Cut the remaining nectarine halves into thirds. Place 2 pieces in the hollow center cavity formed by the nectarine halves. With a serrated knife, even the tops of the nectarine pieces level with the top of the dishes to provide a flat base when inverting the dishes. Pour pastry cream into each dish to fill. Bake the dishes in the preheated oven for 15 minutes, or until the pastry cream bubbles.

Meanwhile, prepare the blackberry puree: Reserving 24 firm blackberries for the garnish, puree the remaining blackberries in a blender or food processor. Strain through a fine sieve to remove the seeds; set aside.

Top each dish with a pastry circle, cover the circle with a broad spatula, and carefully invert the dish over a tray. Repeat with all the remaining dishes. Let the excess liquid run off into the tray. Transfer each dish to a warm plate pooled with blackberry puree and remove the dish. Garnish with fresh berries and serve hot.

LEMON TART

Jimmy Schmidt

Makes one 10-inch tart

A refreshing tart with an intense lemon flavor.

PASTRY SHELL

2 cups unbleached all-purpose flour

6 tablespoons sugar

Pinch of salt

¾ cup (1½ sticks) cold unsalted butter

1 large egg, beaten

FILLING

2 cups fresh lemon juice

1½ cups granulated sugar

6 large eggs

6 large egg yolks

¼ cup grated lemon zest

¾ cup (1½ sticks) unsalted butter, cut into 12 tablespoons

Sifted powdered sugar and mint sprigs for garnish

PREHEAT THE OVEN TO 375°F. In a medium bowl, mix the flour, sugar, and salt. Cut in the butter with a pastry cutter or 2 knives until the mixture resembles fine meal. Add the egg and mix until just combined. Gather the dough into a ball, then flatten slightly. Wrap with plastic wrap and refrigerate for at least 2 hours.

Roll out the pastry on a lightly floured surface to a thickness of ⅛ inch. Fit into a 10-inch tart pan with 1-inch removable sides; trim the edges. Line the pastry crust with aluminum foil, shiny side down. Fill with pie weights, rice, or dried beans. Bake in the preheated oven until set, about 10 to 15 minutes. Remove the weights and foil and continue baking until the crust is lightly browned, about 5 to 10 minutes.

To make the filling: In a heavy, medium stainless steel saucepan, mix the lemon juice and sugar. Bring to a simmer over high heat. Remove from heat. In a medium bowl, whisk together the eggs, yolks, and lemon zest until light in color. Add the hot lemon-sugar syrup while whisking. Pour the custard back into the saucepan, place over medium heat, and whisk constantly for 8 minutes, or until the custard heavily coats the back of a spoon. (Occasionally stir the custard with a rubber spatula to make sure it is not sticking to the pan.) Remove the thickened custard from heat and whisk in the butter by the tablespoon until silky smooth. Strain through a fine-meshed sieve.

Pour the filling into the prepared pastry shell to the top of the crust. Refrigerate until firm, about 4 hours. To serve, dust the top with powdered sugar. Serve each slice garnished with a sprig of mint.

LEMON TART
with Raspberry Sauce
Kevin Graham
Makes one 11-inch tart

Served with a lime-accented raspberry sauce, this tart is a little sweeter than other renditions.

TART SHELL

1¼ cups unbleached all-purpose flour

½ teaspoon salt

2 teaspoons sugar

½ cup vegetable shortening

About ¼ cup milk or more as needed

FILLING

5 large eggs

5 large egg yolks

1¼ cups sugar

Juice of 5 lemons

Grated zest of 2 lemons

6 tablespoons clarified unsalted butter

(see page 4)

RASPBERRY SAUCE

4 cups fresh raspberries

2 tablespoons honey

2 teaspoons sugar, or to taste

Juice of ½ lime

To MAKE THE TART SHELL: In a medium bowl, stir together the flour, salt, and sugar. Cut the shortening into the mixture with a pastry blender or 2 knives until the texture resembles a coarse meal. Make a well in the center and pour in the milk and stir until all the dry ingredients are moistened. If necessary, add milk 1 tablespoonful at a time until the dough is moist but not sticky. Gather the dough into a ball and cover with plastic wrap. Refrigerate for 30 minutes.

Preheat the oven to 375°F. Turn the dough out onto a lightly floured work surface and roll into a circle about 13 inches in diameter. Carefully wrap the dough around the rolling pin and unroll it over an 11-inch tart pan. Press into the bottom and sides of the pan and roll the pin across the top to cut off the excess dough. Prick the bottom of the crust with a fork and chill for 15 minutes. Just before baking, line the crust with baking parchment or aluminum foil and partially fill with pie weights, dried beans, or rice to weight the dough. Place in the preheated oven and bake for 20 minutes, or until the edges are lightly browned. Remove the weights and parchment or foil and return the pastry shell to the oven for about 5 minutes, or until the center of the crust is brown. Let cool on a wire rack.

TO MAKE THE FILLING: Preheat the broiler. In a double boiler over simmering water, whisk the eggs, egg yolks, sugar, lemon juice and zest rapidly for about 10 minutes, or until the filling thickens and forms stiff ridges when the whisk is drawn through it. Remove from heat and whisk in the butter. Pour into the baked tart shell and spread evenly. Place under the preheated broiler about 3 inches from the heat for 1 minute, or until the top is lightly browned. Refrigerate until ready to serve.

TO MAKE THE RASPBERRY SAUCE: Push the berries through a fine-meshed sieve into a bowl; discard the seeds and pulp remaining in the sieve. Mix in the honey, sugar, and lime juice. Serve at room temperature, or cover and place in the refrigerator for up to 2 days. To serve, cut the tart into wedges and top with raspberry sauce.

PECAN-CHOCOLATE TART

Anne Rosenzweig

Makes one 10-inch tart

A rich pecan tart with a chocolate ganache topping. Plan to make the filling one day ahead of time.

FILLING	1 recipe Basic Pastry
½ cup packed light brown sugar	*(recipe on page 6)*
½ cup packed dark brown sugar	¾ cup (3 ounces) pecans
¾ cup plus 2 tablespoons granulated sugar	
	GANACHE
1 cup dark corn syrup	2 cups heavy (whipping) cream
1 cup light corn syrup	1 pound semisweet chocolate,
5 tablespoons unsalted butter, melted	chopped*
6 eggs	¼ cup clear corn syrup
Vanilla extract to taste	4 tablespoons unsalted butter
Salt to taste	

To MAKE THE FILLING: In the bowl of an electric mixer, stir together the sugars. Add the corn syrups and mix well. Add the butter, eggs, vanilla, and salt and mix well. This filling is best if made 1 day ahead, covered, and chilled.

Preheat the oven to 400°F. On a lightly floured surface, roll the dough into a 12-inch circle. Fit the dough into the pan and trim the edges. Place the pecans in a layer on the pie dough. Pour in the chilled filling and place the tart in the preheated oven. Immediately turn the oven down to 325°F and bake for 1 hour, or until the filling is set; chill.

To make the ganache: In a double boiler over simmering water, place all the ingredients, stirring with a whisk until smooth. Pour over the cooled tart and chill until set.

*The chef recommends Lucerne brand fondant chocolate, available at specialty food stores.

RASPBERRY-FUDGE TART

Jackie Shen

Makes one 9-inch tart; serves 8 to 10

For a refreshing change, the chef suggests an apricot glaze to top this tart.

Basic Pastry *(recipe on page 6)*

4 ounces semisweet chocolate, chopped

½ cup (1 stick) butter, cut into pieces

⅔ cup sugar

1 teaspoon vanilla extract

2 eggs

1 egg yolk

3 tablespoons heavy (whipping) cream

¾ cup apricot preserves or seedless raspberry preserves

4 cups firm fresh raspberries

TO MAKE THE TART SHELL: Preheat the oven to 350°F. On a lightly floured board, roll the dough out into an 11-inch circle ⅛ inch thick. Fit the dough into the pan, and trim and crimp the edges. Bake in the preheated oven for 10 to 15 minutes, or until lightly golden.

Preheat the oven to 325°F. In a double boiler over barely simmering water, melt the chocolate and butter together. Stir in the sugar and vanilla until well blended. Add the eggs and egg yolk and beat until well blended. Add the cream and blend thoroughly.

Pour the filling into the tart shell. Place on a baking sheet and bake in the preheated oven for 20 to 25 minutes, or until the filling is set. Let cool completely. The filling will settle slightly as it cools. Transfer the cooled tart to a serving plate.

In a small saucepan, heat the apricot or raspberry preserves over medium heat until melted. Strain the apricot preserves, if using, through a sieve. Brush half of the glaze over the entire surface of the tart. Arrange the raspberries on the tart in circles, starting at the edge and working toward the center. Brush the berries lightly with the remaining glaze.

RASPBERRY-LEMON TORTE

Michael McCarty

Makes one 8-inch torte

The flavors of raspberries and lemon go together so well — and nowhere better than in this classic cake, which combines fresh whole berries, fresh lemon curd, a light almond-biscuit cake, and a white chocolate-custard tart shell.
—Michael McCarty

LEMON CURD

4 large eggs

4 large egg yolks

1⅓ cups granulated sugar

⅔ cup fresh lemon juice

⅞ cup (2 sticks less 1 tablespoon) unsalted butter, cut into ½-inch pieces

ALMOND BISCUIT

¾ cup (4 ounces) blanched almonds

1 cup plus 2 tablespoons powdered sugar, sifted

6 tablespoons unbleached all-purpose flour

5 large eggs

6 large egg whites

¼ cup sugar

5 tablespoons unsalted butter, melted

PÂTE SUCRÉE-CUSTARD SHELL

1¼ cups unbleached all-purpose flour

⅓ cup sugar

8 ounces (1 stick) cold unsalted butter cut into small bits

5 large egg yolks

1 cup plus 1 tablespoon heavy (whipping) cream

3½ ounces white chocolate, chopped

Grated zest of 1 lemon

12 ounces white chocolate, chopped

6 cups fresh raspberries

To MAKE THE LEMON CURD: In a double boiler, off heat, whisk together the eggs, egg yolks, sugar, and lemon juice until smooth and thoroughly blended. Place over simmering water, add the butter, and cook, whisking thoroughly every 3 minutes or so, until the mixture thickens, about 25 minutes. Remove from heat and pass the lemon curd through a sieve. Let the curd cool to room temperature, then cover and chill in the refrigerator for at least 1 hour.

TO MAKE THE ALMOND BISCUIT: Preheat the oven to 375°F. Butter a 24-by-12-inch cake pan. Line the bottom with baking parchment or waxed paper, then butter and flour the paper. In a blender or food processor, grind the almonds to a fine meal. In the bowl of an electric mixer, mix the powdered sugar, almonds, flour, and 2 of the eggs at slow speed until combined, then beat at high speed for 1 minute. Add the other 3 eggs and continue beating for 3 minutes, then set aside.

In the clean, dry bowl of an electric mixer, beat the egg whites until soft peaks form. Add the granulated sugar and beat until just combined; set aside. With a rubber spatula, mix a small amount of the sugar-almond mixture with the melted butter. Quickly pour the butter mixture into the rest of the sugar-almond mixture. With the spatula, fold a small amount of the egg white mixture into the almond mixture, then quickly but gently fold this mixture into the remaining whites. Pour the batter into the prepared pan and bake until the biscuit is golden and pulls away from the sides, about 12 to 15 minutes; let cool.

TO MAKE THE PÂTE SUCRÉE-CUSTARD SHELL: In a medium bowl, mix the flour and sugar. Cut in the butter with 2 knives or a pastry cutter until the mixture resembles coarse meal. Whisk together 1 of the egg yolks and 1 tablespoon of the cream and stir into the flour and sugar mixture just until the dough comes together. Gather into a ball, wrap in plastic wrap, and chill for 1 hour. Cover a baking sheet with baking parchment or grease it. Let the pâte sucrée dough warm and soften at room temperature for about 30 minutes. On a cool, lightly floured surface, pound the pastry with a rolling pin to flatten it, then roll it out to a circle about 11 inches in diameter and ⅛ inch thick. Place a pastry ring 8 inches wide and 2 inches high on the prepared baking sheet. (If you don't have a pastry ring, the sides of an 8-inch springform pan will work.) Gently roll the pastry around the rolling pin, then unroll it carefully into the pastry ring. Gently press the pastry against the bottom and sides, and trim the edges. Refrigerate for about 1 hour.

Preheat the oven to 350°F. Line the pastry with baking parchment or aluminum foil and fill it with pie weights, rice, or dried beans. Bake in the preheated oven until the pastry turns a light golden color, about 20 minutes. Remove from the oven, leaving the oven on. Let cool, then remove the weights and paper.

In a double boiler over barely simmering water, melt the chocolate. In a medium bowl, whisk together the remaining 4 egg yolks, the remaining 1 cup cream, the chocolate, and lemon zest until smooth. Pour the mixture into the prebaked shell. Bake until the mixture is set and a knife inserted into the center comes out clean, about 20 to 30 minutes. Let cool to room temperature.

TO ASSEMBLE: Remove the ring from the custard tart shell and place the shell on a round cardboard cake platform. Use a pastry ring 5 inches wide to cut 2 round cake layers from the sheet of almond biscuit. Center one layer on top of the custard tart filling. Spoon about half the lemon curd on top and spread it evenly over the biscuit and beyond its edges up to the inside edge of the pastry shell.

Reserving the best-looking berries to decorate the top later, crush 1 cup of the berries with a wooden spoon and spread them evenly on top of the lemon curd, staying within the rim of the biscuit layer below. Center the second biscuit layer on top of the berries.

In a double boiler over barely simmering water, melt the white chocolate. Cut a strip of waxed paper 26 inches long and 3 inches wide and place it on top of a wider sheet of waxed paper on a cool work surface. With a metal spatula, spread the melted chocolate evenly over the strip of waxed paper. Carefully lift the waxed paper strip, place it on a cool work surface, and let the chocolate set for 1 to 2 minutes, or until firm but still slightly wet, shiny, and flexible. Lift the waxed paper strip up from the work surface and wrap it, chocolate side in, around the torte. Put the torte in the refrigerator for about 30 minutes, or until the chocolate is hard.

Spoon the remaining lemon curd into the torte, spreading and packing it down evenly with a rubber spatula. Return the torte to the refrigerator to set for about 1 hour. Before serving, arrange the remaining berries in neat concentric circles on top of the torte inside the rim of chocolate. Carefully peel the waxed paper from the chocolate band before serving.

RHUBARB CRUMB TART

Nick Malgieri

Makes one 10-inch tart

Try this tart with other fruit, berries, sour cherries, or blueberries.
—Nick Malgieri

SWEET PASTRY DOUGH

1 cup unbleached all-purpose flour

¼ cup sugar

Pinch of salt

¼ teaspoon baking powder

4 tablespoons butter, cut into bits

1 egg, beaten

POACHED RHUBARB

1½ pounds fresh rhubarb

1 cup sugar

2 cups water

ORANGE CUSTARD

⅔ cup heavy (whipping) cream

¼ cup sugar

Grated zest of 1 orange

1 teaspoon vanilla extract

4 egg yolks

CRUMB TOPPING

1¼ cups unbleached all-purpose flour

½ cup sugar

¼ teaspoon ground cinnamon

½ cup (1 stick) butter, melted

TO MAKE THE SWEET PASTRY DOUGH: In a medium bowl, combine the dry ingredients and stir well. Cut in the butter with a pastry cutter or 2 knives until the mixture resembles coarse meal. Stir in the egg. Press and squeeze the dough together to form into a ball. Wrap in plastic and chill until firm, about 1 hour.

TO MAKE THE POACHED RHUBARB: Trim away the leaves completely and string the rhubarb if it is well developed and tough-looking. Cut into 2-inch lengths. In a large skillet or sauté pan, bring the sugar and water to a boil. Add the rhubarb, cover, turn off the heat, and let the rhubarb cool completely. Drain well.

To make the orange custard: In a small bowl, whisk together all the ingredients until well blended.

To make the crumb topping: In a bowl, mix the dry ingredients. Stir the melted butter into the dry ingredients. Allow to stand for 1 minute, then break into coarse crumbs by hand.

Preheat the oven to 350°F. On a lightly floured surface, roll out the dough ⅛ inch thick and fit it into a 10-inch tart pan. Arrange the rhubarb evenly on the dough. Pour the orange custard batter over the rhubarb. Scatter the crumb topping over the filling. Bake on the lowest level of the preheated oven for about 40 minutes, or until the filling is set and the crumbs have browned lightly. Let cool on a rack. Unmold and serve at room temperature. Refrigerate any leftovers.

ALFRED PORTALE'S STRAWBERRY TARTLETS

with Lemon Cream, Mint, and Mascarpone Sorbet

Alfred Portale

Makes six 3¼-inch tarts

The richness of the Mascarpone sorbet is perfectly balanced by the strawberry tarts.

BERRIES

2 large bunches of mint, stemmed

30 perfectly ripe strawberries, stemmed

Fresh lemon juice and sugar to taste

PASTRY

2½ cups unbleached all-purpose flour

7 tablespoons unsalted butter cut into small pieces, at room temperature

¾ cup powdered sugar, sifted

Pinch of salt

2 large eggs, beaten

LEMON CREAM

¾ cup plain yogurt

¾ cup low-fat cottage or ricotta cheese

½ cup heavy (whipping) cream

1 teaspoon fresh lemon juice

Mascarpone Sorbet *(recipe follows)*

TO PREPARE THE BERRIES: Reserving 6 sprigs for garnish, cut the mint leaves into fine shreds. Place the berries in a bowl, sprinkle with the mint, and add lemon juice and sugar to taste. Allow the berries to marinate in the refrigerator for several hours. Drain berries and reserve the juice.

To make the pastry: Place the flour on a work surface and make a well in the center. Place the butter in the well. Add the sugar and salt. Mix with your fingers. Add the eggs and continue to mix while gradually drawing the flour in. Using extra flour if necessary, knead the dough several times with the palm of your hand until very smooth. Wrap the dough in plastic and chill in the refrigerator for 2 hours.

Preheat the oven to 350°F. On a lightly floured board, roll the dough out ⅛ inch thick. Cut into six 5½-inch circles. Fit the dough into the pans and trim the edges. Line each pan with aluminum foil and fill with pie weights, rice, or dried beans. Bake in the preheated oven for 15 to 20 minutes, or until golden brown. Let cool, then remove the foil and weights.

Meanwhile, make the lemon cream: In a blender or food processor, blend the yogurt and the cheese until smooth. In the bowl of an electric mixer, whip the cream until soft peaks form. Fold the two mixtures together by hand. Add the lemon juice. Cover and refrigerate for 2 hours.

To serve, fill the tart shells half full with lemon cream. Arrange the berries on top. Set each tart on a large dinner plate. Spoon the berry juice around the tarts. Garnish with a ball of sorbet and a reserved sprig of fresh mint.

Mascarpone Sorbet

½ cup sugar

½ cup water

1 cup (8 ounces) Mascarpone cheese
  at room temperature

1½ cups plain yogurt

2 tablespoon fresh lemon juice

In a small, heavy saucepan, bring the sugar and water to a boil, then let cool completely. In the bowl of an electric mixer, whip the Mascarpone and yogurt together. Mix in the cooled syrup and lemon juice; chill. Pour the chilled mixture into an ice cream maker and freeze according to the manufacturer's instructions.

STRAWBERRY-RHUBARB TARTS

Joachim Splichal

Makes four 4-inch tarts

These lattice-topped tarts are a simple yet elegant summer treat.

SUGAR DOUGH	FILLING
1½ cups unbleached all-purpose flour	¼ cup sugar
½ cup (1 stick) plus 2 tablespoons	1 tablespoon cornstarch
cold unsalted butter,	1 tablespoon water
cut into small pieces	3 cups cubed rhubarb
¼ cup superfine sugar	(about 1¾ pounds)
Pinch of salt	2 baskets strawberries, stemmed and
1 egg, beaten	quartered

To MAKE THE SUGAR DOUGH: Preheat the oven to 400°F. Place the flour in the middle of a pastry board and form a well in the center. Add the butter, sugar, salt, and half of the egg. Form the ingredients into a ball and work until well blended by smearing the dough across the work surface. Repeat this process twice. Roll the dough to a ⅛-inch thickness on a lightly floured surface.

Cut out four 6-inch circles of dough. Fit the dough into the tart pans; trim and crimp the edges. Line the tart shells with aluminum foil and weight with pie weights, rice, or dried beans. Bake in the preheated oven for 35 minutes, or until lightly golden. Remove the foil and weights. Brush the surface of the tarts with the remaining egg. Return the pans to the oven for 5 to 8 minutes, or until golden brown. Remove from the oven, leaving the oven on.

To make the filling: In a medium saucepan, moisten the sugar and cornstarch with the water and bring to a boil. Add the rhubarb and cook for about 15 to 20 minutes, or until the rhubarb is tender. Add the strawberries and remove from heat. Fill the tart shells with the strawberry-rhubarb mixture. Roll out the remaining sugar dough. Cut into ¼-inch strips and arrange in a crisscross pattern over the tops of the tarts. Bake until the tops are golden brown, about 15 minutes.

TROPICAL ISLAND TART

Roy Yamaguchi

Makes one 9-inch tart

Mango, pineapple, raspberries, blueberries, and chopped macadamia nuts blend in this luscious tart.

1 recipe Basic Pastry *(recipe on page 6)*

FILLING

¼ cup fresh cubed pineapple	¼ cup cubed mangoes
3 eggs	¼ cup blueberries
1¼ cups sugar	¼ cup macadamia nuts, toasted and
⅓ cup unbleached all-purpose flour	chopped *(see page 4)*
¾ cup (1½ sticks) unsalted butter	1 teaspoon pure vanilla extract to taste
¼ cup fresh raspberries	

To MAKE THE TART SHELL: Preheat the oven to 350°F. On a lightly floured board, roll the dough out ⅛ inch thick. Fit into a 9-inch tart pan and trim the edges. Bake in the preheated oven for 10 to 15 minutes, or until just slightly cooked and light golden in color. Set aside to cool, leaving the oven on.

To MAKE THE FILLING: In a small, dry skillet over medium heat, sauté the pineapple cubes until any excess juice is cooked off. In the bowl of an electric mixer, beat the eggs, sugar, and flour. In a medium sauté pan or skillet, cook the butter until it becomes golden brown in color with a nutty fragrance; be careful not to burn it. Pour the hot browned butter into the egg mixture. Quickly add the fruits and macadamia nuts. Fold in gently. Add the vanilla extract. Spoon the filling into the prebaked tart shell and bake for 40 minutes, or until set. Let cool before serving.

TURTLE TART

Jackie Shen

Makes one 9-inch tart; serves 8 to 10

Who doesn't love "turtles," the confection made of chocolate, caramel, and nuts?
Here's a version baked in a tart shell.

GANACHE-FILLED TART	CARAMEL FILLING
1 recipe Basic Pastry	½ cup (1 stick) butter
(recipe on page 6)	⅔ cup packed brown sugar
½ cup plus 2 tablespoons heavy (whipping) cream	½ cup heavy (whipping) cream
8 ounces semisweet chocolate, chopped	2 ounces semisweet chocolate, chopped
	Sweetened whipped cream
1 cup (4 ounces) pecan halves	

To make the tart shell: Preheat the oven to 350°F. On a lightly floured board, roll the dough out into an 11-inch circle ⅛ inch thick. Fit the dough into a 9-inch tart pan and trim and crimp the edges. Bake in the preheated oven for 10 to 15 minutes, or until lightly golden.

To make the ganache: In a small, heavy saucepan, bring the cream to a boil. Add the chocolate, remove from heat, and stir with a wire whisk until the chocolate melts completely. Refrigerate in an uncovered bowl for at least 2 hours or overnight.

Reserving 10 pecan halves, chop the remaining pecans. Heat the ganache over medium heat, until about one fourth of the mixture starts to melt. Immediately transfer the ganache to the bowl of an electric mixer and beat until light and fluffy. Add the chopped pecans. Immediately spoon the ganache filling into the tart shell and smooth the top with a spatula; chill thoroughly.

To make the caramel filling: In a medium saucepan, mix the butter, brown sugar, and cream. Bring to a boil over high heat, stirring until all the ingredients are blended. Cook for 5 minutes, or until the mixture reaches soft ball stage (240°F on a candy thermometer, or until a small amount dropped into a bowl of cold water immediately forms a soft ball). Let cool slightly. Pour over the top of the ganache-filled tart and smooth to the edges with a spatula; let cool.

To garnish: In a double boiler over barely simmering water, melt the chocolate. Dip the end of each reserve pecan half in the melted chocolate and place on a sheet of waxed paper to cool. Garnish the tart with whipped cream rosettes and pecan halves before serving.

WARM BOSC PEAR AND PECAN CREAM TART

Hubert Keller

Makes four 5½-inch tarts; serves 4

A beautiful tart to make in the fall, when Bosc pears are in season.

⅓ recipe (8 ounces) Quick Puff Pastry	1 large egg
(recipe on page 3)	2 or 3 Bosc pears
6 tablespoons salted butter	2 tablespoons honey
3 tablespoons sugar	
4 tablespoons pecans	Crème Fraîche *(recipe on page 8)*
	and Caramel Sauce *(recipe follows)*

PREHEAT THE OVEN TO 375°F. On a lightly floured surface, roll the puff pastry ⅛ inch thick. Cut out four 5½-inch circles and place on a baking sheet. Refrigerate while preparing the filling, as cold dough will puff better.

In the bowl of a food processor, mix 3 tablespoons of the butter. Process until the butter is white and smooth. Add the sugar and process for another 20 seconds. Add the pecans and blend well. Add the egg and continue processing until the mixture is homogeneous.

Peel and core the pears and slice them into thin wedges. Spread the creamy pecan mixture on top of the pastry circles to within ½ inch of the edges. Arrange the pear slices on top in overlapping concentric circles. Dot with the remaining 3 tablespoons of butter and drizzle with honey. Bake in the preheated oven for 20 to 25 minutes. Serve immediately with crème fraîche and caramel sauce.

Caramel Sauce

¼ cup water

¼ cup sugar

3 tablespoons heavy (whipping) cream

2 tablespoons unsalted butter, cut into pieces

In a small saucepan, boil the water and sugar until the mixture turns a dark caramel color, about 7 to 10 minutes. Remove from heat and whisk in the cream and butter, being careful of the hot steam rising from the pan. Simmer until thick and bubbly, about 1 minute.

Robert Del Grande ❦ Marcel Desaulniers ❦ Susan

Feniger & Mary Sue Milliken ❦ Ken Frank ❦ Kevin

Graham ❦ Jean Joho ❦ Emeril Lagasse ❦ Emily

Luchetti ❦ Nick Malgieri ❦ Bruce Marder ❦

Michael McCarty ❦ Alfred Portale ❦ Seppi Renggli

❦ Anne Rosenzweig ❦ Jimmy Schmidt ❦ John

Sedlar ❦ Piero Selvaggio ❦ Jackie Shen ❦ Nancy

Silverton ❦ Joachim Splichal ❦ Jacques Torres ❦

Barbara Tropp ❦ Charlie Trotter ❦ Jonathan Waxman

❦ Jasper White ❦ Barry Wine ❦ Alan Wong ❦

SORBETS, ICE CREAMS, AND FROZEN DESSERTS

Robert Del Grande ❦ Marcel Desaulniers ❦ Susan Feniger & Mary Sue Milliken ❦ Ken Frank ❦ Kevin Graham ❦ Jean Rhon ❦ Emeril Lagasse ❦ Emily Luchetti ❦ Nick Malgieri ❦ Bruce Marder ❦ Michael McCarty ❦ ...le ❦ Seppi Renggli ❦ Anne Rosenzwei... ...my Schmidt ❦ John Sedlar ❦ Piero Selvaggio ❦ Jackie Shen ❦ Nancy Silverton ❦ Joachim Splichal ❦ Jacques Torres ❦ Barbara Tropp ❦ Charlie Trotter ❦ Jonathan Waxman ❦ Jasper White ❦ Barry Wine ❦ Alan Wong ❦

Sorbets

ALMOND TUILES
with Coconut-Orange Sorbet
Kevin Taylor

Makes 2 quarts; serves 8

Fresh ginger and lime juice provide the extra kick in this complex sorbet served in an almond cookie.

COCONUT-ORANGE SORBET	ALMOND TUILES
2½ cups sugar	½ cup sugar
6½ cups water	¼ cup unbleached all-purpose flour
¼ cup coarsely chopped peeled fresh ginger	1½ cups (6 ounces) sliced almonds, lightly toasted and crushed *(see page 4)*
1¾ cups sweetened dried coconut flakes	4 egg whites
4 cups fresh orange juice	4 tablespoons unsalted butter, melted
¾ cup fresh lime juice	¼ teaspoon almond extract
	Pinch of salt

To MAKE THE SORBET: In a large, heavy saucepan, mix the sugar, 2 cups of the water, and ginger. Bring to a boil. Reduce heat and simmer slowly for 2 minutes. Let sit for 30 minutes, then strain. In a saucepan, mix the coconut and the remaining 4½ cups water. Bring to a boil and simmer slowly for 2 minutes. Let cool for 30 minutes, then strain. Mix the sugar syrup, coconut juice, orange juice, and lime juice. Place in an ice cream maker and freeze according to the manufacturer's instructions.

To MAKE THE TUILE: Preheat the oven to 350°F. Butter 2 baking sheets. In the bowl of an electric mixer, blend all of the tuile ingredients. Spoon ¼ cup batter per tuile onto the prepared pan, leaving 3 inches of space between the cookies. Dip a fork in water and flatten each tuile to an ⅛-inch thickness.

Bake in the preheated oven for about 15 minutes, or until just evenly brown.

Immediately and as quickly as possible, lift each off the pan with a spatula and lay it over an upside-down cup to form a bowl shape. If the cookies harden before having been removed from the pan, return the pan to the oven for 30 seconds to soften again. To serve, fill each almond tuile with sorbet and serve immediately.

Coconut-Orange Sorbet with Warm Berry Compote

Chop 2 cups fresh berries into ¼-inch pieces. In a medium sauté pan or skillet, sauté the berries in 2 tablespoons Grand Marnier until just warm. Touch a lighted match to the liquid and shake the pan until the flames subside. Pour over the sorbet and serve at once.

APPLE AND HONEY SORBET
with Strawberry Sauce
Thierry Rautureau
Makes 3 cups; serves 6

The apples in this sorbet are first baked with honey.

SORBET | STRAWBERRY SAUCE

SORBET	STRAWBERRY SAUCE
8 unpeeled Granny Smith apples, cored	2 cups strawberries, stemmed
8 tablespoons honey	1 tablespoon honey
½ egg white	

To MAKE THE SORBET: Preheat the oven to 350°F. Place 1 table-spoon honey in the center of each apple and wrap each apple in aluminum foil. Bake in the preheated oven for about 50 minutes, or until the apples are soft. Scoop the baked apples out of their skin and blend in a blender or food processor; let cool. Freeze in an ice cream maker according to the manufacturer's instructions. When about half frozen, add the ½ egg white, then complete freezing.

To MAKE THE SAUCE: Place the strawberries and honey in a blender or food processor; blend until smooth and set aside. When ready to serve, scoop the apple sorbet into glasses and top with the strawberry sauce.

BURGUNDY-CINNAMON SORBET

Hubert Keller

Makes 4 cups; serves 8

Any palate will be refreshed by this bracing sorbet.

2¼ cups red Burgundy wine

¾ cup sugar

1¼ cups water

Eight 4-inch cinnamon sticks

1 tablespoon candied julienne orange rinds
   for garnish (optional)

IN A MEDIUM SAUCEPAN, bring to a boil the wine, sugar, water, and cinnamon sticks. Remove from heat, cover, and let sit for 45 minutes. Strain the Burgundy mixture through a sieve into a medium bowl.

Pour the mixture into an ice cream maker and freeze according to the manufacturer's instructions until firm, about 20 to 45 minutes, depending on the type of machine used. Serve immediately in chilled glasses, garnished with candied julienne orange rind if desired. The sorbet will keep in the freezer, but bear in mind that the longer it is frozen, the heavier it will become.

CIDER SORBET

Jasper White

Makes about 2 quarts

In New England, autumn means apple cider. People argue endlessly about which apples and/or which growers make the best cider, but one thing is for sure: There is no shortage of good cider. The quality of the cider will determine the quality of the sorbet, especially in this point-blank recipe, which uses only cider and simple syrup. You can play with the recipe if you like. Add lemon juice or a bit of apple-jack for a little zing. Substitute hard cider. Or make a spiced cider sorbet by infusing the spices traditionally used in mulled cider. But if you are confident in your local cider, try this recipe as is. It is wonderful and refreshing.

—Jasper White

1½ cups sugar

2¼ cups water

6 cups fresh unfiltered cider

IN A LARGE, HEAVY SAUCEPAN, bring the sugar and water to a boil and continue boiling, uncovered, for 3 minutes, or until the sugar is dissolved. In a large bowl, stir together the cider and the sugar syrup. Chill well. Freeze in an ice cream maker according to the manufacturer's instructions.

CHERRY, ALMOND, AND CHAMPAGNE GRANITA

Barry Wine

Makes about 1½ quarts

Freshly juiced cherries and homemade almond syrup are the keys to this light summer refresher.

½ cup (2½ ounces) blanched almonds	1 cup dry champagne
½ cup sugar	1 teaspoon egg white
½ cup water	Pinch of salt
About 5 pounds fresh sweet cherries, pitted and juiced in a vegetable juicer to yield 5 cups	Fresh fruit and mint sprigs for garnish

IN A BLENDER OR FOOD PROCESSOR, grind the almonds and sugar until fine. Place in a small saucepan and stir in the water. Bring to a full boil over high heat. Lower the heat to medium and simmer the almond syrup for 4 to 5 minutes, or until the sugar is dissolved. Chill well.

In a large bowl, whisk together the almond syrup, cherry juice, champagne, egg white, and salt. Pour into a shallow pan and freeze. Stir the granita at least every 30 minutes, drawing the frozen mixture along the side into the center. For a smoother texture, stir the granita every 20 minutes. Serve garnished with fresh fruit and mint.

ALFRED PORTALE'S
MOSCATELLO GRANITA
with White Peaches and Lemon Verbena
Alfred Portale

Makes 4 cups granita; serves 6

When white peaches ripen, New York City is at its hottest. That's why Alfred Portale created this refreshing ice made with orange dessert wine, white wine, and lemon verbena.

1 bunch lemon verbena (about 30 leaves)	3 cups sugar
	6 white peaches, peeled
1 bottle Setubal or Quady's Essensia orange muscat dessert wine	2 lemons, juiced
1 bottle dry white wine	2 cups fresh raspberries for garnish

PICK OVER THE VERBENA, reserving half of the leaves for garnish and using the other half for the poaching liquid. In a large saucepan, bring half of the bottle of orange muscat, three fourths of the bottle of white wine, one half of the verbena, and ½ cup of the sugar to a boil; remove from heat. Immerse the peaches in the syrup, cover the pan with a clean towel, and poach until the peaches are tender, about 5 minutes. Carefully remove the peaches to a bowl and add just enough poaching liquid to cover. Add to the remaining poaching liquid the remaining orange muscat and white wine, the remaining 2½ cups of the sugar, and the lemon juice. Stir to dissolve the sugar. Pour into a shallow container and freeze for a minimum of 4 hours.

To serve, use a fork to scrape the surface of the frozen granita to form ice crystals and mound it into stemmed glasses. Garnish with a whole white peach, raspberries, and remaining lemon verbena leaves. Serve immediately.

RHUBARB SORBET

Bruce Naftaly

Makes 3 cups

The consistency of this sorbet is remarkably creamy, although it contains no cream.

1 cup water

1 cup sugar, or ⅔ cup honey

12 ounces rhubarb, cut into small pieces

IN A SMALL, HEAVY NONALUMINUM SAUCEPAN, boil the water and sugar or honey for 1 minute. Stew the rhubarb in the sugar syrup over medium heat until completely soft, about 20 to 30 minutes. Puree in a blender or food processor and push through a sieve to obtain a smooth puree; let cool. Freeze in an ice cream maker according to the manufacturer's instructions.

STRAWBERRY SORBET

Joachim Splichal

Makes 1½ quarts

Make this sorbet at the height of strawberry season when strawberries are full of flavor.

4 baskets fresh strawberries, stemmed

2 cups water

2 cups sugar

½ egg white

IN A BLENDER OR FOOD PROCESSOR, puree the strawberries. Strain through a fine sieve to remove the seeds. In a large saucepan, boil the strawberry puree, water, and sugar until it begins to thicken, about 10 minutes. Chill thoroughly. Whisk in the egg white until well blended. Freeze in an ice cream maker according to the manufacturer's directions.

WHITE GRAPE AND CURRANT SORBET

Marcel Desaulniers

Makes 1½ quarts

Perlette, Thompson (also a white seedless grape), Red Flame seedless and Ruby Red seedless grapes make excellent sorbets. Seeded varieties may be used, but they must be seeded before they are pureed. Whether using seedless or seeded, it will take 1¾ pounds of grapes off the stems and free of seeds to produce this recipe.

The currants are heated in wine both to rehydrate them and to keep them chewable in the frozen mixture. A more intensely flavored alcohol could be used to rehydrate the currants but would probably overshadow the sorbet.

Thompson seedless grapes are an indistinctive vinifera variety. They in themselves are subtly flavored, so it is important that the wine used to rehydrate the currants be compatible. Many of the white California jug wines are blended with Thompson seedless and French Colombard, which would be ideal for this recipe if the wine chosen is dry rather than sweet; otherwise the sorbet will be unpleasantly cloying on the palate.
—Marcel Desaunliers

3 cups water

2 cups sugar

2 pounds Thompson, Perlette, Red Flame,
   or Ruby Red seedless grapes, stemmed

½ cup dried currants or Thompson raisins

½ cup dry white wine

In a 6-cup saucepan, heat the water and sugar over medium-high heat. Whisk to dissolve the sugar. Bring the mixture to a boil and cook for 18 to 20 minutes, or until slightly thickened and reduced to 3 cups.

While the sugar and water are reducing to a syrup, puree the grapes in a blender or food processor. Pour the mixture through a sieve, reserving the juice (about 1½ cups) in a stainless steel bowl. Add ¾ cup of the pulp to the strained juice (discard the remaining pulp).

In a 6-cup saucepan, heat the currants or raisins and wine over medium-high heat. Bring to a boil, then lower heat and simmer for 5 minutes. Drain the currants or raisins and add to the grape juice mixture. Pour the boiling syrup into the bowl with the grape juice mixture. Place the bowl in a bowl of ice and whisk occasionally until cool (40 to 45°F), about 15 minutes.

Freeze in an ice cream freezer following the manufacturer's instructions. When almost frozen, transfer the sorbet to a plastic container, securely cover the container, and freeze for several more hours before serving. Serve within 3 days.

Ice Creams

CAJETA ICE CREAM

Kevin Taylor

Makes 1 quart

One taste of this goat milk ice cream and you'll know why CAJETA *is a favored flavor in Mexico, available at any supermercado.*

CAJETA	⅛ teaspoon baking soda
¾ cup sugar	¼ cup sugar
1 cup goat's milk	6 egg yolks
1 cup cow's milk	1½ cups half-and-half
½ teaspoon cornstarch	1 cup heavy (whipping) cream

To MAKE THE CAJETA: In a small, heavy saucepan, melt 2½ tablespoons of the sugar over medium heat, stirring slowly, until it melts and turns a light golden brown; be careful not to burn. Set aside. In a medium bowl, mix the milks. In a small bowl, mix ½ cup of the milk mixture with the cornstarch and baking soda; set aside.

In a medium, heavy saucepan, mix the remaining sugar and ½ cup milk and bring just to the boiling point over medium heat, stirring constantly. While stirring vigorously, add the caramelized sugar all at once. Stir in the cornstarch mixture. Cook over low heat for about 1 hour, stirring occasionally, until the *cajeta* thickly coats a spoon. The *cajeta* will thicken rapidly during the last few minutes, so watch and stir frequently to prevent sticking and burning. Set aside and let cool.

In a small heatproof bowl, blend the sugar and egg yolks; set aside. In a medium saucepan, heat the half-and-half and cream and bring just to a boil. Pour about one half of the cream mixture into the egg mixture and blend well. Pour this mixture into the remaining cream mixture and cook the custard, stirring constantly, over medium-high heat for about 5 minutes, or until it coats a wooden spoon. Remove from heat and strain. Add the *cajeta*. Place the pan in a bowl of ice and stir until cool. Place the cooled mixture in an ice cream maker and freeze according to the manufacturer's instructions.

CARAMEL-PECAN GELATO

Piero Selvaggio (created with Rudy Torres)

Makes about 3 quarts

Toasted chopped pecans make this creamy caramel gelato a standout.

VANILLA BASE	CARAMEL SAUCE
16 large egg yolks	½ cup water
1 cup sugar	1 cup sugar
4 cups heavy (whipping) cream	¾ cup heavy (whipping) cream
4 cups half-and-half	4 tablespoons unsalted butter,
1 vanilla bean split in half lengthwise	cut into bits
	1 cup (4 ounces) pecans, toasted and
	chopped *(see page 4)*

To make the vanilla base: In a large bowl, whisk together the egg yolks and sugar. Scrape the pulp from the vanilla bean and add to the egg mixture. In a large, heavy saucepan over high heat, bring the cream, half-and-half, and vanilla bean to a boil. Remove from heat and slowly pour into the yolk mixture, whisking constantly. Pour back into the saucepan and cook over medium heat, stirring constantly, until the mixture coats a wooden spoon, about 5 minutes. Strain the mixture through a sieve and chill.

To make the caramel sauce: In a small, heavy saucepan, boil the water and sugar over high heat until the mixture turns a dark amber. Meanwhile, heat the cream in a small saucepan. Pour the cream into the caramel as soon as it is ready and stir with a wooden spoon. Stir in the butter. Remove from heat and let cool.

In a large bowl, mix the vanilla base and caramel sauce. Pour into an ice cream maker and freeze according to the manufacturer's instructions. When the ice cream is almost completely frozen, add the chopped pecans.

GELATO
with Toasted Pistachios and Chocolate

Steven Howard

Makes about 2 quarts

A traditional eggless gelato studded with chopped pecans and pieces of chocolate.

3 cups heavy (whipping) cream	1¼ cups sugar
1 cup milk	½ cup pistachios, chopped
½ cup half-and-half	½ cup semisweet chocolate
1 vanilla bean, split in half lengthwise	broken into small pieces

IN A LARGE BOWL, whisk together the cream, milk, and half-and-half. Scrape the pulp from the vanilla bean into the cream mixture and add the bean. Whisk in the sugar until the sugar is dissolved. Strain through a fine-meshed sieve. Freeze in an ice cream maker according to the manufacturer's instructions. Fold in the pistachios and chocolate pieces, cover, and place in the freezer overnight.

CINNAMON ICE CREAM

Stephan Pyles

Makes 2 quarts

Crème fraîche in place of cream gives this cinnamon ice cream a unique flavor.

4 cups milk	1⅓ cups sugar
½ vanilla bean, sliced in half length-wise, or 1 teaspoon vanilla extract	12 egg yolks
5 cinnamon sticks, crushed	1 cup crème fraîche *(recipe on page 8)* or heavy (whipping) cream

FILL A MEDIUM BOWL with ice and set aside for later use. In a medium saucepan, bring the milk to a boil with the vanilla bean, if using, and cinnamon sticks. When boiling, remove from heat. Add the vanilla extract, if using. Cover and let sit for 15 minutes.

Meanwhile, in the bowl of an electric mixer, whip the sugar into the egg yolks and continue whipping until the yolks are pale in color and a ribbon forms on the surface of the mixture when the beaters are lifted. Pour the milk through a fine-meshed sieve into the sugar-yolk mixture while stirring constantly. Return the mixture to the saucepan. Cook over low heat for about 5 minutes until mixture is thickened, and coats a wooden spoon (about 185°F on a candy thermometer). Immediately remove from heat, place the saucepan on top of the bowl of ice, and stir the custard to stop the cooking process. Stir in the crème fraîche or heavy cream and chill completely. Freeze in an ice cream maker according to the manufacturer's instructions.

CINNAMON ICE CREAM
with Raspberry Sabayon and
Tulip Shells

Kevin Graham

Serves 10

It's hard to imagine tulips lovelier than these, filled with cinnamon ice cream and fresh raspberries and served with a champagne-framboise sauce.

RASPBERRY SABAYON	TULIP SHELLS
5 large egg yolks	½ cup plus 2 tablespoons bread flour
½ cup sugar	1 cup powdered sugar
¼ cup champagne	4 tablespoons unsalted butter, melted
2 tablespoons framboise or other	3 tablespoons heavy (whipping) cream
raspberry liqueur	½ teaspoon vanilla extract
1¼ cups heavy (whipping) cream	3 large egg whites
	Pinch of salt

CINNAMON ICE CREAM	
2 cups heavy (whipping) cream	2 cups fresh raspberries
2 cups milk	¼ cup powdered sugar, sifted
¾ cup sugar	10 large fresh mint leaves
3 cinnamon sticks	
10 large egg yolks	

To MAKE THE RASPBERRY SABAYON: In a double boiler over simmering water, whisk the egg yolks, sugar, champagne, and liqueur. Cook for 10 minutes, or until the mixture thickens and coats a wooden spoon, whisking constantly. Place in a mixing bowl set over a bowl of ice and whip until cool.

In the bowl of an electric mixer, whip the cream until stiff peaks form and gently fold into the cooled egg yolk mixture. Cover and refrigerate until ready to use. This may be made up to 2 days in advance.

To make the cinnamon ice cream: In a large, heavy saucepan over medium heat, bring the cream, milk, sugar, and cinnamon sticks to a boil. Remove from heat and remove the cinnamon sticks. In the bowl of an electric mixer, whisk the egg yolks until smooth. Add the hot cream mixture to the yolks a little at a time, whisking constantly. Strain into another large, heavy saucepan and cook, stirring constantly with a wooden spoon, for about 10 minutes, or until the mixture is thick enough to coat the back of the spoon. Remove from heat and let cool to room temperature. Pour into an ice cream maker and freeze according to the manufacturer's instructions. (If you do not have an ice cream maker, place the bowl in the freezer and stir every 10 or 15 minutes until the ice cream sets.)

To make the tulip shells: Preheat the oven to 400°F. Grease 2 or 3 baking sheets with vegetable oil. Invert eight 6-ounce custard cups on a flat work surface near the oven. Into a large bowl, sift together the flour and powdered sugar. Gradually stir in the melted butter. Stir in the cream, vanilla, egg whites, and salt. Drop 1 tablespoonful of batter onto a greased baking sheet and, using the back of the spoon, form a 5-inch circle. Repeat, spacing the circles at least 3 inches apart. Depending on the size of the tray, you may only be able to fit 2 or 3 shells per sheet.

Bake one tray at a time in the center of the preheated oven for 15 minutes, or just until the edges are brown; watch closely to avoid overbaking. Using a spatula, carefully lift one cookie onto an inverted custard cup. Place another custard cup on top. Repeat to make 10 tulip shells, working quickly while the cookies are still hot and pliable, and removing the cookies from the custard cups when cool to use the cups again. The cookie shells are very fragile, so handle them gently. The cookies take only a few seconds to cool, so if they harden up before they've been removed from the pan, they can be placed back in the oven for a few seconds to warm and soften. If not using immediately, store in a large airtight container until ready to use.

To serve, spoon a circle of raspberry sabayon onto each of 10 chilled serving plates. Place a tulip shell in the center of each plate. Fill each shell with cinnamon ice cream and raspberries. Dust with powdered sugar and garnish with a mint leaf.

CINNAMON PECAN ICE CREAM

Susan Feniger and Mary Sue Milliken

Makes 2 quarts

Cinnamon ice cream made with brown sugar and crème fraîche and studded with pecans.

8 egg yolks	Pinch of salt
1¼ cups packed brown sugar	1½ cups crème fraîche
2½ cups milk	*(recipe on page 8)* or sour cream
2 cinnamon sticks	1¼ cups (5 ounces) pecan halves,
1 teaspoon vanilla extract	toasted and chilled *(see page 4)*
1 teaspoon ground cinnamon	

IN THE BOWL OF AN ELECTRIC MIXER, whip the egg yolks and brown sugar until light; set aside. In a medium saucepan, bring the milk and cinnamon sticks to a full, rolling boil. Whisk the boiling milk gradually into the egg yolk mixture and let stand until cool; strain through a fine sieve. Whisk in the vanilla extract, ground cinnamon, salt, and crème fraîche or sour cream.

Freeze in an ice cream maker according to the manufacturer's instructions. When frozen, fold in the chilled pecans. For best flavor and texture, use within 3 to 4 days.

CRÈME ANGLAISE ICE CREAM

Marcel Desaulniers

Makes 1½ quarts

Myers's dark rum is the secret ingredient in this ice cream.

1¾ cups heavy (whipping) cream

1¼ cups half-and-half

½ cup whole milk

1½ cups sugar

¾ cup egg yolks (about 9 large yolks)

¼ cup Myers's dark rum

IN A 2½-QUART SAUCEPAN, heat the cream, half-and-half, and milk over medium-high heat. When the mixture is hot, add ¾ cup of the sugar and stir to dissolve. Bring the mixture to a boil.

While the cream-milk mixture is heating, place the egg yolks and remaining ¾ cup sugar in the bowl of an electric mixer. Beat the eggs on high for 2 to 2½ minutes. Scrape down the sides of the bowl, then beat on high for an additional 1½ to 3 minutes, or until slightly thickened and pale in color. At this point the cream-milk mixture should be boiling. If not, adjust the mixer speed to low and continue to mix until the cream boils. Whisk the boiling cream into the beaten egg yolks. Return this mixture to the saucepan and heat over medium high heat, stirring constantly. Cook the custard until it coats a wooden spoon, (a temperature of 185°F), about 2 to 4 minutes. Add the rum and blend thoroughly. Transfer to a bowl, place in a bowl of ice, and stir until cool (40 to 45°F).

Freeze in a ice cream freezer according to the manufacturer's instructions. Several hours before serving, transfer to a plastic container and place in the freezer. Serve within 3 days.

GRAPE ICE CREAM

Barbara Tropp

Makes 1 quart

When you live near a grape-growing region, as I do, it's easy to become fascinated with the flavors of different grapes. They are as intriguing to the tongue as wine, which is not surprising!

This is a delicate ice cream, totally dependent on the quality of the grape. Small or large, red or green, will not matter; what you need is a bursting-with-flavor grape with a good-tasting skin. I favor seedless organic grapes with thin skins for this recipe; it saves the trouble of seeding and straining, and they taste better.

Grape ice cream is a fleeting beauty. Freeze it shortly after blending, and eat it within a day.
—Barbara Tropp

½ cup plus 1 to 2 tablespoons sugar

Zest of 1 well-scrubbed tangerine, orange, or lemon

12 ounces seedless grapes with thin, tasty skins, stemmed (such as Red Flame or Thompson seedless)

2 cups half-and-half

1½ to 2 teaspoons freshly squeezed ginger juice*

Grape clusters, blood orange slices, or candied kumquat slivers for garnish

IN A BLENDER OR FOOD PROCESSOR, place ½ cup of the sugar. Grate a bit of citrus zest directly onto the sugar, more or less as the spirit moves you. Don't grate any of the bitter white pith. Process for 30 seconds to infuse the sugar with the zest. Add the grapes and process until pureed. Scrape the mixture into a large nonaluminum bowl. Stir in the half-and-half. Taste, then add the remaining sugar if and as needed until the mixture tastes a touch too sweet (in order to be balanced once frozen). Add the ginger juice by half teaspoonfuls until the flavor rounds on your tongue.

Freeze in an ice cream maker according to the manufacturer's instructions. Store with a piece of plastic wrap pressed directly on the surface. Let soften slightly before serving. Garnish with grape clusters, blood orange slices, or slivers of candied kumquat.

To juice ginger, slice a knob of peeled fresh ginger and process in a home vegetable juicer, or grind in a blender or food processor and squeeze the juice through cheesecloth. Strain through a fine-meshed sieve.

LEMON CURD ICE CREAM

Anne Rosenzweig

Makes 2½ quarts

Tart and rich, this ice cream tastes just like frozen lemon curd.

8 eggs	1½ cups (3 sticks) cold butter,
8 egg yolks	cut into small bits
2 cups sugar	6 cups crème anglaise
2 cups fresh lemon juice	*(recipe on page 2)*
Grated zest of 2 lemons	Grated zest of 4 lemons

TO MAKE THE LEMON CURD: In a large saucepan, thoroughly whisk the eggs, yolks, sugar, and lemon juice and zest. Cook over medium heat until warm. Whisk in the butter gradually. Cook and whisk until the mixture thickens and the whisk leaves a trail when it is drawn across the surface; do not boil. The curd will be the consistency of pudding. Strain through a fine-mesh sieve. Cover the surface with plastic wrap and chill.

In a large bowl, mix the chilled curd with the crème anglaise and zest. Freeze in an ice cream maker according to the manufacturer's directions.

POMEGRANATE ICE CREAM

Barbara Tropp

Yields 1 quart

Here's an unusual ice cream with a delicious tang of sourness. The color is soft pink and the texture is very smooth. Garnished with a sprinkle of fresh pomegranate seeds and/or served in a ring of blood orange slices, this is one interesting scoop.

If you don't have a juicer, unsweetened pomegranate juice can be found in natural or Middle Eastern food stores. It has a rather odd smell, which happily disappears in freezing. This ice cream holds its flavor for a day or two. The unfrozen mixture should be frozen promptly. This is a nice à la mode partner with a pastry. If you're serving it on its own, try a drizzle of bittersweet chocolate sauce.

—Barbara Tropp

1 cup unsweetened pomegranate juice,*

    or 1 to 2 pounds (4 to 6) pomegranates

2 cups half-and-half

½ cup plus 1 to 2 tablespoons sugar

1 tablespoon grenadine syrup or crème de cassis

3 to 4 teaspoons freshly squeezed and strained lemon juice

TO JUICE POMEGRANATES: Cut the pomegranates in half and juice with a hand citrus juicer, being careful not to crush the white kernels. They will give a bitter taste to the juice.

In a medium nonaluminum bowl, mix the pomegranate juice, half-and-half, and ½ cup of the sugar. Let sit for 15 minutes, then stir to recombine. Taste and add the remaining sugar if and as necessary so the mixture is a touch too sweet (in order to be balanced once frozen). Stir in the grenadine or crème de cassis, then add the lemon juice by half-teaspoonfuls to taste.

Freeze in an ice cream maker according to the manufacturer's instructions. Store in an airtight plastic container in the freezer, with a piece of plastic wrap pressed directly on the surface. Let soften slightly before serving.

Available in Middle Eastern food markets.

SAMBUCA ICE CREAM

Lydia Shire

Makes 1½ quarts

Even people who don't drink alcohol or coffee may not be able to resist this anise liqueur-flavored ice cream made with ground espresso.

4 cups heavy (whipping) cream

¾ cup sugar

6 egg yolks

¼ cup Sambuca liqueur

1 teaspoon anise oil*

2 tablespoons finely ground espresso

IN THE BOWL OF AN ELECTRIC MIXER, blend all the ingredients except the ground espresso. Mix well and chill. Freeze the mixture in an ice cream maker according to the manufacturer's instructions. When frozen, fold in the ground espresso to form streaks and swirls; do not overmix.

You can find anise oil on the spice rack of better grocery stores or specialty food stores.

SWEET CHERRY SUNDAE

Jimmy Schmidt

Serves 4

On a hot summer's evening it's hard to find a better way to cool off than with vanilla ice cream in a cherry-red wine sauce sweetened with honey.

1 pound sweet cherries, stemmed and pitted

1 cup dry red wine, preferably Pinot Noir, or dry white wine

½ cup honey

4 scoops of your favorite vanilla ice cream or frozen yogurt

4 fresh mint sprigs for garnish

HEAT A LARGE NONSTICK SKILLET over high heat until almost smoking, about 5 minutes. Add the cherries to the pan and cook until tender, about 3 minutes, stirring constantly to prevent excessive browning. Add the wine and honey. Cook until the sauce is thick enough to coat the back of a spoon, about 3 minutes. Transfer to a bowl and set aside.

Place a scoop of ice cream in the center of each serving bowl. Divide the warm cherries and sauce over the ice cream. Garnish with mint and serve immediately.

WILD-BLACKBERRY ICE CREAM

Jasper White

Makes 2 quarts

This recipe can be used as a model for any berry ice cream. If you are using less-seedy berries, you can fold in a cup or two of whole berries at the very end.
—Jasper White

4 cups fresh wild blackberries

2 cups milk

16 egg yolks

1 cup sugar

3 cups chilled heavy (whipping) cream

PICK THROUGH THE BERRIES to remove any stems or leaves. Press the berries through a medium-fine strainer or a food mill. You should have 2 cups of puree; set aside.

In a medium, heavy saucepan, warm the milk. In a large bowl, whisk together the egg yolks and sugar and add the warm milk gradually, stirring constantly until all the milk is added. Return to the saucepan and cook over low heat, stirring constantly, until the custard coats a spoon (170° to 175°F), about 3 to 5 minutes.

Pour the heavy cream into a large bowl. Strain the custard into the cream. Stir in the blackberry puree. Mix well, then chill thoroughly. Freeze in an ice cream maker according to the manufacturer's instructions.

VANILLA BEAN ICE CREAM

John Downey

Makes 2 quarts

Our favorite vanilla bean ice cream ever. It was worth writing an entire book to get John Downey to part with this recipe.

10 large egg yolks

1¼ cups sugar

3 cups heavy (whipping) cream

1 cup milk

One 6- to 8-inch vanilla bean

IN A LARGE STAINLESS STEEL BOWL that will fit into a saucepan, cream the yolks and sugar together until pale yellow in color. Measure the cream and milk into a medium saucepan. Split the vanilla bean lengthwise and, using a small knife, scrape the tiny seeds into the cream, add the vanilla bean, and bring the cream slowly to a boil. Remove from heat and remove the vanilla bean.

Pour the hot cream mixture slowly into the egg and sugar mixture, stirring constantly. Place the bowl over simmering water in a saucepan and continue to cook, stirring constantly, until the mixture thickens enough to coat the back of a spoon. (Dip the spoon into the sauce and run your finger across the back of the spoon; if the sauce quickly recoats the stripe, it is not ready.) As soon as it reaches this point, remove the bowl from the simmering water.

Pour the sauce through a fine-meshed strainer into a bowl to remove any lumps or curdling. Place the bowl in a bowl of ice and stir occasionally until cooled. Freeze in an ice cream maker according to the manufacturer's instructions.

Frozen Desserts

FROZEN NOUGAT
Flavored with Candied Fruits and Pureed Mint

Hubert Keller

Make one 8-cup terrine; serves 15

This recipe should be prepared one day before serving so the unusual flavors can marry and the best consistency can be achieved.

3½ cups heavy (whipping) cream	¾ cup (6 ounces) mixed candied fruit
10 to 12 fresh mint leaves	2 cups fresh or thawed unsweetened
1¼ cups sugar	frozen raspberries
3½ tablespoons water	1 teaspoon fresh lemon juice
½ cup (about 4) egg whites	

IN A DEEP BOWL, chill 3 cups of the cream in the refrigerator. When thoroughly chilled, whip the cream, cover, and refrigerate. In a small, heavy saucepan, bring the remaining ½ cup cream to a boil and blanch the mint leaves in it for about 2 minutes. Blend the mixture in a blender until pureed to a bright green liquid. Strain and refrigerate.

In a small, heavy saucepan, combine 1 cup of the sugar and the water. Cook over medium heat for about 5 minutes until the syrup reaches 240°F or the soft ball stage (a small quantity of the syrup dropped into ice water will form a soft ball).

Meanwhile, in the clean, dry bowl of an electric mixer, place the egg whites and beat slowly at first, then faster until stiff peaks form. Reduce the speed of the beater to low and pour a thin stream of the hot sugar syrup into the egg whites. Continue beating on low speed until the mixture has cooled; chill.

Gently fold the meringue into the whipped cream. Then fold in the candied fruit and the fresh mint cream until well blended together. Pour the mixture into an 8-cup terrine, filling the mold to the rim. Smooth the surface with a spatula. Cover and freeze overnight.

TO PREPARE THE RASPBERRY SAUCE: In a blender or food processor, puree the raspberries along with the remaining ¼ cup sugar and the lemon juice. Strain through a fine-meshed sieve to remove the seeds.

Just before serving, wrap a hot wet towel around the terrine for 1 minute to loosen the edges, then invert the terrine on a flat, chilled plate and unmold. Slice the nougat with a bread knife and serve on plates pooled with raspberry sauce.

FROZEN MACADAMIA NUT BOMBE

with Macerated Fruit and Vanilla Custard Sauce

Stephan Pyles

Serves 10

The center of this impressive dessert is filled with chopped macadamia brittle in a vanilla custard, and the sliced bombe is served with macerated fresh fruit.

2 cups chilled heavy (whipping) cream

½ teaspoon vanilla extract

3 egg whites at room temperature

Pinch of cream of tartar

Pinch of salt

¾ cup sugar

¼ cup water

MACADAMIA NUT BRITTLE

½ cup (2½ ounces) unsalted macadamia nuts

½ cup sugar

3 tablespoons water

VANILLA CUSTARD SAUCE

2 cups milk

1 vanilla bean, split in half lengthwise

⅔ cup sugar

6 egg yolks

¾ cup chilled heavy (whipping) cream or crème fraîche

(recipe on page 8)

Fruits of choice, macerated with

¼ cup sugar or to taste

IN A CHILLED DEEP BOWL, whip the cream and the vanilla extract until almost firm; set aside. In the bowl of an electric mixer, beat the egg whites with the cream of tartar and salt until they are stiff but not dry.

In a medium, heavy saucepan, boil the granulated sugar and water over high heat for 5 minutes to form a thick syrup, about 210°F on a candy thermometer. With the mixer on low, pour the syrup a little at a time into the egg whites. When the syrup is completely incorporated, beat vigorously until smooth. Set the bowl in a bowl of ice and continue to beat until the mixture is thick and cool. Fold into the whipped cream. Spoon the mixture into a 10- or 12-cup mold or bowl and freeze for at least 2 hours. Place another empty 10- or 12-cup bowl in the freezer to chill.

TO MAKE THE MACADAMIA NUT BRITTLE: Preheat the oven to 350°F. Lightly oil a baking sheet. Place the macadamia nuts on a dry baking sheet pan and toast, turning once or twice, until lightly browned, about 5 to 7 minutes. In a small, heavy saucepan, boil the sugar and water over high heat for about 5 minutes to form a light caramel, about 325°F on a candy thermometer. Immediately add the warm macadamia nuts and stir for a few seconds to distribute the nuts throughout the caramel. Pour the caramel onto the prepared pan, spreading it with a spatula. Set aside to cool and harden, then chop into ⅛-inch pieces.

TO MAKE THE VANILLA CUSTARD SAUCE: In a medium saucepan, bring the milk and vanilla bean to a boil. Remove from heat and cover; let sit for 15 minutes. Meanwhile, in a medium bowl whisk the sugar and yolks until pale in color. Bring the milk back to a boil and slowly pour the milk through a strainer into the yolks while stirring. Remove the vanilla bean.

Pour the strained mixture back into the saucepan and cook over low heat, stirring constantly with a wooden spatula. Scrape the sides and bottom and continue cooking for about 10 minutes, or until the mixture reaches 185°F on a candy thermometer and coats the spatula. Immediately remove from the heat, place in a bowl of ice, and stir the mixture to cool. Stir in the cream or crème fraîche, cover with plastic wrap, and chill thoroughly.

When the meringue mixture has set around the edges, take the mold and the empty bowl from the freezer. Scoop out the center of the meringue mixture, leaving a 1-inch layer on the sides and bottom, and place in the chilled bowl. Add the chopped macadamia brittle and 1 cup of the vanilla custard sauce. Mix well. Pour the mixture back into the center of the meringue mold and spread to level it. Return to the freezer for 2 to 3 hours. The center should not be as hard as the edges and should remain a little creamy.

Invert the bowl onto a large plate and place a hot wet towel around the bowl for 1 minute to release the bombe. Slice into 10 portions and serve with the remaining vanilla custard sauce and macerated fruit.

KUMQUAT SEMIFREDDO
Nancy Silverton
Makes one 10-inch semifreddo; serves 8 to 10

My favorite of Nancy Silverton's vast and varied repertoire, this citrusy treat with walnut meringue is served with passion fruit sorbet.

WALNUT MERINGUE	SEMIFREDDO
¾ cup (3 ounces) walnuts, toasted *(see page 4)*	2 egg yolks
½ cup plus 1 tablespoon powdered sugar, sifted	2 teaspoons sugar
	¼ cup kumquat syrup *(recipe follows)*
2 egg whites	½ cup heavy (whipping) cream, whipped
3 tablespoons granulated sugar	3 tablespoons chopped nougatine *(left)*
	1 ounce semisweet chocolate, chopped
NOUGATINE	½ cup candied kumquats, chopped *(recipe follows)*
1¼ cups sugar	
⅓ cup water	
½ cup (2½ ounces) blanched almonds	Passion Fruit Sorbet *(recipe follows)*

To MAKE THE WALNUT MERINGUE: Preheat the oven to 300°F. Line a baking sheet with baking parchment or grease it. In a blender or food processor, grind the walnuts with the powdered sugar until fine. In the clean, dry bowl of an electric mixer, whip the egg whites on low speed until frothy. Increase the speed and whip until soft peaks form. Add the sugar and whip until stiff. Fold the walnut mixture into the egg whites. Spoon into a pastry bag fitted with a No. 3 plain tip. Pipe onto the prepared baking sheet into a solid 8- to 10-inch circle. Bake in the preheated oven until the meringue peels away from the paper, about 25 minutes. Let cool.

TO MAKE THE NOUGATINE: In a medium, heavy saucepan, simmer the sugar and water until light golden. Remove from heat and quickly stir in the blanched almonds. Immediately spread out on a sheet of aluminum foil. Let cool thoroughly, then chop.

TO MAKE THE SEMIFREDDO: In the bowl of an electric mixer, mix the egg yolks and the sugar until light. In a double boiler over simmering water, heat the kumquat syrup. Whisk into the egg yolk mixture. Place the bowl in a bowl of ice and continue to whisk as the mixture cools. When the mixture is cool, fold in the whipped cream, nougatine, chopped chocolate, and candied kumquats.

To assemble, line a baking sheet with baking parchment or waxed paper. Place an 8-inch pastry ring or springform pan form on the prepared baking sheet. Fit a walnut meringue into the ring or form, trimming to fit if necessary. Cover the meringue with the kumquat semifreddo to the top of the ring or form. Freeze until the semifreddo is firm. With a hot, wet towel, heat the pastry ring or form and remove. Refreeze until firm, about 2 hours. Place a 10-inch pastry ring or pan form around the semifreddo and fill in the gap between the semifreddo and the 10-inch ring or form with the passion fruit sorbet; freeze, about 2 hours. When solid, with a hot damp towel, heat the pastry ring or form and remove. Refreeze if necessary. To serve, cut into wedges and serve on top of a pool of melted passion fruit sorbet.

Candied Kumquats and Kumquat Syrup

6 ounces kumquats

⅓ cup sugar

1 cup water

1 tablespoon corn syrup

Slice the kumquats in half and remove and discard the pulp and seeds. In a medium saucepan, bring the sugar, water, and corn syrup to a boil, and add the kumquats. Simmer until the syrup is thick and the kumquats are soft, about 10 minutes. Drain the kumquat syrup from the candied kumquats and reserve.

Passion Fruit Sorbet

¾ cup water

½ cup sugar

3 tablespoons light corn syrup

2 cups passion fruit puree*

1 tablespoon fresh lemon juice

In a large saucepan, heat the water, sugar, and corn syrup until the sugar completely dissolves. Remove from the heat. Stir in the passion fruit puree and the lemon juice; let cool. Freeze in an ice cream maker according to the manufacturer's instructions.

Passion fruit puree is available at finer specialty food stores, or it can be ordered from Made in France; 2748 Clearwater Street, Los Angeles, CA 90039; Telephone (213) 663-6027.

FROZEN MANGO MOUSSE IN COCONUT TUILES

Anne Rosenzweig

Serves 8

From New York City, not Hawaii, comes this tropical mousse flavored with Cointreau and fresh lime juice, and served in coconut cookies.

FROZEN MANGO MOUSSE	COCONUT TUILES
3 pounds ripe mangoes	2 cups sugar
¾ cup superfine sugar	1 cup egg whites (about 8 large egg
1 tablespoon Cointreau	whites)
3 tablespoons fresh lime juice	1 cup unbleached all-purpose flour
2 egg whites	6 cups unsweetened dried coconut flakes
⅓ cup heavy (whipping) cream,	¾ cup clarified unsalted butter
whipped	*(recipe on page 4)*

To make the frozen mango mousse: Peel, pit, and chop the mangoes. Puree in a blender or food processor. In a medium bowl, mix the mango puree, sugar, Cointreau, and lime juice. In the dry, clean bowl of an electric mixer, beat the egg whites until soft peaks form; fold into the puree. Fold in the whipped cream. Freeze in an ice cream maker according to the manufacturer's instructions.

To make the coconut tuiles: Preheat the oven to 325°F. Line 2 baking sheets with baking parchment or aluminum foil and butter the paper or foil. In a large bowl, mix together the sugar, egg whites, flour, and coconut until blended. Using about 1 cup of batter for each cookie, place 4 cookies on each baking sheet, leaving 3 inches between cookies. Coat your hand with the clarified butter and flatten each cookie into a round shape. Bake in the preheated oven until golden, about 10 to 15 minutes. With a spatula, remove the cookies from the baking sheet while still warm and drape each one over an inverted coffee cup to make a cup shape; let cool. (If the cookies harden before they can be shaped, place them back in the oven for a few seconds to warm and soften.) Fill each cup with frozen mango mousse and serve at once.

FROZEN GRAND MARNIER "SOUFFLÉ"

Georges Perrier

Serves 6 to 8

A soufflé like no other. Serve this creamy treat after it sets up in the freezer.

1 cup sugar

⅓ cup water

8 egg yolks

⅓ cup Grand Marnier

3 cups heavy cream, whipped to soft peaks

WRAP A ONE QUART soufflé dish in aluminum foil, giving it a collar 6 inches high.

In a heavy medium saucepan over medium-high heat stir the sugar and water until the sugar is dissolved. Cook for about 5 to 7 minutes until the syrup reaches 250°F or the hard ball stage (a small quantity of syrup dropped into ice water will form a ball that will keep its shape but still be pliable).

In the bowl of an electric mixer place the egg yolks. Whisking vigorously by hand, pour a thin stream of the hot sugar syrup into the egg yolks. Then whip on medium speed until the mixture is cool and very thick, about 15 to 20 minutes. Stir in the Grand Marnier. Fold in the whipped cream. Turn into the prepared soufflé dish. Cover and freeze overnight.

To serve, peel off the aluminum foil to give the effect of a soufflé.

Robert Del Grande   Marcel Desaulniers   Susan
Feniger & Mary Sue Milliken   Ken Frank   Kevin
Graham   Jan Joho   Emeril Lagasse   Emily
Luchetti   Nick Malgieri   Bruce Marder
Michael McCarty   le   Seppi Renggli
  Anne Rosenzwei   ny Schmidt   John
Sedlar   Piero Selvaggio   Jackie Shen   Nancy
Silverton   Joachim Splichal   Jacques Torres
Barbara Tropp   Charlie Trotter   Jonathan Waxman
  Jasper White   Barry Wine   Alan Wong

CUSTARDS, PUDDINGS, AND SOUFFLÉS

Custards

GINGERED COUSCOUS CRÈME BRÛLÉE

Stephan Pyles

Makes eight 4-ounce custards

Couscous scented with cinnamon is incorporated into the custard in this unusual version of the classic dessert.

8 ounces fresh ginger, peeled and thinly sliced

8 egg yolks

1 cup sugar

3 cups heavy (whipping) cream

½ vanilla bean, cut in half lengthwise

Cinnamon Couscous (recipe follows)

3 tablespoons chopped candied ginger

IN A SMALL SAUCEPAN, place the ginger and cover with water. Boil for 30 seconds and drain, reserving the blanched ginger. In a double boiler, whisk the egg yolks and 6 tablespoons of the sugar vigorously over simmering water until the mixture thickens and a ribbon is formed on the surface of the mixture when the beaters are lifted, about 3 to 5 minutes. The mixture should resemble a thick hollandaise sauce. You may need to take the double boiler off the heat briefly a couple of times if the mixture gets too hot and starts to cook too quickly around the edges. Leave the double boiler over the heat most of the time, however, because it is essential that the egg yolks be warmed through at this point.

In a medium saucepan, bring the cream to a boil with the vanilla bean and blanched ginger. Slowly strain into the yolks while stirring. Cook in the double boiler over not quite simmering water for 5 to 10 minutes, stirring occasionally, until the custard is slightly thickened. The heat must be very low, so check the water from time to time to make sure it stays just below a simmer. The custard should never be too hot to the touch. The mixture is cooked when it is thick enough to heavily coat the back of a spoon. Strain through a fine-meshed sieve into a bowl set over ice. Fold in the cinnamon couscous and let cool, stirring occasionally. When cool, spoon into eight 4-ounce ramekins, cover, and chill for at least 2 hours.

To serve, preheat the broiler. Sprinkle 1 tablespoon of the remaining sugar evenly over each crème brûlée. Caramelize under the broiler 3 inches from the heat for 1 minute, or until the sugar browns. Chill again for 20 to 30 minutes. Garnish each crème brûlée with candied ginger.

Cinnamon Couscous

6 tablespoons milk
1 cinnamon stick
Dash of salt
½ cup couscous
1 tablespoon unsalted butter
½ teaspoon ground cinnamon

In a medium saucepan, bring the milk to a boil. Remove from heat, add the cinnamon stick, and let sit for 15 minutes; remove the cinnamon stick. Add the salt to the milk and return to a boil. Remove from heat and add the couscous all at once, stirring until all of the liquid is absorbed. Incorporate the butter with a fork, breaking up any lumps. Add the ground cinnamon; blend thoroughly.

PUMPKIN CRÈME BRÛLÉE

John Downey

Makes 10 custards

Think of this dessert as individual servings of pumpkin pie without the crust and topped with caramelized sugar, and you'll get the idea. The perfect ending to a filling holiday meal.

1¾ pounds fresh sugar pumpkin, or 1½ cups canned pumpkin puree (not pie filling)

6 large egg yolks, beaten

⅓ cup plus 5 tablespoons sugar

½ cup honey

1½ teaspoons ground ginger

½ teaspoon ground cloves

2 teaspoons ground cinnamon

2 teaspoons pure vanilla extract

4 cups heavy (whipping) cream

PREHEAT THE OVEN TO 350°F. If using fresh pumpkin, peel and remove the interior and strings; cut into 1- to 2-inch chunks. Place in a steamer over boiling water and steam until tender, about 10 minutes. Press the pumpkin through a food mill or sieve to extract all fiber, leaving a smooth puree. In a large bowl, mix together the pumpkin puree, egg yolks, ⅓ cup of the sugar, the honey, ginger, cloves, cinnamon, and vanilla. Mix thoroughly, but do not beat in additional air; the mixture should be well blended but not fluffy.

In a medium saucepan, bring the cream just to a boil. Pour it slowly into the pumpkin mixture, stirring constantly with a plastic spatula. Divide the mixture among ten 6- to 8-ounce custard cups. Place the cups in a large baking pan and add warm water to halfway up the sides of the cups.

Bake in the preheated oven for 50 to 60 minutes, or until the custards are set except for a wobbly area about the size of a quarter in the center. The tops will feel firm to the touch around the edges. Set aside to cool. When thoroughly cooled, cover each cup tightly with plastic wrap and refrigerate for 6 hours or overnight.

Preheat the broiler to the hottest setting. Unwrap the cups and sprinkle each with 1½ teaspoons of the remaining sugar. Place under the broiler to caramelize the sugar topping. Watch the browning closely; it should take about 1 to 2 minutes, and the sugar will continue to darken for a few moments after you remove the cups. This dessert is delicious served with thin orange-flavored cookies.

CRÈME BRÛLÉE AND PEARS
Poached with Quinces
Bruce Naftaly
Serves 4

Serve this vanilla-flavored custard in autumn, when pears and quinces are in season.

CRÈME BRÛLÉE	POACHED PEARS
1 cup heavy (whipping) cream	1½ cups dry red wine
2 egg yolks	1 cup sugar
⅜ cup sugar	Reserved vanilla bean half from
1 lengthwise-sliced vanilla bean half	Crème Brûlée
	1 quince, peeled, cored, and quartered
	2 ripe pears

To MAKE THE CRÈME BRÛLÉE: In a small heavy saucepan, bring the cream to a boil over medium heat. Meanwhile, in the bowl of an electric mixer, place the egg yolks and sugar. Scrape the pulp from the vanilla bean (reserve the vanilla bean half) into the mixture and beat until a ribbon is formed on the surface of the mixture when the beaters are lifted. Stir about one fourth of the hot cream into the yolks, then stir the yolk mixture into the remaining cream. Return to low heat and slowly cook until the mixture thickens and coats a spoon, stirring constantly; do not boil. Cover and refrigerate.

TO MAKE THE POACHED PEARS: In a medium saucepan, mix together the red wine, sugar, vanilla bean half, and quince. Peel, core, and cut the pears into attractive slices. Place in the saucepan and poach over medium heat until just tender, about 5 minutes. Cover and refrigerate. (The longer the pears are in the liquid the more flavorful they will become.)

To serve, pour the custard into four 6-ounce heatproof custard cups. Fan out some poached pear slices on top of each custard. Place under a preheated broiler for 1 minute, or until the pears are golden brown.

VANILLA CRÈME BRÛLÉE

Thierry Rautureau

Makes 6 custards

The classic no-frills crème brûlée.

4 cups heavy (whipping) cream
1 vanilla bean, split in half lengthwise, and scraped
10 egg yolks
½ cup plus 2 tablespoons sugar

PREHEAT THE OVEN TO 300°F. Butter six 6-ounce soufflé molds. In a medium saucepan over medium heat, bring the cream and vanilla bean to a boil. Meanwhile, in a large bowl, whisk together thoroughly the egg yolks and ¼ cup of the sugar. Slowly whisk in the boiled cream. Remove the vanilla bean.

Place the soufflé molds in a large baking pan and add warm water to halfway up the sides of the molds. Divide the custard mixture among the molds and cover them with aluminum foil. Bake in the preheated oven for about 40 minutes, or until the custard moves in one mass when shaken very gently. Let cool for about 30 minutes. Remove the molds from the water bath and chill in the refrigerator.

To serve, preheat the broiler. Sprinkle 1 tablespoon of the remaining sugar over the top of each custard. Caramelize the sugar under a preheated broiler 3 inches from the heat for 1 minute, or until a deep golden brown. Let cool for a few minutes and serve.

BANANA-MACADAMIA NUT-KAHLÚA CRÈME BRÛLÉE

Alan Wong

Serves 8

A layer of sliced bananas topped by chopped nuts and coffee liqueur forms the foundation of this crème brûlée from Hawaii.

⅔ cup plus 3 tablespoons sugar	1 banana, sliced
12 egg yolks	⅓ cup (2 ounces) unsalted macadamia
4 cups heavy (whipping) cream	nuts, chopped
1 vanilla bean, split in half lengthwise	1 tablespoon Kahlúa liqueur

IN A DOUBLE BOILER over simmering water, whisk ⅔ cup of the sugar, the egg yolks, cream, and vanilla bean for about 5 minutes, or until the mixture thickly coats the back of a spoon. Set aside and remove the vanilla bean.

Preheat the broiler. Divide the banana slices among eight 6-ounce custard cups. Sprinkle the macadamia nuts and dribble the Kahlúa over the bananas. Pour the cooked custard over the nuts and bananas; let cool. Sprinkle the remaining 3 tablespoons sugar equally over the custards. Place under the broiler, 3 inches from the heat, for 1 to 2 minutes, or until golden brown.

CRÈME BRÛLÉE IN A SWEET TACO SHELL

Vincent Guerithault

Serves 6

Guerithault's signature dessert is a caramelized custard with fresh berries, served in crisp molded cookie.

CRÈME BRÛLÉE	SWEET TACO SHELL
1½ cups plus 2 tablespoons heavy (whipping) cream	½ cup (1 stick) butter at room temperature
¾ cup sugar	⅔ cup powdered sugar sifted
1 vanilla bean, sliced in half lengthwise	4 egg whites
10 egg yolks	¾ cup plus 1 tablespoon unbleached all-purpose flour
	1 cup stemmed and sliced strawberries, whole raspberries, or blueberries, or sliced kiwis
	6 teaspoons sugar

PREPARE THE CRÈME BRÛLÉE 1 day before serving: In a medium, heavy saucepan, bring the cream, sugar, and vanilla bean to a boil. In a medium bowl, beat the egg yolks with a whisk. Whisk the cream mixture into the eggs. Cook the mixture, stirring constantly, for about 10 minutes over low heat, or until it coats a spoon; do not boil. Strain into a stainless steel bowl. Place the bowl in a bowl of ice and stir until cool. Cover and refrigerate for at least 12 hours.

TO MAKE THE SWEET TACO SHELL: Preheat the oven to 350°F. Grease 2 baking sheets. In the bowl of an electric mixer, cream the butter and sugar until light and fluffy. Gradually beat in the egg whites and flour. With a tablespoon, shape the dough into eight 3-inch circles and place them 3 inches apart on the prepared baking sheets.

Bake in the preheated oven for about 7 to 8 minutes, or until golden brown. Meanwhile, turn 6 drinking glasses, each about 2 inches in diameter at the base, upside down on the counter. Remove each hot cookie with a metal spatula and immediately drape it over a glass; repeat to mold all of the cookies; let cool until stiff. (If the cookies harden before they can be shaped, place them back in the oven for a few seconds to warm and soften.)

To serve, preheat the broiler. Remove the vanilla bean from the custard. Fill the bottom of the shells with berries and spoon the custard on top. Sprinkle the top of each custard with 1 teaspoon sugar and place under the broiler for 2 minutes, or until caramelized and light brown. Serve immediately. The "taco shells" become soft very quickly.

CINNAMON-ALMOND CUSTARD

Kim Peoples

Makes one 10-inch tart

This easy-to-prepare pudding is filled with candied lemon peel and bread crumbs and scented with cinnamon, allspice, and ginger.

1 recipe Basic Pastry *(recipe on page 6)*
2 cups (10 ounces) blanched almonds, ground
6 eggs
2 cups half-and-half
1¼ cups sugar
Pinch of salt

1 tablespoon ground cinnamon
1 teaspoon ground ginger
1 teaspoon ground allspice
1 teaspoon baking powder
2 cups dry bread crumbs (about 5 slices)
⅔ cup finely chopped candied lemon peel

PREHEAT THE OVEN TO 350°F. On a lightly floured board, roll the dough out ⅛ inch thick and 12 inches in diameter. Fit the dough into a 10-inch tart pan and trim and crimp the edges. Bake in the preheated oven until very light golden, about 10 to 15 minutes.

Increase the oven heat to 400°F. In a blender or food processor, grind the almonds to a fine meal; set aside. In the bowl of an electric mixer, beat the eggs, half-and-half, sugar, salt, cinnamon, ginger, allspice, and baking powder until thoroughly combined. Stir in the ground almonds, bread crumbs, and candied lemon peel. Pour into the prebaked tart shell and bake in the preheated oven for 40 minutes, or until set; let cool.

CAJETA FLAN

Stephan Pyles

Makes twelve 6-ounce flans

This Mexican custard is made from goat's milk.

½ cup sugar

1½ tablespoons water

1½ cups milk

½ cup heavy (whipping) cream

Cajeta *(recipe follows)*

3 whole eggs

2 egg yolks

PREHEAT THE OVEN TO 325°F. Grease twelve 4-ounce flan molds or custard cups. In a small, heavy saucepan, heat the sugar over low heat. When it begins to melt around the edges, stir slowly but continually. When fully melted, add the water all at once and stir. Divide the caramel evenly among the prepared molds or cups.

In a medium bowl, blend the milk, cream, and ½ cup of the *cajeta*. In a small bowl, lightly beat the eggs and yolks and whisk into the *cajeta*-cream mixture. Pour the mixture into the molds or cups and place them in a larger baking pan. Add warm water to halfway up the sides of the molds or cups. Cover with aluminum foil and bake in the preheated oven for 20 minutes, or until set. Refrigerate for 3 hours before unmolding.

Cajeta

⅓ cup sugar
½ cup goat's milk*
½ cup cow's milk
¼ teaspoon cornstarch
Dash of baking soda

In a small, heavy skillet, heat half the sugar over medium heat for about 7 minutes, stirring as it melts. It should be golden brown and free of lumps. Be careful not to burn; set aside. In a large bowl, mix the milks and pour ¼ cup of the milk mixture into another bowl. Add the cornstarch and baking soda to the second bowl and mix until smooth.

In a large saucepan, add the remaining sugar and the remaining ¾ cup milk and place over high heat. Stirring occasionally, bring the mixture just to the boiling point. Add the caramelized sugar all at once while stirring vigorously. Add the reserved milk-cornstarch mixture; blend thoroughly.

Cook over low heat, stirring occasionally, for 50 to 60 minutes. During the last 15 minutes of cooking, the *cajeta* will begin to thicken. Stir more frequently at this point to prevent sticking.

Cows' milk may be substituted for the goats' milk, but the flavor will be different.

BANANA GRATIN
with Pecan Custard
Kevin Taylor
Serves 4

When you're in the mood for a different kind of crème brûlée, try this vanilla-flavored pecan custard topped with bananas and burnt sugar.

7 egg yolks	2 cups (8 ounces) pecans, toasted and
⅔ cup plus 4 teaspoons sugar	coarsely chopped *(see page 4)*
3 cups half-and-half	2 bananas, halved and cut into
1 vanilla bean, split in half lengthwise	¼-inch-thick diagonal slices

IN THE BOWL OF AN ELECTRIC MIXER, beat the egg yolks and ⅔ cup of the sugar until pale in color; set aside. In a medium saucepan over medium heat, cook the half-and-half, vanilla bean, and 1¾ cups of the pecans just until the mixture comes to a boil. Remove from heat and let sit for at least 30 minutes; remove the vanilla bean. Return the mixture to medium heat and again bring just to a boil. Pour about one fourth of the mixture into the yolk mixture and blend well. Pour this mixture back into the half-and-half mixture and cook over medium-high heat until the custard coats a wooden spoon, stirring constantly. Strain through a fine-meshed sieve. Divide the custard evenly among four 6-ounce custard cups and chill thoroughly.

To serve, preheat the broiler. Top each cup with banana slices overlapped to resemble a flower. Sprinkle 1 teaspoon sugar over each custard and banana and glaze under the broiler 3 inches from the heat for 1 to 2 minutes to form a golden brown crust. Top with the reserved ¼ cup pecans.

CRÊPES AU CHOCOLATE

Jacques Torres

Makes 7 crêpes; serves 7

Crepes flavored with spirits and orange zest, filled with chocolate mousse and served with a warm orange sauce.

CRÊPES

1½ tablespoons oil

1 tablespoon sugar

2 eggs

½ tablespoon Grand Marnier

½ tablespoon rum

⅓ cup plus 2 tablespoons cake flour, sifted

2 tablespoons unsalted butter, melted

1½ cups milk

Grated zest of ½ orange

CHOCOLATE MOUSSE

2¼ ounces semisweet chocolate, chopped

1 egg yolk

2½ tablespoons unsalted butter at room temperature

2 egg whites

1 tablespoon sugar

ORANGE SAUCE

½ cup sugar

½ cup orange juice

2 tablespoons Grand Marnier

To MAKE THE CRÊPES: In the bowl of an electric mixer, beat the oil, sugar, eggs, Grand Marnier, and rum. Add the flour and mix well. Add 1½ tablespoons of the melted butter, the milk, and orange zest. Cover and chill for 30 minutes. Using a nonstick 8-inch pan on high heat, brush the pan with a small amount of the remaining butter. Pour ¼ cup of batter in the center and tilt the pan to spread the batter evenly. Cook for a few seconds on each side, or until lightly browned. Repeat, using the remaining melted butter as needed, to cook the remaining batter.

To MAKE THE CHOCOLATE MOUSSE: In a double boiler over barely simmering water, melt the chocolate until smooth. In the bowl of an electric mixer, cream the egg yolk and the butter until pale in color. Add the melted chocolate and stir until smooth. In the clean, dry bowl of an electric mixer, beat the egg whites with the sugar until stiff peaks form. Carefully fold into the chocolate mixture; cover and chill.

TO MAKE THE ORANGE SAUCE: In a medium saucepan over medium heat, stir the sugar, orange juice, and Grand Marnier. Cook until thickened, about 10 minutes.

TO SERVE: Preheat the oven to 350°F. Fill a pastry bag with the chocolate mousse. Pipe about 2 tablespoons onto one half of each crepe and fold in half. Place on a heatproof plate and heat in the preheated oven until the mousse is warm, about 5 minutes. Serve with warm orange sauce.

WILD RICE TUILES AND MARBLEIZED WHITE CHOCOLATE MOUSSE

Barry Wine

Serves 8

Ground wild rice gives a nutty flavor to these thin cookies, which are filled with a mousse of white chocolate marbled with an espresso cream.

WILD RICE TUILES

4¼ cups wild rice

1½ tablespoons granulated sugar

½ cup powdered sugar, sifted

5 tablespoons unbleached all-purpose flour

2 large eggs

Pinch of salt

2 tablespoons unsalted butter, melted

ESPRESSO MARBLE

⅓ cup heavy (whipping) cream

2 tablespoons granulated sugar

1 tablespoon instant espresso powder

2 ounces white chocolate, chopped

1 tablespoon unsalted butter

WHITE CHOCOLATE MOUSSE

½ cup heavy (whipping) cream

3 tablespoons granulated sugar

5 ounces white chocolate, chopped

2 tablespoons unsalted butter

1½ cups heavy (whipping) cream, whipped to soft peaks

2 cups fresh raspberries or other berries in season for garnish

To MAKE THE TUILES: Preheat the oven to 325°F. In an electric spice grinder or blender, grind the wild rice to a fine meal. Cream together the sugars, flour, ground wild rice, eggs, and salt until smooth. Stir in the melted butter and let the batter sit for about 30 minutes. Drop the batter by half-tablespoonfuls on a nonstick baking sheet, spreading each into a 3- to 4-inch disk with the back of a spoon; make sure the disks are 3 to 4 inches apart. Bake in the preheated oven for 5 to 7 minutes, or until the outside ¼ inch of each cookie is light brown. Remove with a spatula and let cool on wire racks.

TO MAKE THE ESPRESSO MARBLE: In a saucepan, bring to a boil the cream, sugar, and instant espresso. Meanwhile, in a blender or food processor, finely grind the chocolate and butter. Pour the hot cream mixture over the chocolate and butter in the blender or processor with the motor running. Continue to process until the chocolate is completely melted and a smooth white ganache is formed. Pour the espresso base into a large bowl and let cool.

TO MAKE THE WHITE CHOCOLATE MOUSSE: In a small saucepan, bring the cream and sugar to a boil over high heat. Meanwhile, in a blender or food processor, finely grind the chocolate and butter. When the cream has come to a boil, pour it over the chocolate and butter in the blender or processor with the motor running. Continue to process until the chocolate is completely melted and a smooth white ganache is formed. Pour the white chocolate base into a large bowl and let cool.

To finish, gently whisk the cooled white chocolate mousse into the whipped cream. When fully incorporated, quickly fold in the espresso marble, taking care to leave a marbleized pattern throughout the mousse. Pour the finished mousse into a container and refrigerate for several hours before serving.

To serve, place a tuile just off the center of the plate. Using 2 large spoons, form a spoonful of mousse into a small oval-shaped quenelle. Place the quenelle on top of the tuile and lean another tuile over it. Form another quenelle. Place this second quenelle next to the tuile to anchor it. Then stand a tuile vertically against the second quenelle. Repeat to make 8 servings. Garnish with fresh berries for color and a tart flavor contrast.

Puddings

MARK'S INDIAN PUDDING CUSTARD

Jasper White

Serves 8

This dish, just recently created by Mark Cupolo, the baker at my restaurant, is lighter than any Indian pudding you ever tasted but is true in flavor to the original dish. Unlike the original Indian pudding, this is best served cold.
—Jasper White

6 cups milk	1 cup maple sugar*
½ cup yellow cornmeal	½ teaspoon ground cinnamon
2 tablespoons unsalted butter	½ teaspoon ground ginger
1 teaspoon salt	½ teaspoon ground nutmeg
1⅓ cups heavy (whipping) cream	
4 eggs	Sweetened whipped cream and
	toasted nuts for garnish (optional)

IN A LARGE, HEAVY SAUCEPAN, bring 4 cups of the milk, the cornmeal, butter, and salt to a boil, stirring constantly to prevent sticking or scorching. Reduce heat and simmer very slowly, uncovered, for 30 minutes, or until quite thick, stirring often.

Meanwhile, preheat the oven to 325°F. In a medium bowl, mix the remaining 2 cups milk, the cream, eggs, maple sugar, cinnamon, ginger, and nutmeg, and whisk thoroughly; keep cold. Remove the thickened cornmeal from heat and whisk in the cold custard mixture. Mix completely, then strain through a coarse-meshed sieve to remove any lumps. Divide the mixture among eight 6-ounce custard cups; wipe off any spills or drops on the cups. Place the cups in a large baking pan and add warm water to halfway up the sides of the custard cups.

Cover the cups loosely with aluminum foil and bake in the preheated oven for about 40 minutes, or until the custard is set around the edges and slightly jiggly in the center when shaken.

Chill thoroughly and serve in the cups as is, or with a small dollop of whipped cream. Garnish with toasted nuts if desired.

Available in natural foods and specialty food stores.

WHITE CHOCOLATE RICE PUDDING TAMALES

with Rum Cream

Stephan Pyles

Makes 12 tamales

Unlike any other rice pudding you have seen, this version contains grated white chocolate and is steamed in corn husks, then served with a warm rum-flavored sauce.

1 cup white rice	½ teaspoon ground nutmeg
1½ cups water	½ cup golden raisins, soaked in rum
10 tablespoons sugar	to cover for 10 to 15 minutes
4 eggs, lightly beaten	12 ounces white chocolate, grated
2 cups heavy (whipping) cream	26 dried corn husks, soaked in water
½ cup milk	for at least 30 minutes*
1 teaspoon vanilla extract	
1 teaspoon ground cinnamon	Rum Cream *(recipe follows)*

PREHEAT THE OVEN TO 300°F. In a medium saucepan, bring the rice, water, and 2 tablespoons of the sugar to a boil over high heat. Cover and cook over low heat until tender, about 15 to 20 minutes. Spoon the rice into a large bowl and add the remaining sugar, eggs, cream, milk, vanilla, cinnamon, nutmeg, and raisins; mix thoroughly. Pour the mixture into a 9-inch baking pan and cover with aluminum foil. Bake in the preheated oven for 30 to 35 minutes, or until set. Remove from the oven and let cool, then mix in the grated white chocolate.

To assemble the tamales, drain and pat dry the corn husks. Tear twenty-four ¼-inch strips from 2 of the husks. These strips will be used to tie the tamales.

Place 2 husks together with the large ends overlapping by 2 inches. Spread about 6 tablespoons of the rice pudding mixture down the middle of the 2 corn husks, leaving 1 inch uncovered at each end. Fold in the long sides of the corn husk, then roll up the husk. Twist and tie each end with a corn husk strip. Repeat this procedure for the remaining tamales. Place the tamales in a steamer and steam over slowly boiling water for 5 to 7 minutes, or until heated through; the water should not come to a rolling boil. Serve warm with warm rum cream.

Rum Cream

2 egg yolks

½ cup sugar

2 cups heavy (whipping) cream

2 tablespoons dark rum

In the bowl of an electric mixer, blend the egg yolks and sugar; set aside. In a medium saucepan, bring the cream and rum to a boil, and pour half of the hot liquid into the eggs and sugar, beating vigorously. Pour this mixture back into the remaining cream, stirring vigorously to incorporate. Cook over medium heat until the mixture coats a spoon, about 5 minutes; strain.

*Available in the Mexican food section of most grocery stores or at Latino food stores or specialty markets.

STICKY COCONUT PUDDING
with Warm Macadamia-Rum Toffee Sauce
Mark Militello

Makes 6 individual puddings or one 9-inch pudding

Chopped dates make this pudding sticky and delicious. A generous amount of rum toffee is poured on top and heated till bubbly just before serving.

STICKY COCONUT PUDDING	MACADAMIA-RUM TOFFEE SAUCE
1 cup water	1 cup packed light brown sugar
½ cup (4 ounces) dates, pitted and finely chopped	6 tablespoons heavy (whipping) cream
⅔ cup unsweetened dried coconut flakes	½ cup (1 stick) plus 1 tablespoon unsalted butter
1 teaspoon baking soda	½ teaspoon vanilla extract
4 tablespoons unsalted butter at room temperature	3 tablespoons dark rum
¾ cup plus 2 tablespoons sugar	¼ cup unsalted macadamia nuts, toasted and chopped *(see page 4)*
2 eggs	
1¼ cups unbleached all-purpose flour	
⅛ teaspoon baking powder	
½ teaspoon vanilla extract	

To MAKE THE PUDDING: Preheat the oven to 350°F. Butter six 6-ounce custard cups or one 9-inch round cake pan. In a saucepan bring to a boil the water, dates, and coconut. Remove from heat and add the baking soda; set aside. In the bowl of an electric mixer, cream the butter and sugar together. Add the eggs one at a time, beating well. Into a small bowl, sift the flour and baking powder. Carefully fold into the egg mixture. Stir in the date and coconut mixture and the vanilla. Pour into the prepared custard cups or cake pan and bake in the preheated oven for 30 to 40 minutes, or until set.

Just before the pudding(s) are done, make the sauce: In a saucepan, bring the sugar, cream, butter, vanilla, and rum to a boil and simmer for 3 minutes. When the pudding(s) are done, generously pour the sauce over the pudding(s), sprinkle the nuts over the top, and return to the oven until the sauce has soaked in and is brown and bubbling, about 5 minutes.

CRISPY QUINOA PUDDING
with Pine Nuts, Carrot Sorbet, and Gingered Carrot Coulis

Charlie Trotter

Serves 6

I like to think of this as "thinking man's" rice pudding. It is much lighter than most rice puddings, and the flavor of the quinoa grain comes through much more. With the addition of carrot, this really becomes a unique combination of flavors and textures — especially as a dessert. Adding carrot was inspired by Middle Eastern pastries that use its natural sweetness instead of such a heavy reliance on sugar or honey. Also, I think ginger is the perfect touch to accentuate both the grain and the carrot, and it really ties them together as well.

—Charlie Trotter

CARROT SORBET

1 cup carrot juice

Grind of black pepper

¼ cup sugar

CANDIED CARROT

1 medium carrot

1 cup sugar

1 cup water

2 cups peanut or grapeseed oil

CARROT SAUCE

¼ cup carrot juice

Grind of black pepper

Dash of salt

¼ teaspoon minced peeled fresh ginger

¼ teaspoon cornstarch

QUINOA

⅔ cup quinoa*

1⅓ cups water

¼ cup dried blueberries or dried cherries

½ cup Crème Anglaise *(recipe on page 2)*

1 egg

1 tablespoon white flour

½ cup (2 ounces) pine nuts, toasted *(see page 4)*

1 or 2 teaspoons butter

2 teaspoons peanut oil

Crème Anglaise *(recipe on page 2)*, optional

¼ cup reserved toasted pine nuts *(above)* for garnish

$\mathcal{T}$O MAKE THE CARROT SORBET: In a small bowl, mix all the ingredients. Freeze in an ice cream maker according to the manufacturer's instructions.

TO MAKE THE CANDIED CARROT: Slice the carrot into 18 very thin, 4-inch-long lengthwise slices. In a medium, heavy saucepan, bring the sugar and water to a boil. Add the carrot slices and reduce the heat to medium. Simmer for 15 minutes, or until the slices are somewhat translucent. With a slotted spoon, remove the carrots from the syrup and place in a sieve to drain and cool. In a deep, heavy saucepan, heat the oil to 325°F, or until a slice of carrot dropped in the hot oil sizzles immediately; do not let the oil smoke. Carefully drop the carrot slices into the hot oil. They will sink to the bottom briefly, then sizzle a bit and rise. When the sizzling begins to taper off, the slices are done. Immediately remove them from the oil with a slotted spoon and drain on a screen or paper towels. As they cool, separate them and lay them flat on a baking sheet to harden.

TO MAKE THE CARROT SAUCE: In a small saucepan, warm the carrot juice, black pepper, salt, and ginger over medium heat. Sprinkle the cornstarch into the saucepan and whisk until slightly thickened.

TO MAKE THE QUINOA, rinse the grain and place it in a heavy, small saucepan with the water. Bring to a boil, then cover and simmer over low heat for about 10 minutes, or until all the water is absorbed. Stir in the blueberries or cherries.

In a medium bowl, thoroughly mix together the quinoa, ½ cup crème anglaise, egg, flour, and ¼ cup of the toasted pine nuts (reserve the remaining nuts for garnish). Divide among six 6-ounce timbale molds or custard cups. Melt the butter with the peanut oil in a nonstick sauté pan or skillet over medium heat. Unmold each timbale into the hot pan and cook on both sides until lightly browned, about 1½ minutes on each side.

TO SERVE: Place 3 candied carrot slices on the center of each plate. Place the warm quinoa timbale on the candied carrot. Place 2 or 3 scoops of carrot sorbet around each timbale and drizzle the carrot sauce around each. (If a richer effect is desired, drizzle a little crème anglaise around the plate as well.) Sprinkle a few toasted pine nuts on each plate.

Quinoa is a small delicate grain and can be found in specialty food and health food stores.

CHOCOLATE, PORT, AND PINE NUT TIMBALE

with Port Wine Sauce

Steven Howard

Serves 12

Unmolded custards rich with chopped chocolate and pine nuts, are coated with chocolate ganache and served in a port wine custard sauce.

¾ cup (3 ounces) pine nuts	¼ cup apricot jam
6 ounces unsweetened chocolate, chopped	6 tablespoons port wine
	1⅓ cups pastry flour
6 ounces semisweet chocolate, chopped	9 egg whites
1 cup (2 sticks) unsalted butter at room temperature	Port Wine Cream Sauce *(recipe follows)*
1¾ cups sugar	Chocolate Ganache *(recipe on page 5)*
9 egg yolks	White chocolate shavings for garnish

PREHEAT THE OVEN TO 350°F. Butter twelve 4-ounce timbale molds or custard cups. In a blender or food processor, grind the pine nuts to a fine meal; set aside. In a double boiler set over barely simmering water, melt the chocolates together; set aside. In the bowl of an electric mixer, cream the butter and sugar at medium speed until pale in color. Add the egg yolks and mix thoroughly. Stir in the apricot jam, port, and melted chocolates. Sift the flour into the mixture and stir it in. Stir in the ground pine nuts. In the clean, dry bowl of an electric mixer, beat the egg whites until stiff peaks form; fold into the batter. Scoop the batter into the prepared molds or cups and bake in the preheated oven until set, about 30 to 40 minutes. Let cool to room temperature. Unmold each timbale onto a plate flooded with port wine cream sauce, coat with warm ganache, and garnish with shavings of white chocolate.

Port Wine Cream Sauce

4 cups milk

1 cup port wine

12 egg yolks

1 cup sugar

In a large, heavy saucepan, mix the milk and port wine. Bring to a simmer over medium heat. Meanwhile, in the bowl of an electric mixer, beat the egg yolks and sugar until smooth. Whisk in the hot milk mixture. Pour into the large saucepan and simmer over medium heat, stirring constantly until the mixture thickens enough to coat the back of a spoon, about 5 minutes.

CHOCOLATE CROISSANT PUDDING

with Wild Turkey Sauce

Joachim Splichal

Serves 8

A rich custard, studded with toasted croissant and chopped chocolate and served with a bourbon-flavored crème anglaise.

PUDDING	WILD TURKEY SAUCE
4 cups heavy (whipping) cream	1 cup milk
1 vanilla bean, sliced in half lengthwise	1 cup heavy (whipping) cream
10 egg yolks	5 egg yolks
¾ cup plus 1 tablespoon sugar	⅓ cup plus 2 teaspoons sugar
1 croissant, toasted and cut into pieces	2 tablespoons Wild Turkey or other
2 ounces bittersweet chocolate,	bourbon to taste
chopped	

To MAKE THE PUDDING: Preheat the oven to 200°F. In a medium saucepan, heat the cream and vanilla bean over medium heat. Meanwhile, in the bowl of an electric mixer, beat the egg yolks and sugar until slightly thickened and pale in color. When the cream begins to boil, pour it into the egg yolk mixture and blend. Return the custard mixture to the saucepan and heat over medium-high heat, stirring constantly until it thickens. Strain to remove the vanilla bean and any lumps.

Mix the croissant and chocolate pieces together and distribute among eight 6-ounce individual soufflé molds. Divide the custard among the molds. Place the molds in a baking pan and add warm water to halfway up the sides of the molds. Bake in the preheated oven for 45 minutes, or until firm; let cool.

To make the Wild Turkey sauce: In a small saucepan, bring the milk and cream to a boil. Meanwhile, in the bowl of an electric mixer, mix the egg yolks and sugar until smooth. Pour the boiling milk into the egg yolk mixture and whisk until smooth. Return to the saucepan and cook over medium heat, stirring constantly until the mixture thickens and coats a wooden spoon, about 5 minutes. Add bourbon to taste. Strain the sauce and chill.

BREAD PUDDING

Jonathan Waxman (created with Toni Chiappetta)

Serves 10 to 12

This moist bread pudding is topped with caramelized Mascarpone cream.

1½ cups sugar	2¼ cups milk
1 tablespoon ground cinnamon	2¼ cups heavy (whipping) cream
1 pound (about 2 loaves) brioche or other egg bread	1 vanilla bean, split in half lengthwise
	6 eggs
½ cup (1 stick) butter, melted	Caramelized Mascarpone Cream *(recipe follows)*

PREHEAT THE OVEN TO 350°F. Butter an 8-inch Pyrex dish. Mix together ½ cup of the sugar and the ground cinnamon. Sprinkle in the buttered dish. Remove the crusts from the bread and cut the bread into ½-inch cubes. Toss in the melted butter and place on a baking sheet. Bake in the pre-heated oven for approximately 10 to 15 minutes, or until golden brown; let cool.

In a large, heavy saucepan scald the milk and cream with the vanilla bean. In a large bowl, whisk together the eggs, and the remaining 1 cup sugar. Add the scalded cream-milk mixture. Whisk until just combined and strain through a fine-meshed sieve. Place the toasted bread in the prepared Pyrex dish and pour the custard over the bread. Cover the mixture with plastic wrap, with the wrap directly touching the surface of the mixture, and let sit until the bread is soft, or overnight in the refrigerator.

To bake, preheat the oven to 300°F. Remove the plastic wrap and place the Pyrex dish in a larger baking pan. Add warm water to halfway up the sides of the dish. Cover with aluminum foil and bake in the preheated oven for about 1 hour, or until the edges are set. Remove the foil and continue to bake until lightly browned and the center is barely set, about 15 minutes. Remove from the water bath and let the pudding come to room temperature. Serve warm or at room temperature with caramelized Mascarpone cream.

Caramelized Mascarpone Cream

1½ cups sugar
1¾ cups heavy (whipping) cream
1½ cups (12 ounces) cold Mascarpone cheese

In a medium, heavy saucepan, heat the sugar over medium heat, stirring constantly until golden, about 5 minutes. Remove from heat and stir in ¾ cup of the cream. Return to heat and bring to a full boil; remove from heat.

In a medium bowl, whisk the Mascarpone and the remaining 1 cup cream together. Whisk in the caramelized sugar to taste.

BAKED LEMON PUDDING

Lydia Shire

Serves 6 to 8

Whipped cream and gingersnaps complete this tangy, warm dessert.

1 cup (2 sticks) butter at room temperature	¾ cup fresh lemon juice
1 cup sugar	1 cup milk
6 egg yolks	1 cup buttermilk
¼ cup unbleached all-purpose flour	1½ cups heavy (whipping) cream
1 teaspoon salt	6 egg whites
	Gingersnap cookies

PREHEAT THE OVEN TO 350°F. Butter an 8-by-10-inch pan. In the bowl of an electric mixer, cream the butter and sugar until light and fluffy. Add the egg yolks slowly and beat well; mix in the flour and salt. In a large bowl, blend the lemon juice, milk, buttermilk, and ½ cup of the heavy cream. Pour this mixture into the batter and beat for 1 or 2 minutes, or until smooth. In the clean, dry bowl of an electric mixer, whip the egg whites until soft peaks form; fold into the batter.

Pour the batter into the prepared pan and place in a larger baking pan. Add warm water to halfway up the sides of the pudding pan. Bake in the preheated oven until golden brown and set, about 45 minutes to 1 hour. Lightly whip the remaining 1 cup cream and serve the pudding warm, with whipped cream and gingersnaps.

Soufflés

ESPRESSO-CARDAMOM SOUFFLÉS

Gray Kunz

Makes 4 individual soufflés

Cardamom, a classic ingredient of savory Indian dishes, plays a sweet role in this soufflé.

½ cup brewed espresso	2 egg yolks
1 teaspoon ground cardamom	4 egg whites
¾ cup sugar	Sifted powdered sugar and finely
2 tablespoons butter at room temperature	ground coffee for dusting

IN A SMALL SAUCEPAN, heat the espresso, cardamom, and 2 tablespoons of the sugar until the sugar is dissolved. Strain into a small bowl and let cool to room temperature. In the bowl of an electric mixer, whip the butter with the espresso-cardamom mixture until foamy.

Preheat the oven to 375°F. Butter four 6-ounce ceramic soufflé cups. In a double boiler over simmering water, whip the egg yolks with 6 tablespoons of the sugar until frothy. Remove from heat and continue whipping until cool; set aside. In the clean, dry bowl of an electric mixer, whip the egg whites with the remaining 4 tablespoons of the sugar until stiff peaks form. Fold in the egg yolk mixture. Fill the prepared soufflé cups with the batter and bake in the preheated oven for 6 minutes, or until golden. Dust the soufflés with powdered sugar and finely ground coffee. Serve immediately.

CANDIED GINGER SOUFFLÉ

Steven Howard

Serves 6

This spicy soufflé uses both candied and fresh ginger.

½ cup plus 1 tablespoon sugar	8 eggs, separated
2 cups milk	6 crystallized ginger pieces, minced
½ cup unbleached all-purpose flour	1 teaspoon cream of tartar
1 teaspoon grated fresh ginger	
1 tablespoon butter	Crème Anglaise *(recipe on page 2)*

IN A MEDIUM SAUCEPAN, whisk together ½ cup of the sugar, milk, flour, and grated ginger. Bring to a boil, stirring constantly, until thickened. Whisk in the butter and egg yolks, and return to a boil. Remove from heat and beat in ⅛ cup of the egg whites and the crystallized ginger; let cool.

Preheat the oven to 375°F. Butter a 9-inch soufflé dish or six 6-ounce ramekins. In the clean, dry bowl of an electric mixer, beat the remaining egg whites with the cream of tartar and remaining 1 tablespoon of sugar until stiff peaks form. Fold in the cooled egg yolk mixture. Pour into the prepared pan. Bake in the preheated oven for 25 minutes, or until the soufflé is set and the top is evenly colored. Serve immediately with crème anglaise.

GRANDMA'S OMELET SOUFFLÉ

with Strawberries

Hubert Keller

Serves 2

This is a very simple and delicate dessert with an aroma of fresh eggs, sizzling butter, and fresh fruit, which sharpens your senses even more!
—Hubert Keller

3 eggs, separated	2 tablespoons butter
3 heaping tablespoons sugar	8 to 10 strawberries, stemmed
Grated zest of 1 orange	and sliced
2 tablespoons Grand Marnier, kirsch,	
Curaçao, or almost any liqueur	Sifted powdered sugar and fresh mint
you please	leaves for garnish

BEAT THE EGG YOLKS very thoroughly with 2 tablespoons of the sugar, orange zest, and liqueur until thick and pale in color. Whip the egg whites and the remaining sugar until they are stiff but not dry. Add half the egg whites to the egg yolks and mix gently. Fold in the remaining whites.

In a 10-inch nonstick sauté pan or skillet, heat the butter over medium heat. Rapidly pour in the egg mixture. The outer surface next to the edge of the pan will brown at once, and the rest will puff up after 2 to 3 minutes. Cover the sauté pan with a lid for about 1 minute, or until set and light brown.

Spoon half of the strawberries into the center of the omelet. Take the omelet pan in one hand and a warmed serving dish in the other. Holding the pan close to the dish, slide the omelet out, folding it over once as you do so. Spoon the remaining strawberries around the soufflé. Sprinkle with powdered sugar and garnish with fresh mint.

PEAR AND CRANBERRY SOUFFLÉ

with Ginger Sauce

Nick Malgieri

Serves 6

An autumn soufflé, perfect after a holiday repast.

SOUFFLÉ	GINGER SAUCE
1½ pounds ripe, fragrant pears such as Bartletts or Anjous	1 cup milk
	1 cup heavy (whipping) cream
One 12-ounce bag (3 cups) cranberries	½ cup sugar
	One 2-inch piece fresh ginger, peeled and thinly sliced, or ½ teaspoon ground ginger
1 cup sugar	
½ cup water	
6 egg whites	6 egg yolks

To MAKE THE SOUFFLÉ: Preheat the oven to 400°F. Butter and sugar a 6-cup shallow gratin dish. Peel, core, and slice the pears. In a large saucepan, bring to a boil the pears, cranberries, sugar, and water. Lower heat, and simmer about 10 minutes, until thick and jamlike. Puree in a blender or food processor; let cool.

In the bowl of an electric mixer, beat the egg whites on medium speed until they hold a firm peak. Fold in the cooled pear mixture by hand and pour the batter into the prepared gratin dish. Bake the soufflé in the preheated oven for about 15 to 20 minutes, or until puffed and slightly firm.

WHILE THE SOUFFLÉ IS BAKING, PREPARE THE GINGER SAUCE: In a medium saucepan, mix the milk, cream, sugar, and ginger, and bring to a boil. Remove from heat and let sit for 5 minutes, then return to a boil. Meanwhile, in a small bowl, beat the yolks until liquid. Beat one fourth of the boiling liquid into the yolks; beat the yolk mixture into the boiling liquid and continue beating until the sauce thickens, about 30 seconds. Strain the sauce into a bowl and stir for 1 minute to cool it slightly. When the soufflé is done, serve it immediately with the sauce.

STRAWBERRY SOUFFLÉ
with Strawberry-Orange Sauce
Nick Malgieri
Serves 6

Vary this soufflé with other fruit or berries. Use 2 cups of strained pureed fruit as a substitute for the strawberries.
—Nick Malgieri

SOUFFLÉ	STRAWBERRY-ORANGE SAUCE
4 cups fresh strawberries	2 cups fresh strawberries
¼ cup water	2 tablespoons sugar
¾ cup sugar	3 tablespoons orange juice
6 large egg whites	1 tablespoon orange liqueur
Pinch of salt	

TO MAKE THE SOUFFLÉ: Preheat the oven to 400°F. Stem and puree the berries. In an 8-cup saucepan, combine the water and sugar and bring to a boil over high heat. Cook until the syrup thickens and reaches 290°F (the soft crack stage) on a candy thermometer (when a small amount is dropped into ice water it will separate into hard threads that will bend), about 3 minutes. Increase heat and add 2 cups strawberry puree (reserving any remaining puree for the sauce), stirring to dissolve any sugar that may have hardened when the puree was added. Bring to a boil and let cool.

Whip the egg whites with the salt until they hold a soft peak. Fold in the cooled strawberry puree. Pour the batter into a buttered and sugared 8- to 9-cup shallow gratin dish. Bake in the preheated oven for about 15 minutes, or until well risen and lightly colored.

WHILE THE SOUFFLÉ IS BAKING, PREPARE THE STRAWBERRY-ORANGE SAUCE: In a blender, combine the sauce ingredients, adding any reserved strawberry puree, and blend. Pour into a saucepan, bring to a boil, and cook for 1 or 2 minutes to reduce slightly. When the soufflé is done, serve it immediately with the sauce.

Robert Del Grande ❦ Marcel Desaulniers ❦ Susan
Feniger & Mary Sue Milliken ❦ Ken Frank ❦ Kevin
Graham ❦ Jean Joho

COOKIES

Emeril Lagasse ❦ Emily
Luchetti ❦ Nick

Bruce Marder ❦
Michael McCarty ❦ ... ❦ Seppi Renggli
❦ Anne Rosenzweig ❦ Jimmy Schmidt ❦ John
Sedlar ❦ Piero Selvaggio ❦ Jackie Shen ❦ Nancy
Silverton ❦ Joachim Splichal ❦ Jacques Torres ❦
Barbara Tropp ❦ Charlie Trotter ❦ Jonathan Waxman
❦ Jasper White ❦ Barry Wine ❦ Alan Wong ❦

ALMOND BISCOTTI

Piero Selvaggio (created with Rudy Torres)

Makes 30 cookies

These almond-studded cookies are perfect with tea or coffee or as a light dessert.

1¼ cups sugar	1 tablespoon unsalted butter at
1 cup cake flour	room temperature
1 cup unbleached all-purpose flour	1 teaspoon vanilla extract
⅛ teaspoon baking soda	¼ teaspoon almond extract
⅛ teaspoon salt	¾ cup (4 ounces) whole unblanched
2 large eggs, beaten	almonds

PREHEAT THE OVEN TO 300°F. Butter and flour 4 baking sheets. In the bowl of an electric mixer, combine the sugar, flours, baking soda, and salt. Then beat in the eggs, butter, vanilla extract, and almond extract just until blended. Stir in the almonds. Turn out onto a lightly floured surface and roll into logs 4 inches in diameter and 12 inches long.

Bake in the preheated oven until golden, about 1 hour. Let cool. Transfer to a cutting board and cut about ¼ inch thick with a serrated knife. Place back on the baking sheet and bake until golden brown, about 25 to 30 minutes. Let cool on wire racks then store in an airtight container.

BISCOTTI

Alfred and Helen Portale

Makes 30 to 40 cookies

Raisins and vermouth make the difference in these otherwise traditional anise-scented biscotti.

1¾ cups cake flour	1 teaspoon vanilla extract
2 cups unbleached all-purpose flour	1 cup (7 ounces) hazelnuts, toasted
2¼ cups sugar	and skinned *(see page 4)*
1 teaspoon baking powder	1½ cups golden raisins soaked in 1
Pinch of salt	cup sweet vermouth
1½ teaspoons ground aniseed	1 egg yolk
5 eggs	2 tablespoons milk

PREHEAT THE OVEN TO 350°F. Line 2 baking sheets with baking parchment or grease them well. In a large bowl, sift together the dry ingredients twice. In a medium bowl, beat together the 5 eggs, vanilla, nuts, raisins, and vermouth. Make a well in the flour mixture and in the center pour in the beaten egg mixture. Mix until blended.

Scoop out one fourth of the batter and place on a lightly floured work surface. Roll into 4 logs, 6 inches in diameter and 12 inches long. Transfer the logs to the prepared pans. (Two logs will fit on each pan.) In a small bowl, beat the egg yolk and milk together and brush onto the logs. Bake in the preheated oven for about 20 minutes, or until golden brown.

Transfer the logs to a cutting board. Cut each into ¾-inch diagonal slices. Place the slices back on the baking sheet and bake a second time for 10 minutes. To test, break open one cookie and check to see if it is moist but not wet. Let cool on wire racks, then store in an airtight container.

HAZELNUT-PISTACHIO BISCOTTI

Steven Howard

Makes 30 to 40 cookies

Candied grapefruit rind and cinnamon are surprises in these complex flavored treats.

5 cups unbleached all-purpose flour	1 tablespoon vanilla extract
3¾ cups sugar	1 teaspoon almond extract
2½ teaspoons baking powder	3 cups (15 ounces) hazelnuts
1 tablespoon ground cinnamon	1 cup (4 ounces) shelled unsalted
6 eggs, beaten	pistachios
5 egg yolks, beaten	½ cup chopped candied grapefruit
Grated zest of 1 orange	rind
Grated zest of 1 lemon	1 egg white, lightly beaten

$\mathcal{P}$REHEAT THE OVEN TO 350°F. Line 2 baking sheets with baking parchment or grease them well. Into the bowl of an electric mixer, sift the flour, 3½ cups of the sugar, the baking powder, and cinnamon. Beat in the eggs and egg yolks, orange and lemon zests, and vanilla and almond extracts until a sticky dough forms. Stir in the nuts and grapefruit rind, and mix until well incorporated.

Turn the dough out onto a lightly floured surface and knead the dough into a cylinder. Cut into 4 equal parts and roll each into a log. Place 2 logs on each prepared pan. Press each log down to a 4-inch thickness, forming a rectangle, and brush with the egg white. Sprinkle the logs with the remaining ¼ cup sugar and bake in the preheated oven for 20 minutes, or until the logs are evenly browned and the tops spring back to the touch. Let cool to room temperature. Cut each log into 1-inch slices and bake again, cut-side down for 10 minutes, or until lightly browned. Let cool on wire racks, then store in an airtight container.

DOUBLE-CHOCOLATE BISCOTTI

Emily Luchetti

Makes 4 dozen cookies

Luchetti's chocolate-espresso biscotti are dipped in melted white chocolate after baking.

2⅔ cups unbleached all-purpose flour

1 cup unsweetened cocoa powder

1½ teaspoons baking soda

¼ teaspoon salt

2 cups sugar

1½ tablespoons finely ground espresso

4 ounces bittersweet chocolate, chopped

5 large eggs

1½ teaspoons vanilla extract

2 cups (10 ounces) hazelnuts, toasted and skinned *(see page 4)*

1 pound white chocolate, finely chopped

PREHEAT THE OVEN TO 325°F. Lightly grease 3 baking sheets. In a large bowl, mix together the flour, cocoa powder, baking soda, salt, sugar and ground espresso. In a blender or food processor, finely grind the bittersweet chocolate with 1 cup of the dry ingredients. In a medium bowl, lightly whisk together the eggs and vanilla extract. Place the dry ingredients, the ground chocolate mixture, and the hazelnuts in a blender or food processor; slowly add the eggs on low speed and mix until the dough comes together. Or, you may mix the ingredients together with a wooden spoon.

On a lightly floured board, roll the dough into 3 logs about 15 inches long. Place one on each prepared pan and bake in the preheated oven for about 25 to 30 minutes, or until the sides are firm, the tops are cracked, and the logs are no longer wet-looking on the inside. Remove the pan from the oven and lower the oven temperature to 300°F.

Cut the logs into ¼-inch-thick slices. Place them, cut-side up, on a greased baking sheet and bake for 15 minutes or until dry and firm. Let cool. While the biscotti are cooling, melt the white chocolate in a double boiler over barely simmering water. Line a baking sheet with baking parchment or waxed paper. With a knife, spread some white chocolate on one cut side of each biscotti. Place the biscotti, white chocolate-side down, on the lined baking sheet. Let cool completely on wire racks, then store in an airtight container.

CHOCOLATE CHIP SHORTBREAD

Barry Wine

Makes 25 to 30 cookies

Traditional shortbread cookies, made irresistible by the addition of bittersweet chocolate chips.

½ cup (1 stick) unsalted butter at room temperature

½ cup superfine sugar

3 tablespoons unsweetened cocoa powder

1 cup unbleached all-purpose flour

⅛ teaspoon baking powder

Pinch of salt

2 ounces bittersweet chocolate, coarsely chopped into chips

PREHEAT THE OVEN TO 325°F. Line 2 baking sheets with baking parchment or grease them well. In the bowl of an electric mixer, cream the butter and sugar until light and fluffy. Into a small bowl, sift the cocoa powder, flour, baking powder, and salt. Blend the dry ingredients into the butter mixture until just blended. Stir in the chocolate. Turn out onto a lightly floured work surface and knead lightly to combine.

Roll out the dough between 2 pieces of baking parchment or waxed paper to a ½-inch thickness and chill. When firm, cut into ½-by-2-inch rectangles. Bake on the prepared pan in the preheated oven for approximately 20 minutes, or until light golden. Let cool on wire racks, then store in an airtight container.

CHOCOLATE VALENCIENNES

Marcel Desaulniers

Makes about 3½ dozen cookies

These easy-to-prepare, buttery chocolate cookies are a nice change of pace from chocolate chip cookies.

4 ounces semisweet chocolate, broken into ½-ounce pieces

¼ heaping cup packed light brown sugar

¼ cup granulated sugar

¼ cup water

4 tablespoons unsalted butter

½ cup cake flour, sifted

PREHEAT THE OVEN TO 325°F. Line 1 or more baking sheets with baking parchment or use nonstick baking sheets. Place the chocolate in a stainless steel bowl. In a 6-cup saucepan over medium-high heat, heat the sugars, water, and butter to a boil. Pour the boiling liquid over the chocolate and stir until smooth. Add the sifted cake flour and stir until smooth.

Drop the batter by level teaspoonfuls onto the prepared or nonstick pans. The batter will spread quite a bit during baking, so only place 6 cookies on each baking sheet. Bake 1 baking sheet at a time in the center of the preheated oven for 7 to 10 minutes, or until cookies are light brown. Let cool until crisp, then transfer to a wire rack to cool completely. Keep at room temperature until ready to serve. Store in an airtight container.

COCONUT HAYSTACKS

Kim Peoples

Makes 40 to 50 cookies

Bits of chocolate make these childhood favorites taste even better than you remembered.

12 egg whites	3 tablespoons unsalted butter at room
¼ cup sugar	temperature
½ teaspoon salt	1 teaspoon vanilla extract
1⅔ cups unsweetened shredded	8 ounces semisweet chocolate,
coconut	chopped into bits

PREHEAT THE OVEN TO 375°F. Line 1 or more baking sheets with baking parchment or grease them well. In a large bowl, mix together theegg whites, sugar, salt, and 1⅓ cups of the coconut; let sit for 1 hour. Mix in the butter, vanilla, and remaining ⅓ cup coconut. Add the chocolate pieces, mixing just enough to incorporate. Using a tablespoon, drop the batter in mounds about 2 inches apart on the prepared pan(s). Bake in the preheated oven for 10 to 15 minutes, or until golden brown. Let cool on wire racks, then store in an airtight container.

JILLY'S CHOCOLATE-CHUNK COOKIES

Emeril Lagasse

Makes 26 large cookies

My youngest daughter Jilly, who is eleven going on thirty, is a big fan of these chocolate chip cookies, which she and I make often together.
—Emeril Lagasse

1 cup (2 sticks) unsalted butter at room temperature	½ teaspoon baking soda
	½ teaspoon salt
¾ cup sugar	1 cup (4 ounces) nuts, chopped (mix
¾ cup packed brown sugar	two of your favorites half and half:
1 egg	pecans, walnuts, almonds,
1 teaspoon vanilla extract	macadamias, etc.)
2¼ cups unbleached all-purpose flour	7 ounces semisweet chocolate,
1 teaspoon baking powder	chopped into chunks

PREHEAT THE OVEN TO 350°F. In the bowl of an electric mixer, cream together the butter, sugars, and egg until light and fluffy. Mix in the vanilla, flour, baking powder, baking soda, and salt to form a stiff dough. Stir in the nuts and chocolate. Form the dough into balls with 2 soup spoons and place them 2 inches apart on ungreased baking sheets. Bake for about 23 minutes, or until lightly browned. Let cool on wire racks, then store in an airtight container.

WHITE CHOCOLATE– MACADAMIA NUT COOKIES

Vincent Guerithault

Makes 48 cookies

It takes only one or two of these nutty, buttery cookies to satisfy.

1 cup plus 2 tablespoons unbleached all-purpose flour	¼ cup granulated sugar
½ teaspoon baking soda	1 large egg
¼ teaspoon salt	1 teaspoon vanilla extract
½ cup (1 stick) unsalted butter at room temperature	9 ounces white chocolate, coarsely chopped
½ cup packed light brown sugar	5 ounces (1 cup) unsalted macadamia nuts, coarsely chopped

PREHEAT THE OVEN TO 375°F. Line baking sheets with parchment paper or grease them well. Into a medium bowl, sift together the flour, baking soda, and salt; set aside. In the bowl of an electric mixer, cream the butter with the sugars until light and fluffy. Beat in the egg and vanilla. Reduce speed and beat in the flour mixture just until blended. Stir in the chocolate and macadamia nuts.

Drop the dough by tablespoonfuls about 2 inches apart onto the prepared baking sheets; flatten with the palm of your hand. Bake in the preheated oven for 4 to 6 minutes, or until firm. With a spatula, turn the cookies and bake another 4 to 6 minutes, or until lightly golden. Let cool on wire racks, then store in an airtight container.

DOUBLE-CHOCOLATE SCOOTERS

Susan Feniger and Mary Sue Milliken

Makes 72 large cookies

These dome-shaped brownielike cookies are flavored with a hint of espresso and filled with plump rum-raisins. We think they're called "scooters" for the speed with which they'll disappear.

8 ounces unsweetened chocolate, chopped	1 teaspoon salt
	8 eggs
8 cups (48 ounces) semisweet chocolate chips	3 cups sugar
	4 teaspoons vanilla extract
1 cup (2 sticks) unsalted butter	3 teaspoons finely ground espresso
1 cup unbleached all-purpose flour	1¼ cups raisins, plumped in rum to
1 teaspoon baking powder	cover for 10 to 15 minutes and drained

PREHEAT THE OVEN TO 300°F. Grease baking sheets. In a double boiler over barely simmering water, melt the unsweetened chocolate, ¾ cup semisweet chocolate chips, and butter, and stir until smooth. Remove from heat and let cool to room temperature. In a small bowl, mix the flour, baking powder, and salt together.

In the bowl of an electric mixer, beat the eggs with the sugar until the mixture is pale in color. Beat in the vanilla and ground espresso. Fold the chocolate mixture into the egg mixture, then fold in the flour mixture. Stir in the remaining 7¼ cups chocolate and the raisins. Let sit for 15 minutes. The batter will be very wet. Drop by heaping teaspoonfuls about 2 inches apart onto greased baking sheets and bake in the preheated oven for 8 to 10 minutes, or until the cookies are puffed, shiny, and cracked on top. Let cool on wire racks, then store in an airtight container.

COCONUT LACE COOKIES

Jonathan Waxman (created with Toni Chiappetta)

Makes 4 dozen cookies

You may remember a simpler version of these cookies from childhood. In this variation, Waxman adds coconut.

1½ cups sugar

¼ cup unbleached all-purpose flour

2 cups shredded coconut

1 egg white

1 teaspoon vanilla extract

1 cup (2 sticks) butter, melted

PREHEAT THE OVEN TO 350°F. In a large bowl, mix together the sugar, flour and coconut. In a small bowl, whisk the egg white and vanilla extract together lightly. Mix the melted butter into the dry ingredients, then add the egg white and mix until all is incorporated. Drop by tablespoonfuls onto parchment-lined baking sheets, leaving plenty of space between cookies as they spread a lot; place no more that 4 to 6 cookies per sheet. Bake in the preheated oven until light golden brown. Let cool and carefully remove from the tray. Store in an airtight container.

CRISP PEANUTIEST COOKIES

Kim Peoples

Makes 36 cookies

Peanut butter cookies with a double surprise: whole peanuts and coconut flakes.

½ cup (1 stick) butter at room temperature

½ cup crunchy peanut butter

1½ cups packed brown sugar

¾ cup granulated sugar

2 eggs

2½ cups unbleached all-purpose flour

1 teaspoon baking soda

½ cup dried unsweetened coconut flakes

¾ cup (5 ounces) unsalted Spanish peanuts skinned *(see page 4)*

PREHEAT THE OVEN TO 350°F. Butter 2 baking sheets. In the bowl of an electric mixer, cream the butter and peanut butter. Gradually add the sugars and beat until light and fluffy. Add the eggs and mix well. Add the flour and baking soda, and mix well. Stir in the coconut and peanuts. Drop by tablespoonfuls onto the prepared baking sheets. Bake in the preheated oven for 12 to 15 minutes, or until golden. Let cool on wire racks, then store in an airtight container.

MARK'S BUTTERSCOTCH ICEBOX COOKIES

Jasper White

Makes 4 dozen cookies

Mark Cupolo, the pastry chef at my restaurant, makes cookies every day that we serve, compliments of the house, at the end of the meal. Mark makes so many great cookies I couldn't decide which recipe to ask for, so I left it up to him. This is one of his favorites — and mine too.

—Jasper White

¾ cup (1½ sticks) unsalted butter at room temperature
1 cup packed light brown sugar
1 egg
1 teaspoon vanilla extract
2 cups sifted pastry flour or unbleached all-purpose flour

1 teaspoon baking soda
½ teaspoon salt
¼ cup pecan halves, toasted and finely chopped *(see page 4)*

IN THE BOWL OF AN ELECTRIC MIXER, cream the butter and brown sugar until light and fluffy. Be sure to scrape down the sides of the bowl. In a small bowl, whisk together the egg and vanilla. Beat into the butter and sugar mixture, again scraping down the bowl to ensure thorough mixing. Into a medium bowl, sift together the flour, baking soda, and salt. Add to the other ingredients and mix until combined. Stir in the chopped nuts. Using plastic wrap, shape the dough into a log about 1½ inches in diameter. Chill for at least 1 hour.

Preheat the oven to 350°F. Lightly butter 1 or more baking sheets. Slice the chilled dough about ¼ inch thick. Place the slices on the prepared baking sheet(s) and chill for at least 10 minutes. Bake in the preheated oven for 10 to 12 minutes, or until lightly browned. Cool thoroughly on wire racks and store in an airtight container.

PECAN GEMS

Patrick O'Connell

Makes 1 dozen cookies

*The nicest thing about pecan gems is that they're not overly sweet —
just chewy treats.*

DOUGH	FILLING
½ cup (1 stick) butter at room temperature	1 tablespoon butter at room temperature
1½ cups (12 ounces) cream cheese at room temperature	⅔ cup packed brown sugar
1 cup unbleached all-purpose flour	1 egg
	1 teaspoon vanilla extract
	1 cup (4 ounces) pecans

TO MAKE THE DOUGH: In the bowl of an electric mixer, beat the butter and cream cheese together until smooth. Thoroughly mix in the flour; the dough will be soft. Shape the dough into a ball, wrap it in plastic, and chill for 30 minutes.

Preheat the oven to 350°F. Butter 12 muffin cups. Divide the dough among the muffin cups. Form a small well in the center of each piece of dough.

TO MAKE THE FILLING: Mix together the butter, sugar, and egg until fluffy. Add the vanilla and pecans and mix thoroughly. Spoon the filling into the well of each piece of dough. Bake in the preheated oven for approximately 12 to 15 minutes, or until lightly browned. Let cool on wire racks, then store in an airtight container.

RUSSIAN TEA CAKES

Jonathan Waxman (created with Toni Chiappetta)

Makes 50 cookies

These buttery cookies are made with either walnuts or pecans, then dusted with powdered sugar.

1 cup (4 ounces) walnuts or pecans	1 cup (2 sticks) unsalted butter at room temperature
2 tablespoons granulated sugar	
2 cups unbleached all-purpose flour	1 teaspoon vanilla extract
Pinch of salt	2 cups powdered sugar, sifted

PREHEAT THE OVEN TO 350°F. Line baking sheets with baking parchment or grease them well. In a blender or food processor, grind the nuts and granulated sugar to a fine meal. Pour into a bowl and mix in the flour and salt. In the bowl of an electric mixer, cream the butter with the vanilla extract until light and fluffy. Mix in the flour mixture until the dough comes together. Wrap in plastic wrap and chill for a minimum of 1 hour.

On a lightly floured work surface, roll tablespoonfuls of the dough into balls. Place them 1 inch apart on the prepared pans. Bake in the preheated oven for 10 minutes. Turn the pan(s) around and continue baking for about 5 minutes, or until light golden brown; let cool slightly. While still warm, roll each cookie in the powdered sugar 2 times. Let the cookies cool on wire racks, then store in an airtight container.

STRUFFOLI

Nick Malgieri

Makes 72 cookies

A popular Italian Christmas pastry, struffoli are tiny, crisp fritters bound with caramel. In some regions it is traditional to prepare the caramel with honey, but I find that sugar caramel holds up better and is less sweet.
—Nick Malgieri

DOUGH	CARAMEL
1½ tablespoons unsalted butter at room temperature	1½ cups sugar
1½ cups unbleached all-purpose flour	1 teaspoon fresh lemon juice
3 large eggs	½ cup (2½ ounces) pine nuts, toasted *(see page 4)*
1 teaspoon vanilla extract	
	Candied fruit for garnish
6 cups vegetable oil for frying	

To MAKE THE DOUGH: In a large bowl, cut the butter into the flour with a pastry cutter or your fingers. In a medium bowl, beat the eggs and vanilla together and stir into the flour. Let stand for 1 minute so that the flour absorbs the liquid. On a generously floured surface, lightly knead the dough until smooth. Wrap the dough in plastic and let sit for 1 hour at room temperature.

Divide the dough into 6 to 8 pieces and roll each into a rope about ½ inch in diameter. Cut each rope into ½-inch lengths. Leave the pieces of dough to dry for a few minutes.

In a large, heavy pot, heat the oil to 350°F, or when a test piece of dough browns within 60 seconds; the oil should not smoke. Fry the pieces of dough in 2 or 3 batches for 3 to 5 minutes, or until a deep golden color. Drain the fritters on paper towels. Place the fritters in a large buttered bowl. Butter a large platter and a pair of rubber gloves.

While the fritters are still warm, prepare the caramel: In a medium, heavy saucepan, mix the sugar and lemon juice. Place over medium heat and cook, stirring occasionally, for about 3 to 5 minutes, or until the sugar melts and caramelizes to a light golden color. Do not allow the caramel to become too dark.

Pour the caramel over the fritters in the bowl and quickly add the pine nuts. Stir rapidly to coat the fritters and the pine nuts evenly with the caramel. Turn the mixture out onto the buttered platter.

Wearing the rubber gloves, quickly and carefully shape the mass of fritters into a ring with a hole in the center to resemble a Christmas wreath. Decorate with candied fruit. Loosen the wreath from the platter before the caramel hardens completely.

CHOCOLATE BROWNIES

Seppi Renggli

Makes sixty 3-by-5-inch brownies

These traditional walnut-studded brownies will sell out first at any school bake sale.

3½ cups (7 sticks) unsalted butter

7 ounces unsweetened chocolate, chopped

7 ounces semisweet chocolate, chopped

15 eggs, beaten

3½ cups powdered sugar

4 cups bread flour

2 tablespoons vanilla extract

5½ cups (22 ounces) walnut pieces

PREHEAT THE OVEN TO 350°F. Butter and flour four 9-by-13-inch cake pans. In a double boiler over barely simmering water, melt the butter and chocolate, mixing until smooth. In the bowl of an electric mixer, beat the butter-chocolate mixture and eggs for about 5 minutes. Mix in the sugar, flour, and vanilla extract. Stir in the walnuts. Pour into the prepared pans and bake in the preheated oven for 30 minutes, or until a toothpick inserted in the center comes out clean. Let cool in the pan on a wire rack, then cut. Store covered in the pan or cut and individually wrapped in plastic wrap.

Robert Del Grande ❧ Marcel Desaulniers ❧ Susan

Feniger & Mary Sue Milliken ❧ Ken Frank ❧ Kevin

Graham ❧ Jean Joho ❧ Emeril Lagasse ❧ Emily

CANDIES

Luchetti ❧ Nick ❧ Bruce Marder ❧

Michael McCarty ❧ le ❧ Seppi Renggli

❧ Anne Rosenzweig ❧ Jimmy Schmidt ❧ John

Sedlar ❧ Piero Selvaggio ❧ Jackie Shen ❧ Nancy

Silverton ❧ Joachim Splichal ❧ Jacques Torres ❧

Barbara Tropp ❧ Charlie Trotter ❧ Jonathan Waxman

❧ Jasper White ❧ Barry Wine ❧ Alan Wong ❧

CHOCOLATE BRITTLE

Kim Peoples

Makes 2½ pounds candy

This easy-to-prepare candy won't last as long as the fifteen minutes it takes to prepare.

24 ounces milk chocolate, chopped
2 cups (8 ounces) walnuts, toasted *(see page 4)*
1¾ cups raisins

IN A DOUBLE BOILER over barely simmering water, melt the chocolate. Stir in the walnuts and raisins. Spread onto a baking sheet lined with baking parchment or waxed paper. Refrigerate until firm, then break into pieces. Serve as candy or use to garnish ice cream dishes.

CHOCOLATE TRUFFLES

Kevin Graham

Makes about 4 dozen truffles

Chocolate truffles demystified, by one of New Orleans's finest chefs. He spikes them with Chambord.

1 cup (2 sticks) unsalted butter

2 cups heavy (whipping) cream

28 ounces semisweet chocolate, chopped

½ cup Chambord liqueur

½ cup unsweetened cocoa powder

½ cup powdered sugar, sifted

IN A LARGE SAUCEPAN, heat the butter and cream until almost boiling. Remove from heat and stir in the chopped chocolate until it is melted, smooth, and glossy. Stir in the Chambord. Transfer to a bowl and cover with plastic wrap placed directly on the surface of the mixture. Let cool to room temperature. Refrigerate for about 24 hours, or until very firm.

Shape the mixture into balls using a teaspoon or melon baller. Chill until firm. In a shallow dish, mix the cocoa and powdered sugar. Roll the truffles in the cocoa mixture until completely coated. Store refrigerated in an airtight container for up to 2 weeks.

DARK CHOCOLATE TRUFFLES

Vincent Guerithault

Makes 50 truffles

The success of this simple recipe depends on the quality of the chocolate used.

2 pounds semisweet chocolate, chopped

2 cups (4 sticks) unsalted butter

½ cup heavy (whipping) cream

½ to 1 cup unsweetened cocoa powder

IN A DOUBLE BOILER over barely simmering water, stir the chopped chocolate, butter, and cream over low heat until all the ingredients are melted and the mixture is smooth. Pour the mixture into a 9-by-13-inch baking pan and refrigerate until hard, a minimum of 4 hours. With a mini melon baller, scoop the mixture into balls. Roll the balls in the cocoa powder and refrigerate. The mixture remaining in the baking pan can be melted, poured into a smaller pan, and scooped into balls again.

ESPRESSO TOFFEE

Kim Peoples

Makes 30 to 40 pieces

This mocha-flavored chewy toffee features toasted pecans.

2 cups sugar

1½ cups (3 sticks) unsalted butter

½ cup water

¼ cup corn syrup

¼ cup finely ground espresso

1 cup (4 ounces) pecans, toasted *(see page 4)*

4 ounces semisweet chocolate, chopped

BUTTER A 9-BY-13-INCH CAKE PAN. In a medium, heavy saucepan, boil the sugar, butter, and water with the corn syrup until it starts to change color. Lower heat and cook until the mixture reaches 310°F on a candy thermometer or the hard crack stage (when dropped into ice water the syrup will separate into threads that are hard and brittle). Remove from heat and add the ground espresso and the nuts; stir briefly. Pour onto the prepared pan. While the toffee is hot, sprinkle the chocolate over the top. As the chocolate melts, spread with a spatula evenly over the toffee. Let cool and break into pieces.

TAMALES OF THE DEAD

John Sedlar

Makes 6 candies

The caramel lime sauce is the perfect foil for these rich chocolate tamale-shaped candies featuring a raised pattern created by wrapping the chocolates in corn husks while they cool.

In Mexico, a sweet tamale, called "the tamale of the dead," stuffed with dried fruits and nuts, is served on Dia de los Muertas (the Day of the Dead), October 31 and November 1, as a sweet remembrance of loved ones. This is our version, made with chocolate.

—John Sedlar

1 cup heavy (whipping) cream	**CARAMEL LIME SAUCE**
10 ounces semisweet chocolate, chopped	¼ cup water
	1 cup sugar
6 dried corn husks*, cut into 1½-by-3-inch pieces	1 tablespoon corn syrup
	¾ cup heavy (whipping) cream
	½ cup fresh lime juice
	Unsweetened cocoa powder for dusting
	Dyed corn husks *(method follows)*

IN A MEDIUM SAUCEPAN, heat the cream. Remove from heat and stir in the chopped chocolate until the chocolate has melted completely and is fully blended with the cream. Chill until set but still soft to the touch, 45 minutes to 1 hour.

Spoon 4 tablespoons of the chocolate mixture onto each piece of dried corn husk. Wrap the husk around the chocolate lengthwise and tuck the open end in to form a package. Wrap plastic wrap tightly around the tamale to hold the husk in place. Chill until solid, about 45 minutes.

Meanwhile, make the caramel sauce: In a heavy, medium skillet, heat the water, sugar, and corn syrup without stirring over medium-high heat until the sugar melts and turns a medium caramel color, about 10 to 15 minutes.

Remove from heat and add the heavy cream. Allow the mixture to bubble. When the caramel settles, stir with a wooden spoon. Return to heat and stir until all the sugar is melted. Remove from heat and add the lime juice. Let cool (the sauce will separate). Mix before serving.

Unwrap each tamale and peel the corn husk off, leaving a raised husk pattern; discard the husk. Dust the chocolate lightly with cocoa powder. Lay a chocolate tamale over the bottom portion of each dyed husk. Spoon the caramel sauce alongside the tamale.

Dyed Corn Husks

6 dried corn husks*
½ cup warm water tinted with 30 drops red food coloring

Wash the corn husks and let them soak in warm water to cover for 10 minutes. Remove from the water. Tear six ¼-inch strips from one of the husks. Place the bottom 2 inches of the wide end of each of the remaining husks into a bowl of the tinted warm water. Let soak until colored, about 2 hours. Remove and drain on paper towels. Gather together the non-dyed end of each husk and tie with a strip of corn husk. Pat off excess water with a towel.

Available in the Mexican food section of most grocery stores or at Latino food stores or specialty markets.

WALNUT PRALINE TRUFFLES

Barry Wine

Makes 30 to 35 truffles

As the ganache of these truffles contains no butter, it is particularly soft and luscious. The added contrast of the pralinéed walnuts results in an explosion of chocolate coupled with a crunchy bite.
—Barry Wine

PRALINÉED WALNUTS

1 cup sugar

½ cup water

2 cups (8 ounces) walnut pieces

GANACHE

1¼ cups heavy (whipping) cream

1 tablespoon instant espresso powder

12 ounces semisweet chocolate, chopped

2 tablespoons applejack

1 tablespoon vanilla extract

Pinch of salt

COATING

24 ounces semisweet chocolate, chopped

2 tablespoons mild vegetable oil, such as canola or grapeseed

½ cup unsweetened cocoa powder

To MAKE THE PRALINÉED WALNUTS: Grease a 9-by-13-inch cake pan. In a large, heavy saucepan, mix the sugar and water. Cook over medium heat, stirring, to dissolve the sugar. When the syrup comes to a boil, cover the pan with a lid and cook for 3 to 4 minutes to prevent the syrup from crystallizing. When the sugar just begins to color, add the walnuts. Stir constantly to coat the walnuts evenly, and continue cooking until the walnuts and sugar turn a deep brown. Turn the pralinéed nuts out onto the prepared pan and place in the freezer to cool. When the nuts are completely cold, chop them finely in a blender or food processor; cover and set aside.

TO MAKE THE GANACHE: In a small saucepan, bring the cream and espresso to a boil. In a medium bowl, place the chopped chocolate and pour the hot cream over it. Mix until the chocolate has completely melted. Mix in the applejack, vanilla, and salt; set aside in a cool place until the ganache is the consistency of room-temperature butter. Place the ganache in a pastry bag fitted with a plain tip. Pipe into 1-inch kisses on baking parchment or waxed paper and refrigerate until firm.

To finish, scoop a small handful of walnut praline in one hand and place a kiss in the center. Roll the kiss between your palms, coating it evenly with the praline and forming it into a ball. Repeat with each truffle, then cover with plastic wrap and place them in the freezer until very firm, 1 to 4 hours or overnight.

In a double boiler over barely simmering water, melt the semisweet chocolate with the oil. Stir until smooth. Insert a toothpick firmly into one of the frozen truffles, then dip it into the melted chocolate and oil mixture. Coat the truffle completely with chocolate, then tap the pick against the edge of the bowl several times to remove any excess. Stick the bottom of the toothpick into a 10-by-10-inch piece of Styrofoam, or place the truffle on a ¼-inch-grid wire rack with a tray underneath to catch any chocolate drips; repeat this process with each truffle. Chill for 20 minutes, or until the chocolate has set.

When the dipped truffles are firm to the touch, add several to a pie pan filled with cocoa. Roll the truffles in the cocoa to coat them evenly, then remove them to a separate plate. Store the coated truffles in the refrigerator while finishing the rest. Remove the finished truffles from the refrigerator at least 20 minutes before serving for the best flavor and texture.

Robert Del Grande ❦ Marcel Desaulniers ❦ Susan

Feniger & Mary Sue Milliken ❦ Ken Frank ❦ Kevin

Graham ❦ Jean Joho ❦ Emeril Lagasse ❦ Emily

Luchetti ❦ Nick Malgieri ❦ Bruce Marder ❦

Michael McCarty ❦ Alfred Portale ❦ Seppi Renggli

❦ Anne Rosenzweig ❦ Jimmy Schmidt ❦ John

Sedlar ❦ Piero Selvaggio ❦ Jackie Shen ❦ Nancy

Silverton ❦ Joachim Splichal ❦ Jacques Torres ❦

Barbara Tropp ❦ Charlie Trotter ❦ Jonathan Waxman

❦ Jasper White ❦ Barry Wine ❦ Alan Wong ❦

Robert Del Grande ❦ Marcel Desaulniers ❦ Susan

Feniger & Mary Sue Milliken ❦ Ken Frank ❦ Kevin

Graham ❦ Jean Joho ❦ Emeril Lagasse ❦ Emily

CAKES

Luchetti ❦ Nick ❦ Bruce Marder ❦

Michael McCarty ❦ le ❦ Seppi Renggli

❦ Anne Rosenzweig ❦ Jimmy Schmidt ❦ John

Sedlar ❦ Piero Selvaggio ❦ Jackie Shen ❦ Nancy

Silverton ❦ Joachim Splichal ❦ Jacques Torres ❦

Barbara Tropp ❦ Charlie Trotter ❦ Jonathan Waxman

❦ Jasper White ❦ Barry Wine ❦ Alan Wong ❦

AMARETTI CAKE

Lydia Shire

Makes one 10-inch single-layer cake

An almond-flavored cake with a hint of chocolate, to serve with an anise-flavored ice cream.

1 cup (2 sticks) unsalted butter at room temperature	3 ounces bittersweet chocolate, grated
1 cup granulated sugar	½ cup cake flour
5 eggs, separated	Sifted powdered sugar for dusting
Six 4-inch almond biscotti cookies	Sambuca Ice Cream *(recipe on page 141)*

PREHEAT THE OVEN TO 325°F. Butter a 10-inch springform pan. In the bowl of an electric mixer, cream the butter and sugar until light and fluffy. Gradually add the egg yolks and beat until pale in color. In a food processor or blender, grind the cookies to a fine meal. In a medium bowl, mix the ground cookies, grated chocolate, and flour, then fold into the butter mixture. In the clean, dry bowl of an electric mixer, beat the egg whites until soft peaks form. Fold the egg whites into the batter.

Spoon the batter into the prepared springform pan and bake in the preheated oven for about 1 hour, or until a knife inserted in the center comes out clean. Let cool, then remove from the pan. Sprinkle with powdered sugar and serve with Sambuca ice cream. Store at room temperature, well wrapped, for up to 3 days.

APPLE-RAISIN SPICE CAKE
with Caramel Sauce
Stephan Pyles

Makes one 10-inch single-layer cake; serves 10

A moist old-fashioned treat served with a luscious caramel sauce.

1½ cups vegetable oil	¼ teaspoon ground ginger
2 cups sugar	½ teaspoon salt
3 eggs	1 pound unpeeled apples, cored and
1 cup cake flour	chopped (3½ cups)
2 cups unbleached all-purpose flour	¾ cup (3 ounces) pecans, toasted
1½ teaspoons baking soda	*(see page 4)*
½ teaspoon ground nutmeg	1 cup raisins, plumped in bourbon to
½ teaspoon ground cinnamon	cover for 10 to 15 minutes, drained
¼ teaspoon ground cloves	
¼ teaspoon ground mace	Caramel Sauce *(recipe follows)*

PREHEAT THE OVEN TO 325°F. Butter and flour a 10-inch springform pan. In the bowl of an electric mixer at medium speed, beat the oil and sugar until light and fluffy, about 5 minutes. Add the eggs, one at a time, beating well. In a medium bowl, sift the flours, baking soda, spices, and salt, and gradually fold into the sugar-oil mixture; blend thoroughly. Add the apples, pecans, and raisins, and blend well with a spatula.

Pour the batter into the prepared pan and bake in the preheated oven for 1½ to 2 hours, or until a knife inserted in the center comes out clean. Let cool, then remove from the pan. Drizzle room-temperature caramel sauce over the cake to serve.

Caramel Sauce

⅓ cup granulated sugar

1 cup packed light brown sugar

¼ cup pure maple syrup

¼ cup dark corn syrup

1 cup heavy (whipping) cream

In a heavy, medium saucepan, mix all the ingredients. Cook over high heat for about 5 minutes, or until the mixture reaches 220°F on a candy thermometer and has thickened but not reached the soft ball stage. Let cool for 20 minutes.

BANANA CAKE
with Coconut Custard
Susan Feniger and Mary Sue Milliken
Makes one 9-inch layer cake; serves 8 to 10

Save your plane fare. Bring the tropics home with this moist satisfying cake.

	COCONUT CUSTARD
1 cup (2 sticks) unsalted butter at room temperature	One 13½ ounce can coconut milk*
1½ cups sugar	2 cups milk
3 eggs	1 cup sugar
½ cup buttermilk	½ cup cornstarch
2 to 3 bananas (1¼ pounds), mashed (1⅓ cups)	8 egg yolks
2½ cups sifted cake flour	3 bananas, sliced
1 teaspoon baking powder	¼ cup fresh lemon juice
¾ teaspoon salt	2 tablespoons sugar
¾ teaspoon baking soda	1 cup unsweetened dried coconut
½ cup (2 ounces) pecans, finely chopped	flakes, preferably the wide-cut variety found in natural foods stores, toasted *(see page 4)*

T O M A K E T H E C A K E: Preheat the oven to 350°F. Butter two 9-inch round cake pans and line the bottoms with baking parchment or waxed paper; butter the paper. In the bowl of an electric mixer, beat the butter and sugar together until light and fluffy. Add the eggs one at a time and continue to beat until very pale in color. Add the buttermilk and mashed bananas and mix well.

In a medium bowl, sift together the flour, baking powder, salt, and baking soda. Add to the batter and mix at low speed until moistened, then beat for 1 minute at medium speed. Fold in the pecans and pour the batter evenly into the prepared cake pans. Bake in the preheated oven for 25 to 35 minutes, or until a toothpick inserted in the center comes out clean. Let cool for 5 minutes, then remove from the pans and let cool thoroughly on wire racks.

To make the coconut custard: In a medium, heavy saucepan, mix the coconut milk and milk thoroughly. In a small bowl, mix ½ cup of the sugar with the cornstarch until free from lumps. Mix together with the egg yolks, remaining sugar and 1 cup of the milk mixture; set aside.

Bring the remaining milk mixture to a boil. Pour into the egg-sugar mixture, whisking constantly. Return this mixture to the saucepan and continue stirring. Over medium heat, cook until bubbles start to form on the surface of the custard. Remove from heat and spread onto a baking sheet tray lined with baking parchment or waxed paper. Cover the top of the custard with baking parchment or waxed paper to prevent a skin from forming. The paper should touch the surface of the custard. Cool in refrigerator.

To assemble, in a large bowl, gently toss the banana slices in the lemon juice and sugar. Trim the top of the first layer of cake so that the surface is level, then spread with a thin layer of custard. Arrange the banana slices over the custard in a single layer. Place the second layer of cake over the bananas and spread generously with the custard. Garnish liberally with the toasted coconut flakes.

* *Available in Asian markets, natural foods stores, or specialty markets.*

BLUEBERRY SOUR CREAM CAKE

Robert Zielinski

Makes one 9-inch cake

Crowned with blueberries, this cake is easy to prepare, yet visually stunning.

About 1¼ cups unbleached all-purpose flour	1 large egg
1 cup sugar	2 cups sour cream
1½ teaspoons baking powder	2 large egg yolks
½ cup (1 stick) unsalted butter, cut into small pieces, at room temperature	4 cups blueberries

PREHEAT THE OVEN TO 350°F. Lightly butter a 9-inch round springform pan. In the bowl of an electric mixer, blend 1 cup of the flour, ½ cup of the sugar, and the baking powder. Add the butter and mix until smooth. Add the egg and blend until combined. The dough will be very soft. Gather into a loose ball using the extra flour as necessary. Cover and refrigerate for at least 30 minutes.

In the bowl of an electric mixer, beat the sour cream and remaining ½ cup sugar until the sugar is almost dissolved. Add the yolks one at a time until well blended. Press the dough evenly into the bottom and 1 inch up the sides of the prepared pan. Add half of the blueberries and cover with the sour cream mixture. Bake in the preheated oven for about 35 to 40 minutes, or until the center is set. Let cool at room temperature for 45 minutes, then refrigerate for 3 to 4 hours. Remove the springform ring and place the remaining blueberries on top of the cake.

CARROT CAKE
Jackie Shen

Makes one 9-inch layer cake; serves 8 to 10

A traditional carrot cake, studded with coconut, pineapple, and walnuts.

CAKE	CREAM CHEESE ICING
1 cup mild-flavored oil such as canola or grapeseed oil	1 cup (8 ounces) cream cheese at room temperature
4 eggs	¾ cup butter (1½ sticks) at room
2 teaspoons vanilla extract	temperature
2 cups sugar	3 cups powdered sugar, sifted
2 cups unbleached all-purpose flour	1 teaspoon vanilla extract
2 teaspoons baking soda	
3 teaspoons ground cinnamon	½ cup unsweetened dried coconut
6 to 8 carrots (1 pound), peeled and shredded (3 cups)	flakes, toasted *(see page 4)*
½ cup unsweetened dried coconut flakes	
½ cup drained crushed pineapple	
½ cup (2 ounces) walnuts, chopped	

To MAKE THE CAKE: Preheat the oven to 350°F. Butter two 9-inch cake pans and line the bottoms with baking parchment or waxed paper. Butter the paper and dust the inside of the pans with flour.

In the bowl of an electric mixer, blend well the oil, eggs, vanilla, and sugar. Add the flour, baking soda, and cinnamon, and mix well. Stir in the carrots, coconut, pineapple, and walnuts; mix until well blended. Divide the batter between the prepared pans and bake in the preheated oven for 35 to 45 minutes, or until a toothpick inserted in the center comes out clean. Let the cakes cool in the pans for 10 minutes before turning onto wire racks. Let cool completely before icing.

To make the cream cheese icing: In the bowl of an electric mixer, beat the cream cheese until light and fluffy. Add the butter and beat again until fluffy. Add the sugar and vanilla and beat once more.

Place one cake layer on a platter or cardboard circle. Spread the top with icing. Place the top layer over the iced layer; ice the top and sides. Mask the sides of the cake with toasted coconut. Chill before slicing.

CARROT CAKE

Anne Rosenzweig

Makes one 9-by-13-inch cake

*A classic carrot cake with a difference: It's served with poached apricots
instead of icing.*

3 cups unbleached all-purpose flour

3 cups sugar

1 teaspoon salt

1 tablespoon baking soda

1 tablespoon ground cinnamon

1½ cups soybean oil

4 eggs

1 tablespoon vanilla extract

1½ cups (6 ounces) walnuts, chopped

1½ cups unsweetened dried coconut flakes

4 to 6 carrots (8 ounces), peeled and shredded (1⅓ cups)

¾ cup drained crushed pineapple

Poached Apricots *(recipe follows)*

PREHEAT THE OVEN TO 350°F. Butter and flour a 9-by-13-inch cake pan. Into the bowl of an electric mixer, sift the flour, sugar, salt, baking soda, and cinnamon. Add the oil, eggs, and vanilla; beat well. Stir in the walnuts, coconut, carrots, and pineapple; pour into the prepared cake pan. Bake in the preheated oven for 30 to 40 minutes, or until firm to the touch. Let cool, then remove from the pan. Serve with poached apricots on the side.

Poached Apricots

1 cup (5 ounces) dried apricots

¾ cup sweet Riesling wine

1 vanilla bean, split lengthwise

In a small nonaluminum saucepan over medium heat, bring to a simmer all of the ingredients. Cook for 5 to 10 minutes, or until the apricots just become plump. Let cool.

CHOCOLATE BREATHLESS

Kevin Graham

Makes 12 meringues

Chocolate mousse with a hint of rum, alternating with layers of crunchy chocolate meringue.

CHOCOLATE MOUSSE	CHOCOLATE MERINGUE
1 pound semisweet chocolate, chopped	7 large egg whites
3 cups heavy (whipping) cream	¾ cup granulated sugar
4 large eggs, separated	1 heaping cup plus 2 tablespoons powdered sugar
⅓ cup water	¾ cup unsweetened cocoa powder
⅓ cup dark rum	Sifted powdered sugar for dusting
⅓ cup granulated sugar	

To MAKE THE CHOCOLATE MOUSSE: In a double boiler over barely simmering water, melt the chocolate. Meanwhile, in the bowl of an electric mixer, whip the cream into soft peaks. Place the egg yolks in a bowl, then whisk in the water and the rum. When thoroughly blended, stir in the melted chocolate. In the clean, dry bowl of an electric mixer, whip the 4 egg whites until foamy. Add the sugar and continue to beat until stiff peaks form. Fold the beaten egg whites into the chocolate mixture, then fold in the whipped cream. Cover and place in the refrigerator.

TO MAKE THE CHOCOLATE MERINGUE: Preheat the oven to 150°F. In the clean, dry bowl of an electric mixer, beat the 7 egg whites until foamy. Add the granulated sugar and continue to beat until stiff peaks form. Into a medium bowl, sift together the powdered sugar and cocoa, then fold gently into the meringue; do not overmix. Spoon the mixture into a pastry bag fitted with a ½-inch plain tube.

Line 2 baking sheets with baking parchment or waxed paper. Pipe thirty-six 2-inch circles onto the sheet about 1 inch apart. Pipe long lines with the rest of the meringue. Place in the preheated oven, leave the door ajar by 1 inch, and bake for about 1½ hours, or until firm. Let cool on the pan. The meringue can be made 1 day in advance and kept in an airtight container.

To assemble: When the meringue is cool, chop the lines into ½-inch pieces and set aside. Place a meringue circle on a flat work surface and top with a layer of chocolate mousse. Add another meringue circle, then more mousse. Complete the stack with another layer of meringue. Frost the top and sides of the stack with the mousse, then sprinkle the chopped meringue pieces on top. Repeat with the remaining meringue discs to make 12 servings in all. To serve, place one breathless on each dessert plate and dust the tops lightly with powdered sugar.

CRANBERRY NUT BREAD

Steven Howard

Makes three 9-inch loaves

A cool-weather treat filled with poppy seeds and walnuts.

1¼ cups (2½ sticks) unsalted butter at room temperature

2½ cups sugar

8 egg yolks

1 tablespoon vanilla extract

3 cups unbleached all-purpose flour

2 teaspoons baking soda

1 teaspoon baking powder

½ cup poppy seeds

1¼ cups sour cream

2 cups (8 ounces) cranberries

2 cups (8 ounces) walnuts

12 egg whites

PREHEAT THE OVEN TO 350°F. Butter and flour three 9-by-5-inch loaf pans. In the bowl of an electric mixer, cream the butter and sugar. Mix in the egg yolks and vanilla and beat well. Sift in the flour, soda, baking powder, and poppy seeds, and beat into the mixture. Stir in the sour cream, then the cranberries and walnuts. In the clean, dry bowl of an electric mixer, whip the egg whites until stiff peaks form; fold into the batter.

Spoon the batter into the prepared loaf pans and bake in the preheated oven for 1 hour, or until a toothpick inserted in the center comes out clean and the center springs back to the touch. Let cool, then remove from the pan.

CRANBERRY-BLACK WALNUT POUND CAKE

Jasper White

Makes one 9-inch loaf cake

Some find the flavor of black walnuts gamey, others irresistible. Here's a gentle introduction to the taste of black walnuts blended with other flavors.

A pound cake is a dense cake that was originally made with a pound of butter, a pound of sugar, a pound of eggs, a pound of flour, and nothing else. Many different flavors and garnishes can be used, but the key to a good pound cake is the butter. Very fresh butter of the highest quality available is called for.
—Jasper White

1½ cups (3 sticks) unsalted butter at room temperature

3¾ cups (1 pound) powdered sugar, sifted, plus more for dusting

6 whole eggs

1 tablespoon fresh lemon juice

1 teaspoon vanilla extract

2 cups sifted cake flour

2 tablespoons grated lemon zest

1 cup (4 ounces) black walnut pieces*, coarsely chopped

1 cup (4 ounces) fresh or thawed frozen cranberries, coarsely chopped

PREHEAT THE OVEN TO 300°F. Lightly butter and flour a 9-inch loaf pan. In the bowl of an electric mixer, cream the butter and the powdered sugar until light and fluffy. Add the eggs one at a time, continuing to beat. Add the lemon juice and vanilla. Stir in the flour, then the lemon zest, walnuts, and cranberries.

Pour into the prepared cake pan and bake in the preheated oven for about 1 hour and 30 minutes, or until a toothpick inserted in the center comes out clean. Let cool on a wire rack for 10 minutes, then unmold and place on a rack to cool thoroughly. Sprinkle with powdered sugar and serve at room temperature.

Available at specialty food stores or from Missouri Dandy Pantry, 212 Hammons Drive East, Stockton, MO 65785; Telephone 1-800-872-6879.

GINGER SHORTCAKE

Nancy Silverton

Makes 10 shortcakes

A shortcake with a warming bite of ginger, served with a tangy huckleberry compote.

2¾ cups unbleached all-purpose flour	⅔ cup crystallized ginger, washed, dried, and chopped
2 tablespoons plus 1 teaspoon sugar	
1 tablespoon plus 1 teaspoon baking powder	1½ cups heavy (whipping) cream
¾ cup (1½ sticks) cold unsalted butter, cut into small bits	Huckleberry Compote *(recipe on page 33)*

PREHEAT THE OVEN TO 375°F. Into the bowl of an electric mixer, sift the flour, sugar, and baking powder. Add the butter and toss until it is evenly coated by the dry ingredients. Mix on low speed for 5 to 10 minutes, or until the mixture is the consistency of fine meal and pale yellow in color. Stir in the chopped ginger. Pour in the cream and mix until the dough just comes together in a mass.

Turn the dough out onto a lightly floured surface and knead gently 3 or 4 times until it forms a smooth ball; don't overwork. Roll the dough out to a ¾-inch thickness. With a 3-inch biscuit cutter, cut out 7 or 8 biscuits. Gather the scraps up, roll out again to a ¾-inch thickness, and cut 2 or 3 more biscuits. You should have 10 biscuits. Place on a baking sheet lined with baking parchment and chill until ready to bake. (The biscuits can be cut out, covered, and refrigerated for up to 3 hours before baking.) Bake in the preheated oven for 10 to 20 minutes, or until the biscuits are golden brown. Serve at room temperature, with warm huckleberry compote spooned over the top.

LEBKUCHEN SWISS SPICE CAKE

with Lemon Icing

Seppi Rengli

Makes one 11-by-15-inch cake

A traditional moist Swiss cake made with honey, candied fruit, and kirsch.

CAKE	½ teaspoon salt
½ cup sugar	3 tablespoons chopped citron
1 cup honey	3 tablespoons chopped candied
½ cup (2½ ounces) unblanched	orange peel
almonds, coarsely chopped	Grated zest of ½ lemon
1 egg	2 tablespoons kirsch
2½ cups sifted unbleached	
all-purpose flour	**LEMON ICING**
2 teaspoons ground cinnamon	1 egg white
½ teaspoon ground mace	1½ cups sifted powdered sugar
½ teaspoon ground cloves	⅓ cup fresh lemon juice
½ teaspoon baking soda	

To MAKE THE CAKE: Preheat the oven to 325°F. Butter and flour an 11-by-15-inch cake pan. In a medium, heavy saucepan over medium heat, dissolve the sugar in the honey. Bring the syrup to a foaming boil and add the almonds. Immediately remove the pan from heat and let the syrup cool completely, by which time the almonds should be well browned. Beat in the egg.

Into a bowl, sift the flour with the spices, soda, and salt. Stir into the mixture in the saucepan. Stir in the citron, candied orange peel, grated lemon zest, and kirsch. Spread the batter in the prepared baking pan and bake in the preheated oven for 20 minutes, or until the top of the cake is well browned. Set aside while making the lemon icing.

To make the lemon icing: In the clean, dry bowl of an electric mixer, beat the egg white until soft peaks form. Add the powdered sugar in small amounts until the mixture is thick but spreadable. Stir in the lemon juice. Coat the cake with icing while the cake is still warm.

PEAR UPSIDE-DOWN SPICE CAKE

Jasper White

Makes one 9- or 10-inch cake

Both spice cakes and upside-down cakes are part of New England's culinary heritage. This recipe combines the two and uses pears, which are plentiful in the region in fall. The best known of the upside-down cakes, though, is pineapple. Pineapple can be substituted for the pears in this recipe.

An upside-down cake is baked with fruit on the bottom. Then it is unmolded, and the fruit ends up on top. Baking the cake in an ovenproof nonstick skillet makes unmolding, which when not successful ruins the presentation, almost foolproof. The skillet I use is oval, and it makes for an interesting shape cake. If you do not have such a pan, use a 9-inch cake pan, but be careful when unmolding.
—Jasper White

PEARS	1 cup sifted cake flour
6 Bosc, Anjou, or Bartlett pears	1 teaspoon baking soda
6 tablespoons unsalted butter	½ teaspoon salt
⅓ cup granulated sugar	1 teaspoon ground ginger
2 tablespoons water	1 teaspoon ground cinnamon
½ cup packed light brown sugar	1 teaspoon ground nutmeg
	4 egg whites
SPICE CAKE	1 teaspoon ground cinnamon
6 tablespoons unsalted butter at room	1 teaspoon ground nutmeg
temperature	4 egg whites
3 tablespoons packed light brown	
sugar	Sweetened whipped cream or crème
2 eggs, separated	anglaise *(recipe on page 2)*
½ cup molasses	for topping

O MAKE THE PEARS: Peel, core, and cut the pears into ½-inch slices. In a hot sauté pan or skillet, toss the pears with 2 tablespoons of the butter and the granulated sugar until they are soft but still hold their shape and the sugar is dissolved, about 5 minutes. Add the water and remove from heat; set aside.

In a 9- or 10-inch ovenproof nonstick skillet, cook the brown sugar and the remaining 4 tablespoons butter over low heat until a syrup forms, about 2 minutes. Arrange the pears in a circular pattern over the syrup. Do this carefully and artistically; remember, the pears will be on top!

TO MAKE THE SPICE CAKE: Preheat the oven to 350°F. In the bowl of an electric mixer, cream the butter and brown sugar until light and fluffy. Beat in the egg yolks from the separated eggs (take the 2 whites from the separated eggs and add to the 4 egg whites and reserve). Stir in the molasses. Into a bowl, sift together the flour, baking soda, salt, ginger, cinnamon, and nutmeg. Fold into the batter; do not overmix.

In the clean, dry bowl of an electric mixer, beat the 6 reserved egg whites until stiff peaks form. Fold into the batter one third at a time. Spread the batter evenly over the pears in the skillet. Bake in the preheated oven for about 25 minutes, or until the center of the cake springs back when touched. To unmold, place a serving plate over the pan and turn it upside down, inverting the cake onto the plate. Serve warm or at room temperature with whipped cream or crème anglaise.

Pineapple Upside-Down Cake

Substitute 1 pineapple for the pears. Peel the pineapple, slice it ¾ inch thick, cut each slice in half, and remove the core. Continue as for the pears.

POUND CAKE
with Apricots and Pistachios
Robert Del Grande

Makes two 9-inch loaf cakes

A moist pound cake sweetened with homemade apricot jam and honey, studded with toasted pistachios.

1 cup dried apricots	1½ cups lightly packed unbleached all-purpose flour
½ cup Riesling or sweet white wine	
1 cup (2 sticks) unsalted butter at room temperature, cut into small pieces	1 teaspoon ground cinnamon
	1 teaspoon baking powder
	1 teaspoon salt
1 cup sugar	1 cup (4 ounces) shelled unsalted pistachios, toasted, skinned and finely chopped *(see page 4)*
1 tablespoon pure vanilla extract	
¼ cup honey	
6 eggs, separated	

PREHEAT THE OVEN TO 350°F. Butter two 9-by-5-inch loaf pans. In a small saucepan, bring to a boil the apricots and wine. Lower the heat and simmer for 30 minutes. Transfer to a blender or food processor and puree to form a thick jam.

In the bowl of an electric mixer, blend the butter and sugar at a medium speed until the butter is light and creamy. Add the vanilla and honey, and mix at a low speed to incorporate. With the mixer running, add the egg yolks one at a time and mix until fully incorporated.

In a small bowl, mix the flour, cinnamon, baking powder, and salt. Add the mixture to the butter-egg mixture and mix until just incorporated. Add the pureed apricots and chopped pistachios to the batter, and mix to incorporate.

In a large bowl, whip the egg whites until they hold soft peaks. Stir one third of the egg whites into the batter to lighten it; then fold in the remaining egg whites. Pour the batter into the prepared loaf pans and bake in the preheated oven for about 1 hour, or until a toothpick inserted in the center comes out clean. Let cool on a wire rack for 10 minutes, then remove from pan and place on a rack to cool thoroughly.

STRAWBERRY MERINGUE CAKE

Nick Malgieri

Makes one 10-inch layer cake; serves 8 to 10

A three-layer genoise cake with a strawberry filling, topped with almond-studded meringue and strawberries.

"This is an ideal cake for the summer since it contains neither whipped cream nor buttercream. The fruit filling and meringue are light and will not melt in hot weather."
—Nick Malgieri

GENOISE LAYER

4 large eggs

Pinch of salt

⅔ cup sugar

½ cup cake flour

3 tablespoons cornstarch

LEMON-KIRSCH SYRUP

⅓ cup water

¼ cup sugar

2 tablespoons fresh lemon juice

2 tablespoons kirsch

STRAWBERRY FILLING

4 cups (1 pound) strawberries

½ cup sugar

1 tablespoon fresh lemon juice

1 tablespoon kirsch

2 tablespoons cornstarch

MERINGUE TOPPING

¾ cup egg whites (about 6 large whites)

1 cup sugar

⅓ cup sliced almonds, toasted (*see page 4*), for garnish

To make genoise layer: Preheat the oven to 350°F. Butter a 10-inch round cake pan. Line the bottom of the pan with baking parchment or waxed paper and butter the paper. Into the bowl of an electric mixer, break the eggs and whisk in the salt, then the sugar. Place the bowl over a pan of simmering water and whisk until just lukewarm. Return to the mixer and whip until cold and increased in volume, about 4 to 5 minutes. Mix the cake flour and cornstarch and sift over the egg whites in 3 or 4 additions, folding it in with a rubber spatula. Pour the batter into the prepared pan and level it off. Bake in the preheated oven for about 30 minutes, or until the cake is risen, golden, and beginning to shrink away from the sides of the pan. Unmold immediately and let cool on a wire rack.

TO MAKE THE LEMON-KIRSCH SYRUP: In a small pan, mix the water and sugar and bring to a boil; let cool. Stir in the lemon juice and kirsch.

TO MAKE THE STRAWBERRY FILLING: Reserve 6 of the best strawberries for decoration. Rinse, stem, and slice the remaining berries. In a small saucepan, bring to a boil 1 cup of the berries with the sugar; remove from heat. Combine the lemon juice, kirsch, and cornstarch and stir into the strawberry mixture. Return to a boil, stirring, and cook for 2 minutes. Remove from heat, let cool, and stir in the remaining sliced berries.

TO MAKE THE MERINGUE TOPPING: In the bowl of an electric mixer, combine the egg whites and sugar. Whisk over simmering water until the egg whites are hot and the sugar is dissolved. Remove from heat and beat on medium speed until cold and risen in volume, but not dry.

TO ASSEMBLE: Preheat the oven to 400°F. Divide the cooled genoise into 3 layers with a sharp serrated knife. Place 1 layer on a cardboard circle or platter and coat with one third of the syrup, using a brush. Spread with half the filling. Repeat with a second layer. Place the third layer of genoise over the filling and moisten with the syrup. Spread the cake with the meringue and pipe a decoration on the top of the cake, using a star tube. Place the cake on a baking sheet and place in the preheated oven for about 3 or 4 minutes, or until the meringue is lightly browned; let cool. To serve, decorate with the reserved strawberries and toasted almonds.

CHOCOLATE-PISTACHIO-RASPBERRY CAKE

Nick Malgieri

Makes one 10-inch layer cake; serves 8 to 10

*A two-layer cake made with pistachios and filled and topped with chocolate
ganache, raspberries, and whipped cream.*

PISTACHIO BISCUIT

4 eggs, separated

¾ cup sugar

1 cup (4 ounces) unsalted pistachios,
skinned *(see page 4)*

½ cup unbleached all-purpose flour

Pinch of salt

GANACHE FILLING

8 ounces bittersweet chocolate,
chopped

2 ounces milk chocolate, chopped

1 cup heavy (whipping) cream

FRAMBOISE SYRUP

⅓ cup water

⅓ cup sugar

⅓ cup framboise liqueur

WHIPPED CREAM

1½ cups heavy (whipping) cream

2 tablespoons sugar

2 tablespoons framboise liqueur

Shaved milk chocolate

4 cups fresh raspberries

½ cup (2 ounces) unsalted pistachios

Sifted powdered sugar for dusting

To MAKE THE PISTACHIO BISCUIT: Preheat the oven to 350°F. Butter a 10-inch round cake pan. Line the bottom with baking parchment or waxed paper and butter the paper. In the bowl of an electric mixer, beat the egg yolks with half of the sugar until pale in color; set aside. In a blender or food processor, grind the pistachios finely, combine with the flour, and set aside.

In the bowl of an electric mixer, beat the egg whites on medium speed with the salt until white and opaque. Increase the speed and beat in the remaining sugar, then beat until soft peaks form. Fold the yolks into the whites, then fold in the pistachio-flour mixture. Pour the batter into the prepared cake pan and bake in the preheated oven for 30 to 40 minutes, or until golden. Unmold and let cool on a rack.

TO MAKE THE GANACHE FILLING: Mix the chocolates together in a heatproof bowl. In a small saucepan, bring the cream to a boil and pour over the chocolate. Let stand for 2 minutes, then whisk until smooth. Refrigerate the ganache, whisking several times until cool but not set.

TO MAKE THE FRAMBOISE SYRUP: In a small, heavy pan, combine the water and sugar and bring to a boil. Let cool and stir in the framboise liqueur.

TO MAKE THE WHIPPED CREAM: In a deep bowl, whip all the ingredients until soft peaks form.

TO ASSEMBLE: Split the pistachio biscuit into 2 layers and place on a cardboard circle or platter. Moisten with half of the framboise syrup and spread with most of the ganache, reserving some for decorating. Distribute most of the raspberries on the ganache, reserving the remainder for decorating. Cover with a layer of the whipped cream.

Place the second layer of the biscuit on the cream and moisten it with the remaining frambroise syrup. Cover the outside of the cake with the whipped cream and press the milk chocolate shavings against the side of the cake.

Place the remaining ganache in a pastry bag fitted with a star tip and make a border of rosettes around the edge of the cake; decorate the rosettes with the raspberries and some of the ½ cup pistachios. Chop the remaining pistachios and place them in the center of the cake; dust the pistachios lightly with powdered sugar.

CHOCOLATE MACADAMIA NUT CAKE

Jackie Shen

Makes one 9-inch single-layer cake; serves 8 to 10

A flourless chocolate cake with a hint of orange.

CAKE	GANACHE
5 ounces semisweet chocolate, chopped	½ cup plus 2 tablespoons heavy (whipping) cream
1 cup (5 ounces) unsalted macadamia nuts, toasted *(see page 4)*	6 ounces semisweet chocolate, chopped
¾ cup (1½ sticks) unsalted butter at room temperature	
1 cup sugar	
4 whole eggs	
½ cup white bread crumbs or chocolate cake crumbs	
1 tablespoon grated orange zest	

To MAKE THE CAKE: Preheat the oven to 375°F. Butter a 9-inch round cake pan. Line the bottom with baking parchment or waxed paper and butter the paper lightly. In a double boiler over barely simmering water, melt the chocolate. Stir until smooth and set aside to cool slightly.

Reserve 8 whole macadamia nuts for garnish. In a blender or food processor, grind the remaining nuts to a fine meal. In the bowl of an electric mixer, cream the butter and sugar until light and fluffy. Add the melted chocolate and mix until light and fluffy. Add the eggs one at a time and mix until light and fluffy. Stir in 1 cup of the ground nuts, the bread or cake crumbs, and orange zest until just incorporated. Transfer the mixture to the prepared cake pan and bake on a baking sheet in the preheated oven for 30 to 35 minutes, or until a toothpick inserted into the center of the cake comes out clean. Let cool to room temperature. Invert onto a 9-inch cardboard circle or platter. Let the cake cool completely in the refrigerator.

TO MAKE THE GANACHE: In a small saucepan, bring the heavy cream to a boil and add the chocolate. Remove from heat and stir with a wire whip until the chocolate is completely dissolved. Let cool slightly.

To assemble, place the cooled cake on a wire rack over a baking sheet. Pour the ganache over the top and, with a spatula, smooth the ganache on the top while pushing the excess over the edge to glaze the sides; let cool.

Mask the side of the cake with the remaining ground macadamia nuts by holding the cake with one hand and pressing a small handful of the nuts onto the side with the other hand, letting the excess fall away. Garnish the top with whole macadamia nuts.

WHITE CHOCOLATE AND RASPBERRY CAKE

with Coffee Butter Cream

Barry Wine

Makes one 9-inch round cake; serves 8 to 12

A dramatic white cake layered with fresh raspberries and coffee butter cream, and topped with white chocolate.

WHITE CHOCOLATE TOPPING

1 pound white chocolate, finely chopped

½ cup corn syrup or honey

WHITE CAKE

3 cups sifted cake flour

1 tablespoon baking powder

¾ teaspoon salt

1½ cups sugar

¾ cup (1½ sticks) unsalted butter at room temperature, cut into pieces

1 cup milk at room temperature

1 teaspoon vanilla extract

5 egg whites

COFFEE BUTTER CREAM

6 egg yolks

¾ cup sugar

½ cup dark corn syrup

2 cups (4 sticks) unsalted butter at room temperature

2 tablespoons instant espresso, dissolved in 1 tablespoon warm water

6 cups fresh raspberries

To MAKE THE WHITE CHOCOLATE TOPPING: In a medium heatproof bowl, combine the ground white chocolate and syrup or honey, and melt in a double boiler over barely simmering water. When the white chocolate is completely melted, stir to blend. Allow to cool to room temperature, then spoon onto a piece of waxed paper or plastic wrap. Wrap the chocolate in the paper or plastic and let sit overnight.

To make the white cake: Preheat the oven to 350°F. Butter a 9-inch round cake pan, line the bottom with baking parchment or waxed paper, and butter the paper. Into the bowl of an electric mixer, sift together the flour, baking powder and salt. In a separate bowl with the electric mixer cream the sugar and butter until light. Add the flour mixture and the milk to the butter mixture in 3 parts, whipping the batter briefly after each addition to fully incorporate it. Mix in the vanilla extract. In a separate bowl, with an electric mixer, whip the egg whites until stiff but not dry. Fold gently into the batter. Pour into the prepared cake pan. Bake in the preheated oven for 20 to 30 minutes, or until the cake is evenly golden brown and the center bounces back when touched. Let cool on a rack, then remove from the pan.

To make the coffee butter cream: In the bowl of an electric mixer, whip the egg yolks on high speed until pale in color. In a small, heavy saucepan, combine the sugar and corn syrup. Bring to a full boil, stirring occasionally to dissolve the sugar into the syrup. Add the hot syrup in 3 batches to the yolks, whipping the mixture on high speed for several seconds after each addition. Continue whipping the yolks and syrup at high speed until they have cooled, then slowly add the butter. When all the butter has been incorporated, add the instant espresso.

To assemble, cut the cake in half crosswise, then cut each half again to make 4 layers. Cover one layer with a thin layer of butter cream. Reserve a few of the raspberries for decoration, then arrange a layer of about one third of the raspberries over it. Generously spread the butter cream on another layer of cake and place it over the raspberries butter cream side down. Press firmly to fill in the area around the berries. Repeat, ending with a layer of cake. Frost the top and sides with butter cream.

Cut the now-hard white chocolate topping into chunks and chop it into fine pieces in a food processor or by hand. On a smooth surface, knead the chopped white chocolate topping until smooth and satiny. (The warmth of your hands will cause the topping to soften.) Roll the topping into a circle between 2 pieces of plastic wrap to about a ⅛-inch thickness. The piece of topping should be large enough to generously cover the cake. Remove one piece of the plastic, lift the rolled topping over the cake, and gently press it into place. Trim any excess and chill until firm. Remove the cake from the refrigerator several hours before serving.

To make the berry coulis, puree 4 cups of the raspberries. Strain the puree through a fine sieve to remove the seeds. To serve, set a slice of cake on a plate covered with the berry coulis. Sprinkle with a few whole raspberries.

NICK MALGIERI'S CHOCOLATE-CHESTNUT BÛCHE DE NOËL

Nick Malgieri

Makes one 14-by-6-inch cake; serves 6 to 8

The traditional French Christmas log exists in many variations of flavor and presentation. I like this one because the chocolate cake and chestnut butter cream are not an excessively sweet combination. Also, the marzipan decorations can be prepared well in advance and kept loosely covered until needed.
—Nick Malgieri

CHOCOLATE GENOISE ROLL

4 large eggs

⅔ cup sugar

Pinch of salt

⅓ cup cake flour

⅓ cup cornstarch

3 tablespoons unsweetened cocoa powder

2 pinches baking soda

CHESTNUT BUTTER CREAM

1½ cups (3 sticks) unsalted butter at room temperature

1½ cups sweetened chestnut puree*

2 tablespoons white rum

2 teaspoons vanilla extract

MARZIPAN

1 cup (8 ounces) almond paste, cut into pieces

¼ cup corn syrup

1⅓ cups powdered sugar, sifted

¼ cup unsweetened cocoa powder

Sifted powdered sugar for dusting

To MAKE THE CHOCOLATE GENOISE ROLL: Preheat the oven to 375°F. Butter a 12-by-18-inch jelly roll pan. Line the bottom with baking parchment or waxed paper and butter the paper. In the bowl of an electric mixer, whisk the eggs, sugar, and salt. Place the bowl over a pan of gently simmering water and whisk until the mixture is lukewarm. Remove from heat and beat until cool and increased in volume. Into a medium bowl, sift the cake flour, cornstarch, cocoa powder, and baking soda. Fold into the egg mixture in 3 additions. Pour the batter into the prepared cake pan and spread the batter smooth. Bake in the preheated oven for about 10 minutes, or until the cake begins to pull away from the sides of the pan and the center bounces back when touched. Immediately loosen the edges of the cake from the pan and invert into a sheet of paper or a cloth towel that has been dusted with powdered sugar; let cool on a rack.

To MAKE THE CHESTNUT BUTTER CREAM: In the bowl of an electric mixer, beat the butter until fluffy, then add the chestnut puree and beat until smooth. Add the rum and vanilla and continue beating until light and smooth, about 4 to 5 minutes.

To MAKE THE MARZIPAN: In the bowl of an electric mixer, mix the almond paste, corn syrup, and powdered sugar until smooth. On a work surface, with your hands, shape the marzipan into a cylinder and cut into 1-inch lengths. Roll half the lengths into spheres. Press the cylinders against the spheres to make mushrooms. Smudge with cocoa powder.

To assemble, peel away the paper and invert the genoise layer onto a fresh sheet of paper or a cloth towel that has been dusted with powdered sugar. Spread with half the butter cream. Use the paper or cloth to help roll into a tight cylinder rolling from the long side; chill. Reserve the remaining butter cream for the outside of the bûche.

Remove the rolled cake from the refrigerator and unwrap. Trim the edges diagonally, cutting one edge about 3 inches away from the end. Position the larger cut piece on the bûche two thirds from one end to make a protruding cut branch. Cover the bûche with the remaining butter cream, making sure to curve around the protruding branch on the top. Score the butter cream with a fork or decorating comb to resemble bark. Transfer the bûche to a platter and decorate with the marzipan mushrooms. Sprinkle the platter and bûche sparingly with powdered sugar to give the appearance of snow.

*Available in specialty food stores.

CHOCOLATE-BLACKBERRY TORTE

Jonathan Waxman (created with Toni Chiappetta)

Makes one 10-inch one-layer torte

This blackberry-studded torte is a refreshing twist on the
chocolate-raspberry theme.

12 ounces semisweet chocolate, chopped	9 eggs
1½ cups (3 sticks) unsalted butter, cut into small pieces	½ cup blackberry brandy, or to taste
	6 cups fresh blackberries
1¼ cups unsweetened cocoa powder	
2 cups sugar	1 cup heavy (whipping) cream, whipped, for garnish

PREHEAT THE OVEN TO 325°F. Place a round of baking parchment or waxed paper in the bottom of a 10-inch round cake pan. In a double boiler over barely simmering water, melt the chocolate and butter, stirring occasionally; remove from heat. Into a medium bowl, sift the cocoa and sugar, then whisk into the chocolate-butter mixture. Add the eggs one at a time, mixing with a whisk. Stir in the blackberry brandy. Add 5 cups of the berries last, folding them in very carefully so as not to crush the fruit.

Pour the batter into the prepared cake pan and bake in the preheated oven for about 25 to 30 minutes, or until the sides have risen slightly but the center is not quite set. Let the cake cool completely before removing from the pan. To remove from the pan, run a hot, clean knife around the side of the cake pan. Invert onto a plate, then reinvert onto a serving platter. Serve garnished with the remaining 1 cup fresh blackberries and a dollop of whipped cream.

ESPRESSO CAKE

Piero Selvaggio (created with Rudy Torres)

Makes one 9-inch cake

A double-layer mocha cake filled with mocha mousse and topped with mocha ganache.

CAKE

1½ cups (15 ounces) hazelnuts, toasted and skinned *(see page 4)*

6 ounces semisweet chocolate, chopped

½ cup (1 stick) unsalted butter

4 tablespoons instant espresso powder

6 eggs, separated

¾ cup plus 1 teaspoon sugar

GANACHE

12 ounces semisweet chocolate, chopped

1 cup heavy (whipping) cream

4 tablespoons unsalted butter, cut into bits

1½ tablespoons instant espresso powder

CHOCOLATE MOUSSE

6 ounces semisweet chocolate, chopped

½ cup milk

2 tablespoons instant espresso

2 tablespoons vanilla extract

1¼ cups heavy (whipping) cream, whipped

CHOCOLATE BASE

8 ounces semisweet chocolate, chopped

¾ cup pirouette cookies or cigarette cookies*

Chocolate shavings for garnish

To MAKE THE CAKE: Preheat the oven to 375°F. Butter a 24-by-12-inch cake pan. Line the bottom with baking parchment or waxed paper, then butter and flour the paper.

In a blender or food processor, grind the hazelnuts to a fine meal; set aside. In a double boiler over barely simmering water, melt the chocolate, butter, and espresso, stirring to mix. In the bowl of an electric mixer, beat the egg yolks and sugar at high speed for 5 minutes, or until a ribbon is formed on the surface of the mixture when the beaters are lifted. Lower the mixer speed to medium, pour in the melted chocolate, and mix until blended. In the clean, dry bowl of an electric mixer, beat the egg whites at high speed until stiff peaks form. Stir one fourth of the egg whites into the chocolate mixture, then fold in the remaining egg whites gently. Gently fold in the ground hazelnuts. Pour into the prepared pan and bake in the preheated oven for 12 to 15 minutes, or until the sides pull away from the pan. Let cool, then remove from the pan.

To make the ganache: Place the chocolate in a bowl. In a small saucepan, bring the cream just to a boil; pour over the chocolate. Add the butter and espresso powder and whisk until smooth. Put half of the ganache in the bowl of an electric mixer and chill for at least 30 minutes, or until semi-soft; leave the remaining ganache at room temperature. Beat the chilled ganache until thick and creamy, but do not overmix or the cream will separate.

To make the chocolate mousse: Place the chocolate in a bowl. In a small saucepan, heat the milk and instant espresso over medium heat until it just comes to a boil. Pour over the chocolate and let sit for 3 to 5 minutes to melt. Whisk in the vanilla until smooth. In the bowl of an electric mixer, whip the cream until stiff peaks form; fold into the chocolate mixture.

To make the chocolate base: In a double boiler over barely simmering water, melt the chocolate. In a blender or food processor, grind the cookies until smooth. Stir into the chocolate.

To assemble, place a 10-inch circle of buttered baking parchment or waxed paper on top of a 10-inch cardboard cake round. Set a 9-by-3-inch pastry ring or the ring of a springform pan on the paper. Cut two 9-inch rounds from the cake. Place 1 cake round in the ring. Pour the chocolate base on top and spread evenly. Spread half of the chocolate mousse on top of the chocolate base. Set the second cake round on top of the mousse and top with the remaining mousse, spreading evenly. Spread the whipped ganache over the mousse. Pour on just enough of the room-temperature ganache to cover the mousse. Refrigerate the cake until the ganache becomes firm. With a warm knife, loosen the cake from the ring and remove. Garnish with chocolate shavings.

Available in specialty food stores.

SHAR-PÉI CAKE

Anne Rosenzweig

Makes 9 individual cakes

Named for the dog with all the folds of skin, this devil's food cake prepared in individual servings is covered with a rich chocolate topping that drapes the cake in loose folds.

CHOCOLATE TOPPING

1 cup corn syrup

10½ ounces semisweet chocolate

DEVIL'S FOOD CAKE

½ cup unsweetened cocoa powder

1¾ cups cake flour, or 1½ cups unbleached all-purpose flour

1 teaspoon baking soda

1 teaspoon salt

½ cup vegetable shortening

1¼ cups sugar

2 eggs

1 cup boiling water

1 teaspoon vanilla extract

CHOCOLATE GANACHE

2¾ cups heavy (whipping) cream

27 ounces semisweet chocolate, chopped

Whipped cream or Vanilla Bean Ice Cream *(recipe on page 144)* for garnish

To MAKE THE CHOCOLATE TOPPING: In a medium, heavy saucepan, heat the corn syrup until it liquifies. Remove from heat, add the chocolate, and stir until the mixture leaves the sides of the pan. Pour into a container lined with plastic wrap; let cool until set, then wrap well and let sit overnight.

TO MAKE THE DEVIL'S FOOD CAKE: Preheat the oven to 350°F. Butter and flour a 10½-by-15½-inch jelly roll pan. Into a small bowl, sift together the cocoa, flour, baking soda, and salt. In the bowl of an electric mixer, beat the shortening and sugar until fluffy. Beat in the eggs one at a time until blended. Add the boiling water, vanilla, and sifted dry ingredients all at once; beat until smooth. Pour into the prepared cake pan and bake in the preheated oven for about 15 minutes, or until a toothpick inserted into the center comes out clean; let cool. Using a 3-inch round cookie cutter, cut the cake into rounds.

TO MAKE THE CHOCOLATE GANACHE: In a large saucepan, heat the cream until almost at the boiling point. Remove from heat, add the cream to the chocolate, and mix until smooth. Let cool to room temperature.

To assemble, cut the devil's food cake rounds in half crosswise and spread the top of the first layer with the chocolate ganache. Place a second layer of cake on top of the first and cover the top and sides with the ganache. Roll out the chocolate topping between two pieces of plastic wrap to a 15-by-15-inch square about ¼ inch thick and cut into nine 5-inch square pieces. Drape each one over a cake, making many folds. Tuck the topping under each cake to make a neat package. Serve at room temperature with whipped cream or vanilla ice cream.

FLOURLESS CHOCOLATE CAKE

with Chocolate Ganache Icing

Emeril Lagasse

Makes one 9-inch single-layer cake; serves 10 to 12

A mousse-like chocolate cake covered with creamy chocolate.

8 ounces semisweet chocolate, chopped	2 teaspoons vanilla extract
	½ teaspoon salt
½ cup (1 stick) unsalted butter at room temperature	Chocolate Ganache Icing *(recipe follows)*
5 eggs at room temperature, separated	Fresh raspberries and whipped cream for garnish
¾ cup sugar	

PREHEAT THE OVEN TO 350°F. Butter and flour a 9-inch spring-form pan. In a double boiler over barely simmering water, melt the chocolate and the butter, stirring occasionally, until smooth and creamy; set aside. In the bowl of an electric mixer, beat the egg yolks with the sugar and vanilla until pale in color, stopping to scrape the sides of the bowl once or twice. In the clean, dry bowl of an electric mixer, beat the egg whites with the salt until stiff peaks form. Gradually fold the chocolate into the yolk mixture. Mix one fourth of the egg whites into the chocolate mixture, then gently fold the remaining egg whites into the chocolate mixture.

Pour the batter into the prepared springform pan and bake in the center of the preheated oven until firm but spongy, about 40 minutes. Remove the springform and place the cake on a wire rack to cool completely. To serve, spread the partially set chocolate ganache icing over the sides and top of the cake. Top with raspberries and serve small wedges of cake with a dollop of whipped cream.

Chocolate Ganache Icing

8 ounces semisweet chocolate, chopped
½ cup heavy (whipping) cream

In a double boiler over barely simmering water, melt the chocolate with the cream, stirring constantly until smooth. Allow to cool until partially set to spreading consistency.

FLOURLESS CHOCOLATE WALNUT CAKE

Bruce Marder

Makes one 8-inch single-layer cake; serves 8 to 10

Bruce Marder, a chef who does things a little differently but always successfully, offers this rich chocolate cake filled with chopped walnuts.

4 ounces semisweet chocolate, chopped

1¼ cups (5 ounces) walnuts

¾ cup sugar

3 tablespoons butter at room temperature

4 eggs, separated

Sifted powdered sugar for dusting

PREHEAT THE OVEN TO 400°F. Butter an 8-inch round cake pan. Line the bottom with a round of baking parchment or waxed paper and butter the paper. In a double boiler over barely simmering water, melt the chocolate; set aside to cool slightly.

In a blender or food processor, chop the walnuts with ½ cup of the sugar until the mixture is the consistency of flour. Add the butter and mix until there are no lumps. Mix in the egg yolks one at a time, then add the melted chocolate.

In the clean, dry bowl of an electric mixer, whip the egg whites with the remaining ¼ cup sugar until soft peaks form. Mix one fourth of the egg whites into the chocolate mixture. Fold the remaining egg whites into the chocolate mixture until blended and pour into the prepared cake pan. Place on a baking pan and bake in the preheated oven for 10 minutes. Turn the oven to 350°F and bake the cake for 50 minutes, or until firm but spongy. Let cool. Turn out of the pan onto a platter and let cool. Dust with powdered sugar to serve.

ALFRED PORTALE'S WARM CHOCOLATE CAKE

Alfred Portale

Makes one 10-inch single-layer cake; serves 8 to 10

This flourless mocha cake derives its unusual tenderness from baking in a water bath.

12 ounces semisweet chocolate, chopped

¼ cup Frangelica liqueur

¼ cup freshly brewed strong coffee

1 cup heavy (whipping) cream

5 large eggs

⅓ cup sugar

Ice cream for garnish

PREHEAT THE OVEN TO 325°F. Butter and flour a 10-inch round cake pan. In a double boiler, over barely simmering water, melt the chocolate; set aside. In a medium saucepan, heat the Frangelica and coffee. Add the melted chocolate; do not stir. Set aside at room temperature.

In the bowl of an electric mixer, whip the cream until stiff peaks form. Cover and refrigerate until needed. In a stainless steel bowl set over a saucepan of hot water, whisk the eggs and sugar until warm. Remove from the saucepan and, with an electric mixer, whip the eggs and sugar until soft peaks form and the mixture has tripled in volume. Mix one fourth of the whipped egg-sugar mixture into the chocolate mixture. Fold the chocolate mixture back into the remaining egg-sugar mixture. Fold in the whipped cream until blended.

Pour the batter into the prepared cake pan. Place the pan in a large pan, add warm water to halfway up the sides of the cake pan, and place in the preheated oven for 30 to 40 minutes, or until the cake has risen and small cracks appear on the surface. Let cool for 15 to 20 minutes before serving with vanilla ice cream.

To reheat, preheat the oven to 300°F. Cover the cake loosely with plastic wrap and place in the preheated oven. Turn the temperature off. Let warm for about 10 minutes.

DOUBLE-DARK CHOCOLATE CAKE

with White Chocolate Sauce

Stephan Pyles

Makes one 9-inch single-layer cake; serves 12

A rich flourless chocolate cake made with both semisweet and unsweetened chocolate and served in a pool of white chocolate sauce.

1 cup heavy (whipping) cream

10½ ounces semisweet chocolate, chopped

2 ounces unsweetened chocolate, chopped

5 eggs

⅓ cup sugar

1 teaspoon vanilla extract

White Chocolate Sauce *(recipe follows)*

PREHEAT THE OVEN TO 350°F. Place a round of baking parchment or waxed paper in the bottom of a 9-inch round cake pan. Butter and flour the pan and paper. In a medium saucepan, bring the cream to a boil. Remove from heat, add the chopped chocolates, and stir to blend. Cover the pan and let the chocolate melt for about 5 minutes. When melted, stir to blend completely; set aside.

In a double boiler, place the eggs, sugar, and vanilla extract. Set over simmering water and whip the mixture until warm to the touch, about 1 minute. Remove from heat. With an electric mixer, beat the eggs at high speed until tripled in volume, about 7 to 10 minutes. Whisk one fourth of the egg mixture into the chocolate until completely incorporated, then gently fold in the rest, trying to deflate the eggs as little as possible. Pour the chocolate mixture into the prepared cake pan and place this pan in a larger pan. Add warm water to halfway up the sides of the cake pan.

Bake for 50 minutes in the preheated oven, or until a toothpick inserted in the center comes out clean. Let sit in the water for 30 minutes, or until cool. Invert the cake on a platter and remove the paper. Serve with warm white chocolate sauce. To store, cover and chill. Bring to room temperature before serving.

White Chocolate Sauce

5 ounces white chocolate, chopped
1 cup heavy (whipping) cream

In a double boiler over barely simmering water, melt the chocolate until smooth. Stir in the cream. Serve warm.

HEATH BAR CAKE

Robert Zielinski

Makes one 9-by-13-inch cake; serves 12

Heath Bars and pecans are the topping for this easy-to-prepare cake.

1 cup packed light brown sugar	1 teaspoon vanilla extract
½ cup granulated sugar	2 cups sifted unbleached all-purpose
½ cup (1 stick) unsalted butter at	flour
room temperature	1 teaspoon baking soda
1 large egg, beaten	8 Heath Bars, frozen and chopped
1 cup buttermilk	½ cup (2 ounces) pecans, chopped

PREHEAT THE OVEN TO 350°F. Butter and flour a 9-by-13-inch cake pan. In a large bowl, cream the sugars and butter until light and fluffy. Beat in the egg, then gradually stir in the buttermilk. Beat in the vanilla, flour, and baking soda.

Pour into the prepared pan and sprinkle the chopped Heath Bars and pecans over the top. Bake in the preheated oven for 45 minutes, or until a toothpick inserted in the center comes out clean. Let cool on a rack before removing from the pan.

BÊTE NOIRE

Steven Howard

Makes one 10-inch single-layer cake

This flourless mocha cake has a warm, fudgy heart.

12 ounces unsweetened chocolate, chopped	2 cups sugar
6 ounces semisweet chocolate, chopped	8 eggs
1½ (3 sticks) butter, cut into pieces	½ cup Chocolate Ganache *(recipe on page 5)*
¾ cup freshly brewed coffee	Whipped cream and fresh fruit for garnish

PREHEAT THE OVEN TO 300°F. Butter a 10-inch round cake pan and line the bottom with baking parchment or waxed paper. Butter the paper. In a double boiler over barely simmering water, melt the chocolates and butter, and stir until smooth. In a small saucepan, heat the coffee and 1½ cups of the sugar to a simmer. Add to the chocolate mixture, whisking until completely blended. In a medium bowl, whisk together the eggs and the remaining ½ cup sugar until smooth. Whisk into the chocolate mixture until completely incorporated.

Pour the batter into the prepared cake pan and place the pan in a larger baking pan. Add warm water to halfway up the sides of the cake pan. Bake in the preheated oven for 30 to 40 minutes, or until the cake is set to a warm fudge consistency in the middle. Let cool completely on a rack and remove from the pan. Serve drizzled with ganache and garnished with whipped cream and fresh fruit.

CAJETA CHEESECAKE

Kim Peoples

Makes one 9-inch cheesecake

A complexly flavored cheesecake made with CAJETA, *the rich, sweetened goat milk caramel of Mexico.*

GRAHAM CRACKER CRUST

1⅔ cups graham cracker crumbs
 (about 14 graham crackers)

2 tablespoons sugar

1 teaspoon ground cinnamon

6 tablespoons unsalted butter, melted

FILLING

3 cups (1½ pounds) cream cheese at
 room temperature

1¾ cups sugar

¼ cup cornstarch

1½ teaspoons ground cinnamon

½ teaspoon ground ginger

6 eggs

2 egg yolks

2 teaspoons vanilla extract

1½ recipes *Cajeta (recipe on page 171)*

Preheat the oven to 300°F. To make the graham cracker crust: Butter a 9-inch springform pan. In a medium bowl, mix all the ingredients for the crust until blended. Press into the bottom of the prepared pan.

To make the filling: In the bowl of an electric mixer, cream the cream cheese and sugar until fluffy. Add the cornstarch, cinnamon, and ginger; mix well. Add the eggs and yolks gradually, scraping down the sides of the bowl between additions. Stir in the vanilla and *cajeta*. Pour into the prepared cake pan and bake in the preheated oven for about 1 hour, or until set. Let cool completely before removing from the pan.

COCONUT-CRUSTED BIG ISLAND GOAT CHEESE LAYER CAKE

with Macadamia Nut Praline

Roy Yamaguchi

Makes four 3-inch cakes or one 10-inch cake

A sweetened goat cheese adds dimension to this chiffon cake with a chewy coconut crust and topped with tropical fruit.

CHIFFON CAKE

½ cup water

6 tablespoons vegetable oil

2 eggs

1¼ cups cake flour

1 cup sugar

1¾ teaspoons baking powder

1 cup egg whites (about 8 large whites)

¼ teaspoon cream of tartar

COCONUT CRUST

6 tablespoons unsalted butter, melted

2 cups unsweetened shredded dried coconut

FILLING

½ cup plus 1 tablespoon (4½ ounces) Big Island goat cheese, or any plain mild fresh goat cheese at room temperature

½ cup plus 1 tablespoon (4½ ounces) cream cheese at room temperature

1 cup sour cream

½ cup sugar

2 tablespoons fresh lemon juice

Grated zest of 1 lemon

1 whole papaya or mango, peeled, seeded, and cut into thin slices

Macadamia Nut Praline *(recipe follows)*

To MAKE THE CAKE: Preheat the oven to 350°F. Butter and flour four 3-inch tart pans or a 10-inch round cake pan. In a large bowl, mix the water, oil, and eggs. Sift together the cake flour, ½ cup of the sugar, and baking powder. Add to the egg mixture and mix well.

In the clean, dry bowl of an electric mixer, beat the egg whites until frothy. Gradually add the remaining ½ cup sugar and the cream of tartar while mixing on high speed until soft peaks form. Fold into the flour mixture. Pour the batter into the prepared cake pan. Bake in the preheated oven for 40 minutes, or until a toothpick inserted into the center of the cake comes out clean. Let cool, then remove from the pan.

To MAKE THE COCONUT CRUST: Preheat the oven to 300°F. In a medium bowl, blend the butter and coconut. Press onto the sides of the prepared pans and down towards the center, adding a little at a time until the bottom is evenly covered. Bake in the preheated oven for 10 minutes, or until lightly brown; let cool.

To MAKE THE FILLING: In the bowl of an electric mixer, beat the goat cheese, cream cheese, and sour cream until smooth and creamy. Add the sugar and continue to mix for 3 minutes. Add the lemon juice and lemon zest and mix for another 3 minutes.

To assemble the cake, preheat the oven to 275°F. Cut a ⅛-inch crosswise layer from the chiffon cake and place it over the coconut crust. Reserve the remainder of the chiffon cake for another dessert or discard. Arrange the sliced papaya or mango in a single layer on top of the cake. Spread the goat cheese filling over the fruit. Sprinkle the macadamia nut praline over the filling. Bake in the preheated oven for approximately 25 minutes, or until just slightly firm. Let cool before serving.

Macadamia Nut Praline

1 cup sugar

¼ cup sugar

1 cup (5 ounces) macadamia nuts, toasted and chopped *(see page 4)*

In a small, heavy saucepan, mix the sugar and water. Cook over medium heat until the mixture starts to thicken and turn slightly golden in color, about 5 minutes. Remove from heat and thoroughly stir in the nuts with a wooden spoon. Immediately spread evenly onto a clean, dry baking sheet. Let cool, then chop into bite-sized pieces.

MACADAMIA PRALINE CHEESECAKE

Kevin Taylor

Makes one 9-inch single-layer cake

Crunchy pralinéed macadamia nuts are laced throughout this traditional cheesecake.

MACADAMIA PRALINE

½ cup (2½ ounces) unsalted macadamia nuts

1 cup sugar

CHEESECAKE

3¼ cups (26 ounces) cream cheese at room temperature

½ cup sugar

3 eggs

⅔ cup half-and-half

1 teaspoon vanilla extract

1 teaspoon grated lemon zest

TO MAKE THE MACADAMIA PRALINE: Preheat the oven to 400°F. Lightly butter a baking sheet. Place the nuts on the pan and toast in the preheated oven, turning frequently, for 5 to 10 minutes, or until they just begin to brown; let cool. In a saucepan, melt the sugar slowly over medium heat, stirring constantly, until golden brown, about 10 minutes. Add the nuts and continue cooking for another 30 seconds. Pour out onto the prepared pan. Chill until cool and hard. Chop the praline into bite-sized pieces.

TO MAKE THE CAKE: Preheat the oven to 325°F. Butter a 9-inch round cake pan, line the bottom with baking parchment or waxed paper, and butter the paper. In the bowl of an electric mixer, slowly mix the cream cheese and sugar until smooth. Add the eggs one at a time, blending each in completely.

Add the half-and-half, vanilla extract, and lemon zest to the cream cheese, and blend well. Stir in the macadamia praline until just evenly blended.

Pour the batter into the prepared pan. Place the pan in a larger baking pan and add warm water to halfway up the sides of the cake pan. Bake in the pre-heated oven for 1 hour, or until the center is firm; let cool.

CHEESECAKE

Christopher Gross

Makes 6 individual cheesecakes

These little cheesecakes are served with an enticing honey-champagne sauce and fresh figs and berries.

CHEESECAKE

2½ cups (18 ounces) cream cheese at room temperature

1 cup sugar

6 tablespoons crème fraîche *(recipe on page 8)*

6 tablespoons heavy (whipping) cream

1 egg

1 teaspoon vanilla extract

1 cup (5 ounces) blanched almonds, sliced

SAUCE

½ cup honey

1 cup champagne

GARNISH

12 fresh strawberries, stemmed

30 fresh raspberries

6 fresh blackberries

⅔ cup fresh huckleberries

3 fresh figs, quartered

6 slices kiwi, halved

12 fresh mint leaves

6 fresh mint sprigs

To MAKE THE CHEESECAKE: Preheat the oven to 225°F. Line the bottom of six 8-ounce ceramic or stainless steel mousse molds or custard cups with baking parchment or waxed paper and coat the sides with nonstick vegetable-oil spray or butter.

In an electric mixer on medium speed, beat the cream cheese and the sugar together until completely smooth. Scrape the sides of the bowl well. Continue mixing on low speed and blend in the crème fraîche and heavy cream. Scrape the sides of the bowl again; beat in the egg and blend in the vanilla extract.

Fill each mold two-thirds full with the cheesecake mixture and cover the top with the sliced almonds. Place the molds in a baking pan and add warm water to halfway up the sides of the molds. Bake the cheesecakes in the preheated oven for about 1½ to 2 hours, or until the centers are firm. Let cool to room temperature and refrigerate until ready to serve.

TO MAKE THE SAUCE: In a heavy saucepan, heat the honey, blend in the champagne, and simmer until thickened to a light syrup, about 30 minutes; let cool.

TO GARNISH AND SERVE: Run a warm thin knife around the edge of the molds and carefully turn them out onto 6 plates, removing the paper. Ladle a small amount of the sauce around the outer edge of each plate. Cut half of the strawberries in half and cut the others into fans. Reserve 6 raspberries. Arrange the berries, along with the figs and the half slices of kiwi, around each cheesecake and its pool of sauce. Julienne 2 mint leaves and sprinkle over the sauce for each cheesecake; garnish with a sprig of mint and 1 raspberry.

PRALINE CHEESECAKE

Ken Frank

Makes one 9-inch cake

The great thing about this cheesecake is that, unlike others, it is not too heavy and has the wonderful flavor of hazelnuts. They are positively habit-forming. The crust can be made well ahead of time or even kept in the freezer. Make sure your tart pan is the kind with a removable bottom. Have fun.
—Ken Frank

CRUST

Scant 2 cups unbleached all-purpose flour

½ cup (1 stick) plus 2 tablespoons cold unsalted butter, cut into pieces

3½ tablespoons sugar

Pinch of salt

4 drops vanilla extract

2 egg yolks

FILLING

1¾ cups (14 ounces) cream cheese at room temperature

3 egg yolks, beaten

3 tablespoons sugar

2 tablespoons crème fraîche

(recipe on page 8)

1 teaspoon fresh lemon juice

1 teaspoon vanilla extract

2 egg whites

CARAMEL WHIPPED CREAM

⅓ cup sugar

3 tablespoons water

1¾ cups heavy (whipping) cream

PRALINE TOPPING

¼ cup sugar

2 tablespoons water

¼ cup hazelnuts, toasted and skinned

(see page 4)

To MAKE THE CRUST: Preheat the oven to 350°F. In a mixing bowl, blend the flour, butter, sugar, and salt until the mixture resembles coarse meal. Add the vanilla and egg yolks and combine just until the dough forms a ball. It may be necessary to add a few drops of water, but don't make it too sticky. Wrap tightly in plastic wrap and refrigerate a few hours until hard.

Break the cold hard dough into 4 or 5 pieces and knead them slightly on a lightly floured surface to soften and make the dough easier to handle. Form the dough into a disc. On a lightly floured surface, roll the crust into a circle about ⅛ inch thick and 11 inches in diameter. You may need to dust the crust with flour to keep it from sticking. Use as little flour as possible for a finer crust. Roll up the dough loosely on the rolling pin and lay over a 9-inch tart pan with a removable bottom. Fit the crust into the pan and trim off the excess around the edges. Chill for 30 minutes, or until ready to bake. Place a piece of aluminum foil shiny side down over the crust and fill with 1 inch of uncooked rice or dried beans. Bake in the preheated oven for about 10 to 15 minutes. Remove the weights and foil and continue to bake for 5 minutes or until the crust is golden brown. Let cool to room temperature.

To MAKE THE FILLING: Preheat the oven to 350°F. In the bowl of an electric mixer, combine the cream cheese, egg yolks, sugar, crème fraîche, lemon juice, and vanilla for 30 seconds, or until smooth. In the clean, dry bowl of an electric mixer, whip the 2 egg whites until they form stiff peaks. Quickly but gently fold the whites into the cheese mixture and pour into the prebaked tart shell. Bake in the preheated oven for 30 minutes, or until set and golden brown. Let cool to room temperature, then refrigerate until cold.

To MAKE THE CARAMEL WHIPPED CREAM: In a small, heavy saucepan, cook the sugar with the water until it is a rich brown caramel. Remove from heat and stir in ¼ cup of the cream; let cool to room temperature. The cream should be as thick as honey. In the bowl of an electric mixer, whip the remaining 1½ cups cream until it holds soft peaks. Add the caramel while whipping the cream to stiff peaks.

To MAKE THE PRALINE TOPPING: In a small, heavy saucepan, cook the sugar and water until it is a rich brown caramel. Turn off heat and stir in the hazelnuts. Pour immediately onto a baking sheet lined with a smooth piece of aluminum foil and let cool. When cooled, break the praline into small pieces and chop it in a blender or food processor with a few quick pulses.

To assemble, remove the cheesecake from the tart pan and slide it onto a 9-inch cardboard circle. Mound the caramel whipped cream in the center of the cake. With a long pastry spatula, spread the cream smoothly over the top, tapering from the sides up to a point in the center like a cone. Sprinkle with the powdered praline.

CHOCOLATE MARBLE CHEESECAKE

John Downey

Makes one 9-inch cake; serves 10

When we first developed this recipe in Downey's restaurant, we made it in a big yellow bowl, well oiled. The finished cake was a voluptuous dome, and with its chocolate glaze it looked like a rich Doux de Montagne cheese to enjoy with the wines from dinner. Now we serve it in a more common cheesecake shape, but if you want to try using a heatproof bowl as a mold, select one that is about 12 inches across the top, although the filling will only come up to about a 9-inch-diameter level. To unmold, dip the bowl in hot water briefly.

—John Downey

SHORTBREAD

⅔ cup sugar

2 cups plus 3 tablespoons unsifted pastry flour

1 cup (2 sticks) chilled unsalted butter, cut into ½-inch cubes

GANACHE ICING

2 cups heavy (whipping) cream

3 ounces unsweetened chocolate, chopped

9 ounces semisweet chocolate, chopped

FILLING

2 cups (1 pound) cream cheese at room temperature

12 ounces fresh ricotta cheese

1 cup plus 2 tablespoons sugar

½ teaspoon vanilla extract

½ cup heavy (whipping) cream

3 large egg yolks, beaten

RASPBERRY SAUCE

1 cup fresh raspberries, or one thawed frozen 6-ounce package unsweetened raspberries

Raspberry jam to taste

To MAKE THE SHORTBREAD: Preheat the oven to 325°F. Line a baking sheet with baking parchment or grease it well. Into a medium bowl, sift the sugar and flour together 3 times. Cut in the butter with a pastry blender or 2 knives until the mixture is the consistency of cornmeal. Turn the dough out onto a lightly floured surface and knead the dough just until it begins to crack. Roll out to a ¼-inch-thick circle. Trim the dough, using a 9-inch cake pan as a pattern and cutting around the edge. Place on the prepared baking sheet and bake in the preheated oven until golden brown, about 12 to 15 minutes. Let the shortbread cool completely on the baking sheet or it will break. (If you are making this ahead, wrap it tightly in plastic wrap and store in the freezer.)

To MAKE THE GANACHE ICING: In a medium saucepan, bring the cream to a full boil. Remove from heat and stir in the chocolates until they have melted completely. Whisk until completely smooth and keep warm until ready to use. (Keep the pan covered so a skin won't form. The ganache may be made ahead and rewarmed gently over hot water.)

To MAKE THE FILLING: Cut a circle of baking parchment or waxed paper to fit into a 9-inch round cake pan. Brush the paper well with a mild-tasting vegetable oil on both sides and place it in the pan. Oil the sides of the pan well. In the bowl of an electric mixer, beat together the cheeses, sugar, and vanilla. In a double boiler over simmering water, cook the cream and beaten egg yolks, stirring, until the mixture is thick enough to coat a spoon, about 3 minutes.

Mix about one third of the cheese mixture into the cream mixture and continue to cook and stir until warm and blended. Pour into the remainder of the cheese mixture and beat with a wire whisk until light and fluffy. Pour the cheese mixture into the prepared cake pan. Swirl in ½ cup of the warm chocolate ganache to achieve a marbled effect. Cover the pan tightly with plastic wrap and refrigerate to chill thoroughly.

To MAKE THE RASPBERRY SAUCE: Puree the fresh or thawed raspberries in a blender or food processor. Strain to remove the seeds. Mix in raspberry jam to sweeten.

To assemble, spread one side of the shortbread circle liberally with chocolate ganache. Run a knife around the inside of the cake pan to loosen the filling. Set the shortbread, chocolate side down, on top of the cheesecake filling and press firmly together. Release the filling and the base from the mold onto a wire rack with a baking sheet underneath. Pull off the oiled paper. Making sure the ganache is warm and will pour easily, pour it evenly over the cheesecake to glaze completely. Do not spread the glaze with a knife, but if necessary lift the rack and turn the cake, allowing the glaze to flow where you need it. Chill until ready to serve.

To serve, pool some raspberry sauce on each serving plate. Using a warm knife, cut slices of the cake and place 1 slice on the sauce on each plate.

BUTTER-ALMOND FINANCIER

Nick Malgieri

Makes one 10-inch cake

The name of this traditional French dessert probably comes from its richness. It is an unusual batter where ground almonds, sugar and flour and a large quantity of melted butter are folded into egg whites which have been beaten with sugar. Of course, the egg whites fall and liquify as the butter is folded in, but the Financier rises well, nonetheless.

—Nick Malgieri

1 cup whole, blanched almonds, about 5 ounces	2 tablespoons dark rum
1½ cups sugar, divided	2 teaspoons vanilla extract
1 cup unbleached, all-purpose flour	8 large egg whites (1 cup)
10 tablespoons (1¼ sticks) unsalted butter	1 pinch salt
	¼ cup sliced, blanched almonds

PREHEAT THE OVEN TO 350°F. Butter a 10-inch round pan. Line with a disk of parchment or wax paper, and butter the paper. Place the almonds and ¾ cup of the sugar in a food processor and pulse until the mixture is finely ground. Pour into a bowl and stir in the flour.

Melt the butter and add the rum and vanilla extract. Set aside to cool slightly.

In a clean, dry bowl, beat the egg whites with the salt until they form a very soft peak. Beat in the remaining ¾ cup sugar in a very slow stream, and continue beating the egg whites until they hold a soft peak.

Fold the almond and butter mixtures into the egg whites alternately, ⅓ at a time, beginning with the almond and ending with the butter.

Pour into the prepared pan. Smooth the top and sprinkle with the sliced almonds.

Bake in the preheated oven for about 50 minutes until well-risen and golden. The center of the cake should feel firm when pressed with the palm of the hand.

Cool the Financier briefly on a rack and unmold. If some of the almonds on the surface fall off, replace them on the cake. Dust very lightly with confectioners sugar.

PROFILES

Robert Del Grande ❦ Marcel Desaulniers ❦ Susan Feniger & Mary Sue Milliken ❦ Ken Frank ❦ Kevin Graham ❦ Jean Joho ❦ Emeril Lagasse ❦ Emily Luchetti ❦ Nick ❦ Bruce Marder ❦ Michael McCarty ❦ le ❦ Seppi Renggli ❦ Anne Rosenzweig ❦ Jimmy Schmidt ❦ John Sedlar ❦ Piero Selvaggio ❦ Jackie Shen ❦ Nancy Silverton ❦ Joachim Splichal ❦ Jacques Torres ❦ Barbara Tropp ❦ Charlie Trotter ❦ Jonathan Waxman ❦ Jasper White ❦ Barry Wine ❦ Alan Wong ❦

ROBERT DEL GRANDE

Cafe Annie, Rio Ranch, Cafe Express

Houston, Texas

*F*INE BUT INFORMAL DINING was an important part of my childhood as far back as I can remember. My mother was a superlative, self-
taught cook, and *Gourmet* sat on the coffee table next to *Life*. When my parents
divorced in the fifties, it was only natural that my mother got a job managing
what was universally acclaimed as Houston's finest restaurant, Rudi's, then
located on South Main. The restaurant eventually moved to the Post Oak
Galleria, and my mother moved to New York. Whether it was the absence of
my mother or changing tastes, Rudi's eventually closed. Years later Robert Del
Grande came to Houston and took over Cafe Annie, which became in the eighties what Rudi's was in the sixties. When he outgrew his first location, he found
just the spot he was looking for in the Post Oak Galleria: the site of the former
Rudi's.

Del Grande wasn't born in Texas, but he fell in love with the colliding
cuisines that coalesced into the style we call Southwestern. Del Grande is self-
taught; in fact, he never intended to become a chef. He received his doctorate
in biochemistry at the University of California, Riverside, in 1981 and took a job
at Cafe Annie just for fun before beginning postdoctoral work. But it was his
destiny to become a chef. His mother was a great cook, and good food was
important in the Del Grande household. The combination of an early love for
food and a scientist's investigative style has yielded success for Del Grande at
Cafe Annie and his small restaurant named Cafe Express. Recently named the
James Beard recipient of the award for Best Southwest Chef, Robert Del Grande
will continue to set the standard for modern Southwestern cuisine not only at
Cafe Annie but at his new Rio Ranch Restaurant, which serves a grander version
of Texas Hill Country food.

"When it comes to desserts," says the chef, "we make the batter, we bake
it, and eat it. Our approach is less architectural than some restaurants that build

their desserts. In the European tradition, they create desserts made of parts, which are then assembled, as in the case of a genoise. But we're in America. So I take a direct approach. The dessert has a name, and that name describes the predominant flavor. We serve blackberry pie, caramel custard, and Mom's chocolate cake at Cafe Annie."

For Del Grande, desserts must create a response based on our memories of childhood sweets. "Everybody remembers pound cake from when they were little. But who grew up with opera cake? So at Cafe Annie, our favorite dessert is toasted vanilla pound cake with double-chocolate sauce. It strikes a chord that first got plucked thirty-odd years ago when our customers were young. That's why at my restaurants we don't do any pastry gymnastics, we just do solid cooking." *Great Desserts* includes a variation of Del Grande's pound cake, which includes apricots and pistachios.

MARCEL DESAULNIERS

The Trellis

Williamsburg, Virginia

WHEN I FIRST APPROACHED Marcel Desaulniers to participate in *Great Desserts from the Great Chefs*, I had no idea he was at work on a dessert book project of his own: *Death by Chocolate: The Last Word on a Consuming Passion* (Rizzoli, 1992). Yet despite being preoccupied with testing recipes, researching, and writing text, not to mention running his ever-busy Trellis Restaurant in Williamsburg, Marcel gladly acceded to my request and was the first chef to respond, providing numerous rigorously tested and well-explained recipes.

Such is the character of Marcel Desaulniers, who is always ready to help out with any project that will advance the enjoyment, understanding, or appreciation of food. He serves on many boards at cooking schools and professional associations, and his uncomplicated, yet refined cooking has quietly established a national reputation for Desaulniers's colonial Williamsburg restaurant.

The clientele for his straightforward noontime presentations, typical American lunchtime fare, are mostly tourists. But at night, when the tourists are on their way to Monticello or Washington, the lights are lowered, the tablecloths are laid, and those who have made the Trellis a destination restaurant for the last eighteen years dine on food as well prepared and inventive as that served in any restaurant in America today.

This book includes Desaulniers's crème anglaise ice cream, white grape and currant sorbet, chocolate valenciennes, and double-chocolate walnut tart. His recipes can be time-consuming to prepare, but I have found few recipes better explained. Desaulniers is meticulous about detail, and he takes the time to walk you step-by-step through his recipes so that there can be no doubt about their outcome: an unqualified success every time.

TOM DOUGLAS
Dahlia Lounge
Seattle, Washington

WHEN I MOVED BACK TO SEATTLE after an absence of thirty-eight years, it was a joy to return to a city I had never wanted to leave. But the homecoming was official when, dining at Tom Douglas's Dahlia Lounge one night, I noticed an apple dumpling with caramel sauce and vanilla ice cream on the menu. My mother often served meltingly soft, tart-sweet apples inside a pyramid of pie dough, dusted with cinnamon-sugar and swimming in a sweet sauce of the apple's own juice, reduced and thickened during baking. Could this restaurant dessert be anything like my Mom's, I wondered? It turned out it was, and I left the restaurant feeling I really had come home.

It doesn't surprise me now that Tom Douglas serves such desserts as apple dumplings and coconut cream pie. He's pretty much self-taught. He worked in a series of restaurants beginning with the Hotel Dupont in his native Delaware. By the time he reached Seattle, he was accomplished enough to elevate Cafe Sport to one of the top restaurants in the city. In 1989 he opened the Dahlia Lounge, which isn't really a lounge (no bar, no entertainment), but the name fits. The place has a forties ambience–just the setting for Douglas's homey food.

"Desserts are artsy at fancy restaurants," says Douglas. "We're rustic in our approach. We serve good food, home-style. I guess there's a place for the other kind of dessert. But there are only so many dots of sauce and purees I want to see with my dessert."

You won't see any dots or purees anywhere near Douglas's pear tart with caramel sauce or his lemon pound cake with lemon ice cream. He does serve a crème caramel, but not the "artsy" kind. It's richer and creamier than the flanlike versions you see at "fancy" restaurants.

"Desserts are a homey thing for us," says Douglas. "I guess that's why people come here to eat them. They can recapture sweet memories of growing up."

LISSA DOUMANI

Terra

St. Helena, California

IRTUOSO PASTRY CHEF and child prodigy Lissa Doumani, like Mozart, soloed at age five (her first cake), and made her first original dessert recipe at twelve. She went on to acquire her basic restaurant training from Sally Schmitt of French Laundry restaurant fame. She took a brief detour to become a stockbroker, but she soon came back to cooking. Perhaps Doumani was destined to become a restaurateur, as was her father before he became a wine maker at Stags' Leap Winery.

With little restaurant training but plenty of chutzpah, Lissa Doumani somehow persuaded Wolfgang Puck to give her a job at Spago, where she began as pastry cook under Nancy Silverton. To the surprise of everyone but herself, she rose to become pastry chef when Silverton left for New York.

After a year and a half, Lissa went to work as pastry chef for Roy Yamaguchi's 385 North in Los Angeles. There she started pastry competitions and honed her skills for the time when she would leave to start her own restaurant.

That time came in 1986, when she and her husband, Hiro Sone, former chef at Spago, left for the Napa Valley to plan the opening of Terra. Though running the restaurant as owner, hostess, and business manager keeps her fingers on the computer and not in chocolate butter cream, she is the moving force behind such desserts as a dense chocolate-walnut brownie with bourbon ice cream, tiramisú, sorbets served in a giant tuile and, depending on what is fresh at the market, a "tart of tonight." *Great Desserts* presents Doumani's fruit crostata.

JOHN DOWNEY

Downey's
Santa Barbara, California

*I*F YOU CAN THINK of a more oxymoronic enterprise than a hang-gliding business in New York City, I can't imagine what it would be. Perhaps that's why John Downey abandoned Windborne Hang Gliders in 1976, after one year. His journal notes: "What a thrill! The early days were ridiculously dangerous! Exciting but peaceful when you're soaring. For most customers it was only one lesson and not much follow-through except for a few crazies." It goes to show that mid-life career changes are not always prudent—especially when you're as talented a chef as John Downey.

Working his way up through various kitchen stations onboard Cunard Lines' *Queen Elizabeth* and *QE2*, Downey finally made landfall in New York at Lafayette Restaurant in 1972. After his experiment with Windborne, he went to work for Joe Baum at the World Trade Center. Then he took a real flyer, which turned out to be his best career move yet: moving to California.

Santa Barbara's first establishment to serve ambitious California cuisine was Penelope's, which John was hired to open as chef in 1979. Three years later, he struck out on his own and opened Downey's. The storefront restaurant holds forty-eight guests in a white garden setting with large, colorful paintings. It's the perfect place for Downey's sunny, light creations made with the freshest of organic ingredients.

The light, "not contrived, not architectural" dishes, as Downey puts it, are —again in his own words—"comfortable, the way you would describe your mother's food if she were a good cook." That philosophy holds true for his desserts as well. The butterscotch baked apple in puff pastry (with the best vanilla bean ice cream I've ever tasted) the three-citrus genoise, and the white chocolate-raspberry mille-feuille are among my favorites. In summer Downey takes ripe Santa Barbara peaches and makes a shortcake, a dish that typifies his approach to desserts. "Desserts need to be simple, gutsy, and good, but not something you'd see in a Betty Crocker cookbook." Downey creates a grand look to the desserts, which sit on a table in the center of the dining room and are beautiful enough to tempt even those who might already be full. Downey's desserts aren't as sweet as many restaurant pastries. The flavors, not the sugar, carry the day. Having tasted them all many times, I can only say that it's difficult to choose which of the former wind-sailor's desserts you'd most want (as my eleven-year-old son Cory puts it) to hang with. Included here are his world-best vanilla bean ice cream, the apple in puff pastry to go with it, the white chocolate mille-feuille, and a pumpkin crème brûlée.

SUSAN FENIGER AND MARY SUE MILLIKEN

Border Grill

Santa Monica, California

"I LOVE ETHNIC FOOD," says Mary Sue Milliken, "but not ethnic desserts." That about sums up the approach she and her partner taketo desserts at Border Grill. The ethnic concept is based on their travels to Mexico and Central America where they learned from street vendors and *mamacitas* the secrets of down-home cooking south of the border. At Border Grill, they present these dishes much as you would find them in the interior of Mexico, Guatemala, or Honduras. The food remains authentic— right down to the tortillas made continuously in the front of the restaurant where the aroma captivates you the moment you walk in.

The approach with desserts, in keeping with Milliken's philosophy, is to suggest Mexicano but deliver Americano. The Mexican-chocolate cream pie, with a touch of cinnamon, is the best American chocolate cream pie you can imagine. The lime pie is topped with coconut. And, yes, there are flans.

Don't look for fancy desserts at Border Grill. "I don't do elaborate square-cornered, sturdy desserts," says Milliken. "I concentrate on serving homey desserts that taste good but don't look gorgeous." But they taste gorgeous. The double-chocolate scooters presented in this collection are well named; they'll scoot right out of your kitchen the moment they come out of the oven. We've also included a homey banana cake with coconut custard, cinnamon pecan ice cream, and a Mexican-inspired lime-coconut pie.

KEN FRANK
House of Blues
Los Angeles, California

WHILE THE BLUES ARE "COOKIN" in the first floor performance hall, Ken Frank continues his career as, in his words, "a French chef in America's golden age of cuisine" in the third floor Foundation Room, a private club dedicated to raising money to bring art, music, and culture to underprivileged kids. You'd think a place called House of Blues would serve jambalaya and cafish pie. And it does in its second floor dining room. But Ken Frank has nothing to do with that operation. He continues serving the kind of food he made famous at La Toque (just a few blocks west on Sunset Strip), where for thirteen years as chef-proprietaire he was famous for fresh pasta with black truffles and egg yolk, and some of the best wild mushroom dishes in town.

A few of his famous La Toque desserts followed him to House of Blues. His concorde cake studded with chocolate meringue, chocolate espresso soufflé, and praline cheesecake are favorites at House of Blues. But along with these pastries he serves fresh fruit desserts, mousses, and homemade ice creams.

Just as House of Blues books acts from out of town in its performance hall, Frank invites the very finest chefs from around the country to join him for gigs in the kitchen. And when they're jammin' together, some think they make the sweetest music on all three floors. In this collection, Frank shares with us his praline cheesecake.

KEVIN GRAHAM
Grill Room, Windsor Court Hotel
New Orleans, Louisiana

*D*OES IT SEEM CONTRADICTORY to prepare savory dishes based on a spa cuisine called Body Conscious and then cut loose and offer desserts like chocolate breathless and blueberry cheesecake crumble? Not to Kevin Graham of New Orleans's peerless Grill Room. Desserts are by definition rich. Why eat them unless you're indulging? So by preparing lighter entrees such as Mediterranean fish with dill broth, or Chinese lacquered duck with coffee mandarin glaze, Graham knows there'll be room for more than Jell-O.

Of course, this doesn't stop him from preparing such airy desserts as his confoundingly good citrus soup, but most people think of dessert as a time to splurge. So Graham makes sure they'll have room to enjoy that indulgence. The food is not ascetic, nor is it intended to be, by definition, a dietary regimen. Says Graham, "When we create, we never sacrifice flavor. We spend a little more time than the average kitchen in thinking through and planning how our dishes can be made without the nonnutritive and nonessential elements such as fats, preservatives, salt, and sugar. Using reductions instead of commercial bases and constantly questioning whether a dish really needs that extra cream, whether a sauce needs that roux, allows us to create food that makes us cognizant of the materials we place in our bodies and thus be more in tune with ourselves and our environment."

The chef's philosophy (which wouldn't count for diddley-squat without his unerring taste and execution) seems to be working, because a lot of people are very happy placing Graham-created materials in their bodies. Named one of America's top ten new chefs by *Food and Wine* in 1991, he presides over what the Distinguished Restaurants of North America organization deemed one of the top twenty-five restaurants in the country in 1992.

And presides is just the way Graham would put it. The chef de cuisine, he says, is "merely the man who has the power of veto. Ideas for the menus can come from the lowest echelon, not necessarily from me." To Graham, the creative process is a continual progression, with the kitchen as a think tank.

To that end, the English-born, Hotel Negresco-trained Graham works hand-in-hand with executive pastry chef Shane Gorringe to create the made-from-scratch pastries and ice creams that make the Grill Room shine in a city with an abundance of stars. Graham and company have a penchant for architectural presentations. But none of the Grill Room desserts, such as the chocolate breathless, strawberry-champagne soup, or lemon tart with raspberry sauce, sacrifice flavor for design. Recipes for these three dishes, along with Graham's chocolate truffles, cinnamon ice cream with raspberry sabayon and tulip shells, and fresh berries in champagne and pastis are included in this book.

CHRISTOPHER GROSS

Christopher's, Christopher's Bistro

Phoenix, Arizona

CHRISTOPHER GROSS couldn't decide if he wanted to open a formal restaurant or a casual one. So he opened two dining rooms sharing the same kitchen: the elegant Christopher's and Christopher's Bistro, which, along with Vincent on Camelback and RoxSand, have brought fine dining to Phoenix.

Christopher did not share the same burning desire that Georges Perrier and Jean Joho had to be a chef. But at about the same age, fourteen or so, he began his "apprenticeship" flipping burgers so he could afford a dirt bike. The boy who didn't like food (not just vegetables; he really didn't like much else besides hamburgers) was now surrounded by it.

In his late teens, while working at the old Adams Hotel in Phoenix, he found himself growing interested in sauces in spite of himself. There he was exposed to chefs from Europe and, looking for role models and a career, began to admire their discipline and talent. He knew he'd have to go abroad to get the training necessary to develop further.

After a short stint in an English kitchen, a flurry of letters produced a job at a Michelin two-star restaurant in Paris, where his boss obsessed about such things as the grill marks on a steak. No obsession, no stars, Gross learned. He returned to the States disciplined and trained, and continued to hone his skills at L.A.'s L'Orangerie. Soon he was ready to return to Phoenix to open his own place.

After a few years of developing a unique style on the outskirts of Phoenix at Le Relais, Christopher partnered with one of his best customers to open Christopher's and Christopher's Bistro.

At the black-and-pink-tiled Bistro, you sit in bentwood chairs and eat red lentil soup with duck confit, roasted chicken leg stuffed with wild mushroom mousse, and finish with strawberry croustillant or the chef's signature chocolate tower with fresh fruit and espresso sauce. At Christopher's, however, white damask tablecloths are the setting for a sauté of venison loin with vegetables, wine, pepper, thyme, and hazelnut oil; lamb spiced with coriander, cinnamon, ginger, cloves, and pepper; and monkfish fillet in a balsamic-vinegar reduction. Chocolate hot and cold is a favorite dessert at Christopher's: warm chocolate cake covered in bittersweet chocolate sauce and resting on a base of cool, intense chocolate mousse. For my all-time Christopher's dessert favorite, however, I'd go back to the Bistro and order the banana split, as long as I was dining with three friends. We've presented his classic cheesecake here.

VINCENT GUERITHAULT

Vincent on Camelback

Phoenix, Arizona

$\mathcal{I}$ HAVE ONLY TWO PROBLEMS with Vincent Guerithault: He located his wonderful restaurant in Phoenix where I seldom have occasion to travel; and when I do go there, it's nigh on impossible to make it past his miniature croissants: peerless, buttery, flaky puffs that no chef I've encountered in France or America has come close to matching.

Those quibbles aside, what a joy is Guerithault's traditional French cuisine made with Southwestern ingredients. He's often compared to Los Angeles's John Sedlar, though John started in Santa Fe and added his French training later. Guerithault grew up in France, trained at L'Oustau de Baumanière and Maxim's alongside Wolfgang Puck, and worked under Jean Banchet at Le Français near Chicago. He was then invited to head the kitchen at a restaurant in Phoenix, and it wasn't long before he opened Vincent in 1986.

After a prix-fixe dinner featuring Vincent's wild mushroom-filled chilies with blue cheese sauce, cream of avocado soup, and ratatouille tamales (plus a basket of the aforementioned croissants), it's difficult to imagine having dessert. But I always find room for one, whether it be Vincent's signature berry crème brûlée in a sweet "taco" shell, his lemon crust, or a little something like his white chocolate macadamia nut cookies or a dark chocolate truffle. The French and Southwestern influences even intersect in desserts such as a jalapeño and orange tart with accents of fresh ginger.

For Vincent Guerithault, dessert isn't an afterthought. "You can't overemphasize the importance of dessert," he told me. "It's what people will remember most about dinner at your restaurant, because it's the last thing they eat there."

That message wasn't lost on Mimi Sheraton. She recently named Vincent one of "50 Restaurants Worth the Journey" in *Traveler Magazine*. That'll have to do until Michelin starts awarding stars in America.

Until you make that journey, sample here Guerithault's truffles, white chocolate–macadamia nut cookies, lemon crust, crème brûlée in a sweet taco shell, and if you're adventurous, his honey, jalapeño and orange chutney tart.

STEVEN HOWARD

Walla Walla, Washington

S TEVEN HOWARD should be an inspiration to anyone who aspires to greatness in the kitchen without years of formal training. While many insist culinary school or apprenticeship is the only way to accumulate the knowledge and experience necessary to become an important chef, Steven Howard is proof that the self-taught can achieve greatness. Howard learned by reading, testing, failing, and testing again. "I was able to learn from the masters of the pastry world only from their books," says Howard. "I made many mistakes, but with Lenôtre's first pastry book as my personal bible, I was able to develop my culinary craft."

In 1985, Howard began working for Richard and Larry D'Amico, veteran Minneapolis restaurateurs, at Primavera. It was there that he put into practice what he had learned from books. "In the beginning we did sit-down dinner parties for up to two thousand people. Through the experience of making such a high volume of desserts, I learned quickly what would and wouldn't fly."

When the brothers opened D'Amico Cucina in 1988, they felt Howard was ready to head the pastry department there. This was to be a different operation altogether. "At D'Amico Cucina we created each dessert individually. Prior to serving, the dessert was composed by my pastry crew for maximum impact." At D'Amico Cucina, Howard came up with cannoli with Mascarpone and vanilla; pear and Gorgonzola tart; ricotta cheesecake with candied fruit and cassis; and chocolate bread pudding in a sweet Chianti sauce. My favorite was a lusty fig mousse layered in filo.

"It was here I developed my philosophy of creating desserts with a wide variety of flavors and textures, using local, seasonal ingredients as much as possible. Of course, folks in Minneapolis want more in their desserts than just apples during our six-month winter, so I'm grateful for the produce grown in our coastal and southern states as well as South America."

Steven Howard has now settled in Washington state, where he'll take advantage of the Northwest bounty to create more great desserts. Here we present his cranberry-nut bread, chocolate-covered toasted-pistachio gelato, bête noire, and biscotti as well as his chocolate, port, and pine nut timbale; candied ginger soufflé; and butter pastry with sweet squash filling. We've also included two tart recipes from this prolific chef: chocolate tart and nectarine tart.

JEAN JOHO

Everest

Chicago, Illinois

𝒜MERICA'S FAMILIARITY WITH REGIONAL French cooking was generally limited to dishes from Burgundy, Provence, and Brittany until Jean Joho came to Chicago in the mid-eighties, bringing with him the tastes of his native Alsace. Earthy flavors from ingredients both humble (potatoes, turnips, parsley, cauliflower, and salsify) and sublime (truffles, foie gras, and lobster) are paired by Joho to create the highly individual dishes served in the rarified setting of the Everest, forty stories above Chicago.

Joho began his apprenticeship in the traditional French manner, beginning at age thirteen and finishing with Paul Haeberlin at his three-star L'Auberge de l'Ill. But unlike many of his contemporaries, Joho did not come to the United States directly from France. He traveled through Europe picking up Mediterranean and Central European influences that rounded out his training and helped him develop a unique cuisine.

Joho's ever-changing dessert menu is inspiration- and market-driven. "In winter," says Joho, "I might offer desserts with citrus or bananas or an exotic fruit like mango. But in fall I want to support our local growers by using apples, pears, and quinces grown around here. In summer, nothing helps digestion better after a big meal than fresh local red berries and cherries."

A pioneer at exposing America to unfamiliar flavors in his savory courses, Joho follows suit in his desserts. B.J. (before Joho), few of us had been exposed to dishes such as amber beer crème brûlée, Alsatian-style; Alsace kugelhopf; or cold Pinot Noir de Alsace cherry soup. But Joho makes familiar desserts with equal aplomb, such as crêpes with sautéed apples (albeit with kirsch from Alsace), and blueberry apple crumble. "You won't find a *bavarois* or a genoise on my dessert menu," says Joho. "It's too hard to digest a heavy dessert after a big meal. My desserts are most always fruit-based." But when Joho does decide to make a chocolate dessert, such as his fantasy of chocolate, it is spectacular. Desserts from Joho's menu included here are blueberry apple crumble, and crêpes with sautéed apples.

HUBERT KELLER

Fleur de Lys

San Francisco, California

THE FLEUR DE LYS, the stylized iris of French heraldry, is the ideal symbol for Hubert Keller's restaurant of the same name. Hubert Keller decided from the beginning to create a regal dining room for special occasions. The entry, with its rough-hewn beams, is juxtaposed with a dining room festooned with hundreds of yards of hand-printed red floral fabric that gives the restaurant the feel of a royal garden tent set in the French countryside. And you are treated like royalty by a small regiment of vigilant and attentive tuxedo-clad waitstaff.

Such a setting and service call for elegant food, and although the court of France may have dined on richer fare, I doubt that they had better food than that at Fleur de Lys. Keller calls his cooking "contemporary French cuisine with a Mediterranean touch," and he excels at such dishes as pork tenderloin, lobster, tuna, and veal chops. He also elevates vegetables from the mundane to the sublime, a sign of rare talent in a chef: Fleur de Lys serves a vegetarian prix-fixe menu featuring such dishes as creamy lentils with ginger and sesame oil; artichoke hearts filled with creamy mashed potatoes and spinach; and a napoleon of ratatouille and goat cheese.

The years Keller spent with Haeberlin, Bocuse, Verge, and Maximin show in the savory courses; the years with Lenôtre show in the sweet. From the simple figs and blueberries in an intense citrus broth (the chef's favorite), to pear and pecan tart; Burgundy-cinnamon sorbet; and frozen nougat flavored with candied fruit and pureed mint, Keller's mastery of his mentor's lessons is obvious. The dessert menu is rounded out with classics such as house-made marrons glacés, and homespun favorites such as Grandma's omelet soufflé with strawberries.

Fleur de Lys was described in *Food and Wine* as one of the top twenty-five restaurants in America; *Gault-Millau* says it's the best in San Francisco; and the

Zagat Guide says it is "merely the best... in the U.S." Until you go there to try it for yourself, you can sample Keller's desserts in this collection. We offer two of Keller's light desserts: burgundy-cinnamon sorbet and figs, bananas, and blueberries in citrus broth. Try creating his frozen nougat flavored with candied fruits and pureed mint, grandma's omelet soufflé with strawberries, and warm bosc pear and pecan cream tart.

GRAY KUNZ

Lespinasse

New York, New York

"You won't find any Chrysler Buildings on my dessert plates," states Gray Kunz definitively, referring to the current practice of building architectural desserts high on a plate. On the contrary, Kunz is more apt to build down, creating wonderful dessert soups. Paying close attention to what's in season, he brings forth such sweet summer concoctions as an infusion of vanilla and lemongrass with fresh mango, watermelon, and peach. In autumn his tart, clear, cinnamon-scented apple soup with apple granita and vanilla maple syrup is crisply refreshing. So refreshing, in fact, that we've included it in this book.

Flavors such as vanilla, cinnamon, and lemongrass are essential to Kunz's unique cuisine, rigorously French in technique and presentation, but with subtle shadings from Southeast Asia, Malaysia, and Indonesia. His style, not to be confused with the French-Chinese cooking of Wolfgang Puck at Chinois, comes from memories of growing up in Singapore and his years heading up the kitchen at the Regent in Hong Kong. In between, he learned how to cook from a fellow Swiss, the legendary Fredy Girardet of Crissier near Lausanne.

Kunz is always on the lookout for the exotic. That's why he's a member of an international organization devoted to the preservation and cultivation of rare fruit. On a recent menu, Kunz presented a bracing kalamansi and pineapple soup. The kalamansi, about the size of a kumquat, is a cross between a clementine and a lime.

Other Kunz dessert favorites include soufflés such as espresso-cardamom (included here) or hot passion fruit; a dark espresso mousse with espresso zabaglione and a sweet Mascarpone and bittersweet chocolate sauce; a frozen anise mousse with caramelized bananas and yogurt mousseline with lightly stewed berries; and an apricot tarte tatin served over almond ice cream.

"I want to broaden people's view. I want to educate when I cook," says Kunz. "That's why I'm fond of using unusual spices. And that's why I serve simple desserts. For flavor to be at its peak, you can't lose time assembling something. Lose time and you lose taste. So in my desserts I focus on simplicity. I choose one or two strongly pronounced predominant flavors, with spice accents. I can't deliver peak flavor in some sort of an elaborate construction. It's only the flavor of the dessert that counts."

EMERIL LAGASSE

Emeril's, NOLA

New Orleans, Louisiana

D INERS SOMETIMES COMPLAIN that they eat so much bread at Emeril Lagasse's restaurants that they hardly have room for the food, let alone dessert. But the same talent that produces rich corn bread, spicy buns, and hearty whole-wheat rolls makes Lagasse a great pastry chef.

As a boy growing up in the small town of Fall River, Massachusetts, Lagasse worked at a local Portuguese bakery, where he became adept in the art of bread and pastry baking. As a teen, Emeril turned down a music scholarship to follow his dream of being a chef, and worked his way through the culinary program at Johnson and Wales University, where he received a doctoral degree.

If anyone comes to his New Orleans restaurants sick of bad cooking, this doctor has the cure. He starts with fresh, local ingredients, often from a devoted cottage industry of growers and fishers who give Lagasse just what he needs to create his "new New Orleans cookery." Using as a foundation the deep, rich flavors familiar to lovers of Creole food, he adds Asian, New England, Southwestern, and Mediterranean influences to his original dishes.

The desserts, however, are all-American and all original. His homemade goat cheese cheesecake with Creole cream cheese coulis, and his chocolate-pecan terrine with coffee anglaise sauce are among my favorites.

"My background is baking," says Lagasse. "And with baking, freshness is everything. So in my restaurants we don't go with the pastry cart approach with desserts made God knows when. Ours is an individualized approach. We merchandise our desserts like we would a great bottle of wine. What will go well with the food just consumed?"

Will it be the Boston cream pie, the ice cream sandwich (a seasonal cookie with an unusual ice cream), peanut butter pie, a chocolate polenta cake, or a light mille feuille of Louisiana strawberries? There are a dozen and a half desserts on the menu. Why so many?

Says Lagasse: "We offer a spectrum of desserts on a separate menu. To complete a fine dining experience we'll offer something fruity like a pie or cobbler or simply fresh fruit, a pastry like a pandowdy or Key lime pie, a chocolate dessert, or the house specialty: banana cream pie with banana crust with chocolate drizzles. A dessert for me must be special to end a special dining experience."

We've included Lagasse's banana cream pie, along with Jilly's chocolate chunk cookies and flourless chocolate cake, in this collection.

EMILY LUCHETTI
Stars, Stars Cafe
San Francisco, California

O MY TASTE, San Francisco is the finest restaurant city in America. A fraction the size of New York, Los Angeles, or Chicago, the city by the bay outshines them in all in breadth and depth of great places to eat. So when Emily Luchetti, pastry chef at Stars and Stars Cafe was rated by the San Francisco *Examiner* as one of the top six pastry chefs in the Bay Area, it meant she had to be among America's greats. And a sampling of the recipes in her *Stars Desserts* (HarperCollins, 1991) or the representative desserts in this collection shows why she excels not only at traditional dishes but with revolutionary ones as well.

If you have the good fortune to dine at Stars, you'll find old-fashioned desserts ranging from a blancmange served with fresh berries, to trifles, crêpes, and pandowdies. Figs and raspberries shine in both a gratin and a lemon-Mascarpone cream tart. A refashioned treat of yesteryear is a grown-up sandwich of chocolate-espresso ice cream. And then there's a classic strawberry-rhubarb crisp. My favorite of Ms. Luchetti's cakes is her plum cake flavored with cardamom and served with a vanilla custard sauce.

Emily didn't have a long-simmering passion to become a chef, but grew to love cooking after taking her first kitchen job in a New York executive dining room. Study at the New York Restaurant School and Gerard Pangaud's two-star restaurant in Paris prepared her to be a charter member of the Stars cooking team of Jeremiah Tower and Mark Franz that has dazzled San Francisco since 1984.

Seasons are important to Emily Luchetti. When passion fruit becomes available in the spring, you might find her passion fruit pudding soufflé on the menu. In winter, winter-fruit dumplings (included here), and toasted pecan cake with warm apples and cinnamon double cream share the dessert menu with chocolate paradise (a chocolate soufflé pastry layered with chocolate ganache and served with champagne sabayon). And in summer her mango fantasy cream served with pineapples and bananas is a fantasy fulfilled. For a stunning light dessert we've included her white chocolate-dipped double-chocolate biscotti.

NICK MALGIERI

Peter Kump's New York Cooking School

New York, New York

"NO CHESTNUTS IN JUNE or strawberries in December," insists Nick Malgieri, summarizing the importance of fresh, seasonal ingredients in making winning desserts. The chef elaborates: "Stick to the season at hand. In that way you maximize freshness. All ingredients must be the freshest possible, quickly prepared, and served fresh." Malgieri goes on to say that "the preparation and presentation should not complicate or overwhelm the flavor of the ingredients used." Using these precepts, Nick Malgieri fashions cold-weather desserts such as cranberry-walnut tart and chocolate-chestnut bûche de Noël. And where can you taste such treats? Only by taking a class at Peter Kump's or by cooking them in your own kitchen.

As director of the pastry program at Peter Kump's New York Cooking School and as author of Nick Malgieri's *Perfect Pastry* (Macmillan, 1989) and *Great Italian Desserts* (Little, Brown, 1990), Nick Malgieri devotes himself to perfecting the art of pâtisserie.

After graduating from the Culinary Institute of America, Malgieri apprenticed in Switzerland and France before returning to the States to serve as pastry chef at the Waldorf-Astoria. But making pastries wasn't enough; he wanted to teach. So, in 1979, he began at the New School Culinary Arts Program. Two years later he was chairman of the baking department, developing and teaching the baking curriculum for the New York Restaurant School and authoring the baking section of the Restaurant School's textbook.

Malgieri is especially drawn to the desserts of his forebears, so in 1985 he began to travel to Italy to study the pastry-maker's art. Now Malgieri's research into Italian techniques and recipes for desserts are making the world aware that Italian chefs produce more than just gelato and tiramisú. For example, there's *struffoli*, a popular Italian Christmas pastry of fritters bound with caramel. But Malgieri is equally at home teaching French desserts, such as the above-mentioned bûche de Noël and a *brêton aux pommes* and all-American favorites such as the cranberry-walnut tart: a pungent, not-too-sweet dessert that serves as a perfect finale to a holiday meal. We've included all these desserts in our book so you can sample the breadth of Malgieri's dessert repertoire. In addition we present his chocolate-pistachio-raspberry cake, strawberry meringue cake, and rhubarb crumb tart. For soufflé-lovers, we offer Malgieri's pear and cranberry soufflé and his strawberry soufflé with strawberry-orange sauce.

BRUCE MARDER

West Beach Cafe, Rebecca's, Broadway Deli

Los Angeles, California

HO STARTED CALIFORNIA CUISINE? Alice Waters was certainly among the first, pairing the Golden State's bounty with a Provençal cooking style. But though some would give the credit to Wolfgang Puck or Michael McCarty, Bruce Marder was the first Southern California chef to develop the style known as California cuisine.

Languishing in dental school at the University of Southern California in the early seventies, it probably never occurred to Bruce Marder that he'd someday be filling stomachs instead of teeth.

Marder's first restaurant was West Beach Cafe in Venice Beach, California. He had learned the basics at Chicago's Dumas Père School of French Cuisine and at the Beverly Hills Hotel. But extensive travel and exposure to exotic flavors (he decided to become a chef after eating Indian food prepared by a Dutch woman on the beach in Morocco) and his intuition for what appeals to diners ("Food that tastes good before you do anything to it") gave him an edge on people who thought veal cordon bleu and lobster thermidor would define haute cuisine forever.

Young artists with an appreciation for the ground-breaking cuisine Marder was creating were his first customers. Word spread, and those that represented and/or bought art came to dine next to those who created it, while Marder pioneered the hanging of original contemporary art on his restaurant walls. Artists like Laddie John Dill, John Dill, Peter Alexander, and Chuck Arnoldi sat cheek by jowl with other patrons, enjoying eggplant and tomato pizza, grilled Chilean sea bass, and grilled rare breast of duck ragout. It was at West Beach Cafe that Marder introduced such desserts made-to-order as French apple tart with caramel sauce; strawberries gratin; and chocolate-mousse cake—copies of which soon began appearing all over Los Angeles.

"I think my approach to desserts is the same as it is to the rest of my food," says Marder. "I just keep everything simple. If you get too many ingredients going, it's no good. That's why people like my chocolate soufflé or lemon soufflé, or the hot apple tart with caramel sauce. The desserts are simple, recognizable, and immediately satisfying."

The same philosophy holds true at Rebecca's, which Marder named for his wife and where the chef lives out his fantasy of creating upscale but down-to-earth Mexican desserts such as hearty flans and citrusy tarts. In every venue, Marder's desserts, from the crème brûlée cake to the flourless chocolate-walnut cake (presented here), have set a standard for L.A. restaurants.

The Broadway Deli is a collaborative effort between Marder, Michel Richard, and investor Marvin Zeidler. In this amazingly eclectic restaurant-emporium, French bistro and Jewish deli-food coexist in the restaurant area while, a few feet away, patrons can buy organic produce, French cheeses, imported groceries, or Michel Richard's impeccable pastries. As the Broadway Deli proves, Bruce Marder, as much as anyone in the restaurant business today, gives people the kind of food they want.

MICHAEL McCARTY
Michael's

Santa Monica, New York City

ALTHOUGH HE HAS SHUTTERED ADIRONACKS in Denver
and failed to consummate his long-sought deal to create the Santa
Monica Beach Hotel, Michael McCarty is still smiling. After all, he founded
Michael's, the restaurant that revolutionized cooking in Los Angeles. He can
take credit for launching or advancing the careers of Jonathan Waxman, Ken
Frank, Roy Yamaguchi, Nancy Silverton, and Mark Peel, among others. And he
still runs Michael's in Santa Monica and New York.

Michael's in Santa Monica continues to be the most casually elegant restaurant in America, with its lush sunken garden and gentle waterfall. The food, con-
ceived with Michael's ingenuity and the finest ingredients money can buy, rose
to a peak soon after opening and has never fallen off. That's because no matter
who's at the stove or out in front, Michael McCarty's rigorous training at the
École Hotelier de Paris, the Cordon Bleu, and the Academie du Vin informs
every dish, and every move made by the waitstaff.

I tasted my first great dessert when Jimmy Brinkley was the pastry chef at
Michael's. It was a tarte tatin whose buttery apples melted in my mouth but not
on the crust, which remained as light and flaky as filo dough. Since the departure of Brinkley, many pastry chefs have entered and exited the double doors to
Michael's kitchen, but the desserts, like the savory courses, have remained a constant. The Heath Bar dessert (which Michael says actually reminds him more of
a Sugar Daddy) is a Michael McCarty classic.

McCarty's food is American. But he could have never opened Michael's
without the French training that is so much a part of his style; and his desserts
are often amalgams of his tradition and his training. His rice tart is a combination of American rice pudding and crème brûlée. The strawberry bagatelle is
similar to a strawberry shortcake, but with a white chocolate mousse filling.
Other desserts are purely French (tarte tatin, opera cake) or purely American

(pistachio ice cream, double-chocolate brownies). And for McCarty, the look of the dessert is as important as the flavor, as you will learn by trying any of his desserts from this collection: two fruit gratins, chocolate truffle cake, berry-chocolate mousse cake, raspberry-lemon torte, and Heath Bar cake. Every one is deeply satisfying and stunning in presentation.

MARK MILITELLO

Mark's Place

Miami, Florida

HERE'S ONE IN EVERY REGION: a chef who, more than any of his or her contemporaries, has revolutionized the local culinary scene. It was Michael McCarty in Los Angeles, Anne Rosenzweig in New York, Jean Banchet in Chicago, Alice Waters in the San Francisco Bay area, and Mark Militello in South Florida. And in each area, there were others who helped to elevate American cooking to world-class status in a variety of ways. In South Florida, for example, there was Oliver Saucy and his Max restaurants, Charles Saunders (who now has his own place in Sonoma), and Michael Chiarello (now the chef at Napa Valley's Tra Vigne), all part of the mid-eighties cooking revolution. But no one has done more than Mark Militello to enhance the development and production of fresh fruits and vegetables, some of which, because of South Florida's unique climate, can grow nowhere else in America.

Emblematic of Militello's trail-blazing cuisine is his signature dish: fresh hearts of palm marinated in tangerine and orange juices, citrus honey, and red peppercorns. He gets the hearts of palm from the Seminole Indians, and the citrus and honey from nearby growers. The ingredients were always there; it was the inspiration to use them that was missing. Mark Militello provided that.

He came to Miami after many years of working in kitchens, interspersed with training programs at the Morrisville, New York, Culinary Hotel Program and Florida International University's Hotel School. Then he opened Mark's Place in 1989. By 1992, locals as well as discriminating diners on vacation had made Mark's Place a destination, and the restaurant tied with Philadelphia's Le Bec-Fin as the *Zagat Guide's* highest-rated restaurant in America. And the Distinguished Restaurants of North America organization named Mark's one of the top twenty-five restaurants in America. You'll know why when you sample the sticky coconut pudding with warm macadamia-rum toffee, and the banana macadamia-nut filo tart presented in this collection.

BRUCE NAFTALY

Le Gourmand

Seattle, Washington

*I*F YOU ASK BRUCE NAFTALY what he's proudest of, he will invariably say: "My local Northwest ingredients." Few, if any, of the foods he uses are in any way associated with large commercial enterprises. Sally Jackson provides the rich, fresh-churned butter (as well as the sheep's milk cheese for the blintzes). Dorothy Anciaux, Dave and Judy Duff, Marguerite Margason, and other neighborhood gardeners grow the organic vegetables, herbs, and edible flowers. And Donna Weston searches the Northwest woods for wild mushrooms. For his line-caught salmon, lingcod, sturgeon, and halibut, Naftaly counts on Jim Smith, among others. Naftaly's pantry is replenished daily with an assortment of bags, boxes, and crates of food that look more like what you'd bring home from a farmer's market than from a restaurant-supplier.

Naftaly has cultivated his organic garden of fanatically devoted fishers, foragers, and gardeners as carefully as they tend their own sources. For he knows his success depends on the ingredients they bring him. And he gives them credit on the back of his hand-written seasonal menu, much as a producer does his crew at the end of a film.

Naftaly's cuisine has the same home-grown quality. The above-mentioned blintzes, thick with Jackson's rich cheese, are served in a creamy golden sauce flecked with chives. His sorrel soup tastes of the summer sun. Naftaly serves as an aperitif an herbal infusion with a judicious touch of fresh-picked berry sweetness. And his entrees are always served with a heaping platter of simply prepared, intensely flavorful organic vegetables such as beets with greens, turnips, carrots, green beans, and potatoes.

When it comes to dessert, Naftaly offers dishes such as a creamy blackberry fool flecked with lavender mint, profiteroles in chocolate sauce, a tangy rhubarb ice cream, and seasonal fruit cobblers. The desserts have a rustic look that makes them that much more appealing. And the flavors, provided by just-picked locally grown fruit and Jackson's rich cream and butter, have a homemade immediacy lacking in other restaurant desserts.

For Naftaly, dessert must be simple and unfussy. "Something that sounds simple may taste intriguing," says Naftaly, "which then surprises and delights. Especially if you juxtapose flavors that might not seem like they'd go well together, like pear and rose hips for a sorbet or like crème brûlée with pears and quinces."

You'll find no architecturally constructed desserts sitting atop Naftaly's eclectic collection of plates. The energy goes into maximizing flavors, not presentations. Nor do portions make eating a dessert an ordeal. "The end of a meal should gently revive one's spirits and leave one uplifted and satisfied," says the chef. That's surely the case with the chef's rhubarb sorbet.

Naftaly came to Seattle in 1976 to study voice privately with Carlyle Kelley. But over the past seventeen years, working in a series of restaurants (culminating in his opening of Le Gourmand in 1985), Bruce Naftaly has instead found a unique culinary voice with a distinctive Northwest timbre.

PATRICK O'CONNELL

The Inn at Little Washington

Washington, Virginia

PATRICK O'CONNELL TAUGHT HIMSELF to cook by reading Julia Child and then by cooking for friends. He got his first professional job at the Iranian Embassy in Washington during the tumultuous last days of the Shah. After more embassy jobs, he started a catering business based in the Blue Ridge Mountains town of Washington, Virginia, seventy miles south of the capital, and became an instant success. Soon, however, he tired of the long drives hauling food and equipment back and forth.

"We found that to do the parties right, we wound up carrying potted palms, flowers, food, props, candelabra, tents, lighting, even dancing girls. So we decided to open a restaurant closer to home and let people come to us."

Inspired, but with little planning, O'Connell and partner Reinhardt Lynch bought an old building in the town of Washington and in 1978 opened the Inn at Little Washington. The restaurant drew first on their catering clientele from inside the Beltway looking for a country inn with fine food. Word spread fast. O'Connell's restaurant, by its eighth year, was enthusiastically described by Craig Claiborne as one of the finest in America.

But many complained of the long sleepy drive back to the capital near midnight. The senses, sated by such dishes as shrimp flavored with juniper berries in a mustard and dill sauce, followed by dark and white chocolate gâteau or grilled duck breast with red currants and wild rice, topped off by coeur à la crème with raspberry sauce, lost their edge for the hour-and-a-half drive home. Then came the second inspiration: Convert the upstairs into sleeping accommodations, so guests could retire and perhaps dine at the Inn the next night as well. This time, they planned.

"Whatever I do, I put myself completely into it," says O'Connell. "For us, it wasn't enough to just open a hotel. So we spent two years touring the greatest hotels in the world, spent three days in each one, measuring bathrooms, looking at facilities until we decided on a design that could operate at the same level as the restaurant."

The resultant ten-room inn clearly does operate at that level, and is now one of only twelve American members of the exclusive fraternity of the world's finest small hotels known as Relais et Châteaux. Now, after dining on fresh foie gras sautéed with smoked goose breast, topped off with chocolate pecan grapefruit tart, guest trundle upstairs to rest and perhaps to gather their strength for another significant repast.

Yet it is rare that anyone comes away stuffed from a Patrick O'Connell meal. "Portions should be small and delectable," says the chef. "Especially when it comes to dessert. If you view the dining experience as a theatrical production, dessert becomes the last act or finale. It's an essential component in creating a lingering memory. The planning of a dessert course is very important in the context of the overall menu. Relativity to the seasons should be considered as well."

Thus, in winter, O'Connell's dessert menu features little in the way of fruit other than a warm apple-walnut tart with cinnamon ice cream. Nuts abound, as in the case of his pecan gems and in a trio of little nut tarts (hazelnut, pecan, and pine nut) with homemade caramel, vanilla, and maple ice creams. And chocolate desserts, from the swans of white chocolate mousse swimming in passion fruit puree to the warm Valrhona chocolate cake with a pistachio custard sauce, are well represented. In summer, when Virginia produces luscious berries and stone fruit, the dessert menu reflects the local bounty. In this collection we've presented his pecan gem cookies.

KIM PEOPLES

Red Sage

Washington, D.C.

"**I** GOT MY START IN PASTRY," says Kim Peoples, "the old-fashioned way: by accident, and while living out of my van. I needed money; a restaurant needed a baker's assistant." From there, Kim went on to work at Macy's and the Adam's Mark Hotel. He traveled, and studied with Bocuse, Verges, and Lenôtre. He ran his own kitchen for a while, and worked at a country club. Then he met Jonathan Waxman. Peoples remembers: "With Jonathan's support, the world of pastry began puffing with chocolates, zests, exotic fruits, delicate creams, spices, cakes, and more great chefs."

One of those great chefs was Mark Miller, who invited Peoples to come to Santa Fe to make pastries at Coyote Cafe. It was there that Peoples developed cajeta cheesecake, one of my all-time favorite desserts. And I don't like cheesecake.

When Miller opened Red Sage in Washington, he knew its success depended on having Peoples running the bakery and pastry department. Here Kim developed down-home desserts with a cosmopolitan twist that appeal to the sophisticated crowd in the District. Among Peoples's favorites that we've included in this collection are blueberry tart, cinnamon-almond custard tart, cajeta cheesecake, espresso toffee, crisp peanutiest cookies, coconut haystacks, and chocolate brittle (an irresistible mélange of milk chocolate, toasted walnuts, and raisins) and the aforementioned cajeta cheesecake.

His desserts have visual appeal, but not at the cost of taste. The flavors are direct and intense without a lot of superfluous garnish. In the chef's words:

I work to create a sweet that is not too sweet
Art to the eye, and delicious to eat.

GEORGES PERRIER

Le Bec-Fin

Philadelphia, Pennsylvania

*A*MID THE FLURRY OF CULINARY CHANGES during the last fifteen years that have transformed American cuisine and catapulted it to world-class status, there have been some casualties. Many hide-bound, classically-trained French chefs never saw the changes coming. Their stockpots that once bubbled joyously with rich sauces sit dusty and abandoned.

Other chefs were cooking with their eyes open. "Years ago I made my *beurre blanc* much richer according to the taste of the times. Today my customers, not to mention me, could never eat a sauce like that," says Georges Perrier, who has been cooking what many would argue is the best French food in America for the past twenty-five years at Philadelphia's Le Bec-Fin.

Perrier's desserts have gotten lighter, too. What could be lighter than his floating island? Today his menu features desserts like frozen Grand Marnier "soufflé," framboisier (fresh raspberries with yogurt mousse), and a host of sorbets. His patrons do expect grand, ponderous-sounding desserts such as Perrier's opera cake topped with edible 23-karat gold leaf, marjolaine, and dark chocolate ice cream with caramel nougat. But Perrier's personal favorite after a meal is a fresh fruit or sorbet.

As has been the tradition for as long as anyone cooking today can remember, Perrier's apprenticeship began at the age of fourteen and included such memorable stops as La Pyramide and L'Oustau de Baumaniere. He eventually made his way to Philadelphia where he opened Le Bec-Fin.

He has not gone unrecognized. Paul Bocuse compares him to the best in Lyons; Craig Claiborne, to the finest in America. But Perrier's signal honor is the Silver Toque, the most coveted trophy in the world of haute cuisine, awarded him in 1989 by the Maitres Cuisiniers de France.

Though the sauces have lightened and the menu has broadened, Georges Perrier will always have a very French restaurant complete with one of the most formal dining rooms in America, a legion of tuxedoed waitstaff, and silver-domed service. After a prix fixe or à la carte dinner and a thoughtfully put together cheese course, an astounding thirty-odd creations of Perrier and pastry chef Robert Bennett—like the house favorite frozen Grand Marnier "soufflé," *tarte citron,* and a St. Nizier—come to the table on a three-tiered silver cart, confounding an easy resolution to a peak dining experience. Oh, and another cart is needed for the dozen-or-so house-made ice creams and sorbets.

ALFRED PORTALE

Gotham Bar and Grill, One Fifth Avenue

New York, New York

NEARLY TEN YEARS AGO, Alfred Portale rescued Gotham Bar and Grill from the restaurant wrecking ball. But it's one thing to bring considerable training (his classes at the Culinary Institute of America, plus stints with Jacques Maximin, the Troisgros brothers, and Michel Guerard) to bear on a dying restaurant, revive it, and achieve New York *Times* three-star status during the go-go eighties. Keeping it alive in the recessionary nineties as one of the top ten restaurants in New York is a tribute to Portale's ability to develop as a chef. Now that ability has propelled him into another successful Manhattan restaurant, One Fifth Avenue.

Portale creates new dishes by using his imagination as well as his training, and, according to the chef, "by working to understand the ways that people like to eat, things like time factors, degrees of elegance, and nutritional concerns." All the vegetables and fruits he uses are organically grown. The poultry is free-range, and menus include a variety of low- or non-fat and vegetarian selections.

The desserts show the same kind of attention to pleasing guests. At One Fifth Avenue, Portale brings forth treats such as frozen lemon torte with lemon curd and lemon thyme; warm pear tart on frozen port soufflé; warm ricotta gratin with toasted walnuts, honey, and sage; a glazed banana tart with anise ice cream and crisp *kadaifi* (a baklava-type pastry); and caramelized apple crêpes with a spiced carrot sauce.

At Gotham, Portale creates warm chocolate cake with milk chocolate ice cream; warm banana cake with walnut pastry cream and banana ice cream; and a sweet and sour black plum tart with almond cream and cinnamon ice cream: one of my favorite desserts. I say one, because my most favorite of Gotham's desserts is the warm nectarine strudel with toasted almond cream. I still remember the first time I tasted the crunchy filo dough crust and the perfectly cooked fruit.

That experience seems to be shared by the crowds who come here each day, year after year, in spite of the economy. The memory of artfully presented, clear flavors brings people back to Gotham Bar and Grill and One Fifth Avenue again and again.

Your favorite may be one of the many Portale desserts in this collection, such as his nutty biscotti, warm pear and fig strudel, strawberry tarts with lemon cream, or his refreshing moscatello granita with white peach and lemon verbena.

STEPHAN PYLES

Star Canyon

Dallas, Texas

ESTING THE THREE HUNDRED RECIPES submitted for this book proved a daunting task. Because Andrea and I have full-time jobs, finding the time wasn't easy. So we eventually hired Keith Mathewson, then the pastry chef at the Bellevue Athletic Club, to test recipes. Before we found Keith, we had to devise a strategy. One day a week would be devoted to preparing all the recipes submitted by a single chef. Then came the tasting. We knew we could never eat all of the desserts we'd made. We vowed only to consume a bite or two for a critical appraisal. That commitment was broken on the day we now fondly refer to as Stephan Pyles Day: *The Day We Couldn't Stop Eating Dessert.*

It started like most of our taste testings. A spoon was to be dipped in the first dessert for one taste to experience the flavor, and perhaps a second, if need be, to confirm our findings. We started with gingered couscous crème brûlée, which I proceeded to consume in its entirety. Okay, that was a fluke. Next I tried the cajeta flan—that would be no problem, since I don't like flan. A minute later the flan was gone; only the memory of the creamy, goaty caramel remained.

And on it went, through the double-dark chocolate cake with white chocolate sauce; the white chocolate rice pudding tamales with rum cream; the frozen macadamia nut bombe with macerated fruit and vanilla custard sauce; and the black bottom pie with rye whiskey sauce. To be sure, the portions were small, but each was irresistible.

"I'm a weird bird when it comes to making desserts," says Pyles. "I have mixed signals about pastries. Do I favor the homey recipes of my Mom's West Texas restaurants and serve cobblers and cream pies? Or do I serve pastries in the French manner consistent with my professional training? I think now I have synthesized the two and have a dessert style I can call my own. My food can be spicy, and I think that calls for a rich dessert to balance the heat. But I make the desserts familiar enough so that people aren't intimidated by them."

Stephan Pyles has been making irresistible food since he opened Routh Street Cafe over a decade ago in Dallas, at a time when Texans ate either plain (chicken-fried steak) or fancy (lobster Newburg). He introduced the city to his own brand of cooking, a synthesis of the many styles that intersect in Texas: among them Southern barbecue and Tex-Mex. And he encouraged local growers to plant interesting varieties of vegetables, herbs, and fruits to provide the freshest, most flavorful raw materials for his dishes.

The formal prix fixe Routh Street Cafe is gone. Now, at the woodsy, casual Star Canyon, Pyles serves "new Texas" cuisine. Wood-roasted rabbit enchiladas and sweet potato shellfish tamales share the menu with a variety of dishes all featuring Texas-grown fish, game, gamebirds, and of course, steaks. Much of the food is prepared on the barbeque, in the smoker or on the rotisserie. The desserts include those offered in this collection as well as housemade ice cream and a warm apple cake with *cajeta*.

Andrea and I suggest you try one of Pyles's desserts at a time, such as those mentioned above, or his berry-pecan buckle or apple-raisin spice cake drenched in caramel sauce.

THIERRY RAUTUREAU

Rover's

Seattle, Washington

WHEN I MOVED FROM LOS ANGELES to an island a short ferry ride from Seattle, I knew I would not miss L.A., but I do miss Citrus, Patina, West Beach Cafe, City, Pazzia, and Michael's.

But fortunately, Seattle has Rover's, where Thierry Rautureau creates food as original as that of his former boss, Joachim Splichal. Had Thierry chosen to remain in Los Angeles to open a restaurant, there is no doubt top food critics would sing his praises, and his restaurant would be packed every night. But the smaller crowds and lower decibel level of Rover's come with the evergreen-covered, smog-free, less-hectic territory.

Rover's occupies a renovated house with not much more kitchen space than that of most homes. There's no room for a separate pastry kitchen, so Rautureau has developed dessert classics that can be made in a minimum of work space, like his black and white chocolate mousse with espresso sauce; vanilla crème brûlée; and passion fruit mousse with wild raspberry coulis.

My favorite, though, is his fruit soup of home-macerated Rainier cherries and apricots. Thierry puts up the fruit himself in an elixir of sugar, brandy, vodka, red wine, port, and spices. In another corner of the kitchen, from a small ice cream machine, Rautureau cranks out unusual sorbets such as baked apple and Cabernet Sauvignon, and rich ice creams.

Thierry Rautureau knew what he was giving up by deciding to open a restaurant in Seattle. He chose to move here for the quality of life it afforded him and his family. And whenever I catch myself longing for one of my favorite restaurants in L.A., I remember Rover's, and I'm glad we both made the move. We've included Rautureau's vanilla crème brûlée and his apple and honey sorbet in this collection.

SEPPI RENGGLI

American Harvest, Savories, Sea Grill
Rockefeller Center
New York, New York

ONE NEW YORK CHEF'S career has been inextricably linked with the blossoming of fine cuisine in Manhattan: the humble, playful Swiss, Seppi Renggli. When he started with Restaurant Associates in the sixties, he oversaw such varied kitchens as La Fonda del Sol and the Forum of the Twelve Caesars. Then RA's Paul Kovi left the company to take over the Four Seasons and hired Seppi as chef and partner. Thus began that restaurant's long run as the place that exemplified fine dining in New York.

Seppi *was* the Four Seasons. Though he remained in the background, Renggli spent seventy-two seasons bringing the restaurant to its position of pre-eminence and keeping it there. In 1989, in a swap reminiscent of a baseball trade, Renggli went to command Restaurant Associates' complex at Rockefeller Center, and the chef of the Sea Grill there, Stefano Battistini, moved to the Four Seasons. The trade seems to have helped both clubs. And Renggli has never been happier. He's his relaxed, fun-loving self, constantly teasing his devoted staff and effortlessly turning out winning dishes from the cavernous kitchens beneath Rockefeller Center.

Overseeing kitchens at the American Harvest and Savories as well as the Sea Grill gives Seppi the opportunity to serve a wide variety of desserts for a diverse clientele. Bananas Foster, Key lime pie, carrot cake, pecan pie, chocolate brownies, and deep-dish apple pie are old favorites that somehow seem to be better here than almost anywhere else. Only Renggli has both the skill and the culinary wit to sauté lemon, lime, and orange zest with bananas Foster, to serve Key lime pie with lime sorbet, and carrot cake with both carrot sauce and candied carrots.

Renggli doesn't think of desserts the way most Americans do. "I don't understand cakes and pastries as desserts. They're too heavy after a big meal. In

Europe we might eat such a dessert with coffee or tea at 3 or 4 o'clock, after the lunch has had time to digest. For me a dessert after dinner is something light like a soufflé, crêpes, flambés, or flans. Certainly nothing heavier than some ice cream or sorbet. Or perhaps something really light like a macedoine of fruit or a fruit soup. We serve traditional desserts here, but it doesn't surprise me that often chocolate cake comes back to the kitchen half-eaten, while crêpes never do."

So, you might not find the Swiss spice cake with lemon icing offered here on the restaurant menu. We are happy to say that it was given to us by the chef from his secret recipe file.

ANNE ROSENZWEIG

Arcadia

New York, New York

ANNE ROSENZWEIG never intended to become a chef. But while doing ethnomusicological research in Kenya and Nepal, she found a new consuming passion—food—too strong to deny. Unfortunately, New York's early-eighties old-boy chef network didn't feel the same way about her. Unable to find a paying job, she started out doing scullery work for free.

Eventually her determination paid off, and she was given a job cooking at a New York eatery called Vanessa. There, she attracted the attention of Ken Aretsky, who helped her open Arcadia. This intimate room with a wraparound four-season nature mural is the setting for desserts that defy easy choice. How do you decide between carrot cake shortcake with lemon curd ice cream; baked-to-order apple tart with rum raisin ice cream; an espresso ice cream brownie with peanut brittle; mango mousse in a coconut tuile; or a clementine and champagne sorbet?

Emblematic of Rosenzweig's restless imagination is a recent offering, chocolate Shar-Péi cake, inspired by the dogs of many folds who ply nearby Park Avenue in numbers nearly rivaling those of taxis. Anne was searching for a chocolate dessert that could become as popular as her warm chocolate bread pudding. By experimenting with chocolate toppings (corn syrup provides the flexibility for draping the topping in folds) she came up with an "adult Hostess cupcake," as Rosenzweig refers to it, an almost caramelly-chewy confection of devil's food cake draped with chocolate ganache.

Rosenzweig feels that desserts need some sort of contrast—hot and cold, sweet and sour, or crunchy and soft—to make them work. And they need a bit of whimsy. The Shar-Péi cake, both striking and luxurious, has it all.

Her brunch training at Vanessa may be one of the reasons why Rosenzweig's food is so likable. A brunch chef, unbound by the conventions of what people expect at a particular meal, has the freedom to improvise and experiment with combinations that might otherwise seem forced or contrived.

Along with the Shar-Péi cake, we offer here Rosenzweig's carrot cake, lemon curd ice cream, mango mousse in coconut tuiles, and pecan chocolate tarts.

JIMMY SCHMIDT

The Rattlesnake Club, Très Vite, Cocina del Sol, Buster's Bay, Stelline

Detroit, Michigan

W HEN MICHAEL MCCARTY'S manifest destiny took him east in the eighties, he partnered three Rattlesnake Club restaurants with Jimmy Schmidt in Denver, Detroit, and Washington, D.C. The partnership dissolved, with Schmidt becoming the sole owner of Detroit's Rattlesnake, while McCarty took possession of the Denver and D.C. operations, renaming them Adirondacks.

In time, McCarty shuttered the Denver restaurant, but Schmidt hunkered down in Detroit to devote all his energies to the Rattlesnake Club. There he attracted another partner, one who had been following Schmidt's career since his first Detroit job at the London Chop House.

Now that business partner, Mike Ilitch, chairman of Little Caesar Pizza, has joined forces with Schmidt to open Très Vite, Cocina del Sol, Buster's Bay, and Stelline, all in Detroit.

People are attracted to Jimmy Schmidt quite simply because there are only a handful of people in America who can cook like him. Madeleine Kamman taught Schmidt the basics. But his unique philosophy about ingredients brings out flavors that other chefs might never be aware of. Schmidt pays close attention to the seasons and what grows locally, so he's nearly always working with ingredients at their natural peak of flavor.

"My concept," Schmidt told me, "is to enhance the natural flavors of foods at their seasonal prime. With these ingredients and good technique, you can captivate the taste buds."

Captivating indeed are these sample seasonal desserts from a fall menu: grilled comice pears; pumpkin and maple sugar crème brûlée; pumpkin-pecan pie with nutmeg and cinnamon; lemon tart, and grapefruit and pomegranate tart.

"Winter is a time of satisfaction," says Schmidt. "So I'll serve pear bread pudding with bourbon sauce, or cherimoya and banana fritters bathed in ginger and chocolate." A spring dessert menu features more exotics: ginger-passion fruit crème brûlée and kiwi ice cream, and pressed chocolate cake made with pepper vodka, while summer brings simpler delights such as peach shortcake, sweet cherry sundae, and strawberries macerated in red wine.

To give you an idea of Schmidt's seasonal dessert sensibilities we've included his sweet cherry sundae, pumpkin-pecan pie, and lemon tart.

JOHN SEDLAR

Abiquiu, Bikini
San Francisco, Santa Monica, California

WHEN JOHN SEDLER LEFT St. Estephe to open Bikini Restaurant I wondered if it was a midlife culinary crisis that made him turn from his longtime love of preparing the foods of his native Northern New Mexico for the sweet young Bikini thing where diners could experience flavors from all of the world.

But Sedler soon rekindled the old flame and opened Abiquiu Restaurants in San Francisco and in the patio next to Bikini. There he serves the Southwestern dishes that were so popular for ten years at St. Estephe.

At Bikini he offers simple fresh fruit plates (albeit with the best and most exotic fruits), chocolate desserts, and housemade ice creams. The real dessert experimentation takes place at Abiquiu where you can end your meal with Southwestern petits fours of little chocolate tortes and candied fresh berries and fruits. Or taste the revived version of an old St. Estephe favorite of mine: blue corn crêpes with pumpkin ice cream. Other Abiquiu favorites are Grandma Eloisa's empanaditas filled with sweet pine nut "mincemeat," chocolate-chile ice cream, and the dessert Sedler contributed to this collection: chocolate "tamales" of the dead with caramel-lime sauce.

PIERO SELVAGGIO
Valentino, Primi, Posto
Santa Monica, West Los Angeles, Sherman Oaks, California

SOME SAY THAT CALIFORNIA CUISINE was born when Alice Waters introduced California to the foods of Provence. But without the Italian influence of Piero Selvaggio, California food would not be as richly varied as it is today. Just as Waters dispelled the notion that French food had to be creamy and rich, Selvaggio disabused us of the idea that Italian food had to be limited to spaghetti and lasagna. Selvaggio's Valentino and Primi restaurants introduced foods to California and the rest of the country that today are taken for granted: extra-virgin olive oil, balsamic vinegar, radicchio, arugula, *parmigiano reggiano* and gelato.

"In Italy," says Selvaggio, "people don't want a rich dessert. They prefer fruit, nuts, or a little piece of chocolate. Ice cream is eaten apart from a meal. But because Americans are French-trained when it comes to dessert, they consider a rich dessert the only way to end a great meal. They look at dessert as the climax to a perfect meal. So it's essential to deliver a superior product."

That's why Selvaggio has gone to Italy year after year searching for ideas for the finest in both sweet and savory Italian dishes. And that's why he searches constantly for the finest talent to produce those dishes.

In Culinary Institute of America-trained Rudy Torres, he has found a young, deft hand who understands the subtleties of almond biscotti and can bring the tastes of America and Italy together in caramel-pecan gelato. Torres apprenticed in Italy and brought back recipes such as espresso cake—a Valentino standard today—and an Italianate pumpkin-flavored crème brûlée.

"America is a chocoholic country," says Selvaggio. "So that has to be emphasized on our menu. And even when people pride themselves on eating a low-calorie, low-salt, low-bread meal, they splurge on the luxury of a rich chocolate dessert."

As anyone who has dined at Valentino, Primi, or Selvaggio's newest place, Posto, will tell you, Piero is the consummate host, so it is not surprising that his desserts satisfy all expectations. "We are here to give people a happy experience. And a great dessert means a sweet ending to that rich, happy, experience. That's what I get out of my bed to achieve every day."

And I get out of bed every day in hopes of tasting desserts like those of Torres we've included here: caramel pecan gelato, espresso cake, and almond biscotti.

JACKIE SHEN

Jackie's

Chicago, Illinois

JACKIE SHEN IMMIGRATED to America from Hong Kong to pursue her dream of working in the hospitality industry, and today she's achieved what many in her profession only dream of: her own restaurant.

At Jackie's, she cooks her interpretation of modern French-American cuisine with Chinese touches: filo nest with exotic mushrooms; striped sea bass with shrimp, avocado, and peppers; fillet of whitefish baked with water chestnuts, bamboo shoots, baby corn, and ginger. Her mentor in Chicago was the legendary Jean Banchet, and his training is evident in the exacting standards she sets for purveyors and staff alike. "I know it isn't easy working for me," understates Jackie, "but I've got a responsibility to satisfy the diner who has many choices. I want his first choice to be Jackie's."

Her light touch with entrees leaves room for substantial desserts such as a chocolate "bag" filled with white chocolate mousse in a raspberry sauce, or light ones such as green tea ice cream or simple fruit tarts.

"I don't make my desserts too sweet," says Jackie. "Dessert should be like a final note to a piece of music. There should be a balance, as in the Oriental philosophy of yin and yang. After a wonderful meal, I don't want to ruin it by overdosing my customers with sugar. For example, in my chocolate bag I use bittersweet chocolate. From bittersweet I can extract enough sweetness to satisfy anyone's palate."

Chocolate figures prominently on Jackie's menu. "I serve what my customers want, which is chocolate, chocolate, chocolate! Besides our chocolate bag, we get constant requests for our turtle tart, chocolate-raspberry fudge tart, chocolate macadamia nut cake, and chocolate-banana napoleons. Still, not everyone likes chocolate, so we offer fresh fruit tarts, carrot cake, lemon-lime mousse cake, and fresh berry white satin tart. Presentation is important for the overall enjoyment of the dessert, so we take special pains to make sure our desserts look as good as they taste."

In this collection we've included Shen's carrot cake and some of her chocolate desserts such as chocolate macadamia nut cake, chocolate banana napoleons, turtle tart, and raspberry fudge tart.

LYDIA SHIRE

Biba

Boston, Massachusetts

PEOPLE FLOCK TO LYDIA SHIRE'S BIBA in Boston to taste her rustic yet refined, highly personal yet authentically ethnic food. But her lasting contribution to cooking may well be her commitment to preserving ingredients and recipes that might be lost forever as chefs move toward homogeneity, even in top-flight establishments.

As a vegetarian, I have no plans to taste anything from Shire's gutsy menu category entitled "Offal," which includes tripe, sweetbreads, and other varieties of organ meats rarely encountered on a restaurant bill of fare. But in the spirit of the popular bromide, I'll fight to the death for her right to cook them. Shire is concerned that some "old-fashioned" foods such as these will disappear now that so many restaurant menus look alike.

Lydia Shire's dessert menu also is unique. Such original desserts as brown sugar angel food cake with caramel ice cream; fresh mango "creamcicle" float; and hot fallen bitter-chocolate soufflé are examples. Her beguiling Sambuca ice cream peppered with espresso grounds; amaretti cake with grated bitter chocolate; and baked lemon pudding are featured in this collection. The recipes are simple and straightforward. That's because Shire, who learned from cookbooks before attending Cordon Bleu, knows what it's like for the harried home chef to make something really appealing *á la minute*.

After a "career" as a successful home cook, Shire was given a kitchen job at Boston's Maison Robert when she brought her "resumé," a seven-layer cake, to the restaurant by trolley. Stints at several hotel kitchens in Boston and Los Angeles gave her the necessary professional training to open Biba. But she still remembers what it's like to turn out crowd-pleasing dishes from a home kitchen, which is what will happen when you prepare Lydia Shire's desserts.

"I make my desserts like I make the rest of my food," says Shire. "Gutsy and robust. I like things like caramel, chocolate, and butter because they have the richness that food has to have to make the impact that a dessert should have."

Try a scoop of the Sambuca-espresso ice cream with a slice of amaretti cake, or some baked lemon pudding. You'll get the point.

NANCY SILVERTON

Campanile

Los Angeles, California

LOVE MAKES US DO STRANGE THINGS. When in 1972 Nancy Silverton set eyes on the good-looking herbivore who was running the vegetarian food-service operation at Sonoma State University, she became an overnight vegetarian and offered to work in the kitchen next to him, though she had never cooked before. In time, she ended her relationship with the young man, but not with cooking, which has remained her lifelong passion.

Nancy stayed in Northern California after graduation, working in restaurants. Then, realizing she had a lot to learn, she attended the Cordon Bleu in London. When she returned to the States, she heard about Michael's, a new restaurant opening in Santa Monica that aimed to reform dining in America. She wanted to work there to put to use all she had learned in cooking school, but the only opening in the kitchen was for someone to work on the computer. Taking the "mailroom to board room" approach, Nancy accepted the job. Suddenly there was an opening for an assistant pastry chef. Thus she was able to study under the legendary Jimmy Brinkley, who, as much as anyone, revolutionized restaurant desserts in America. Silverton's Cordon Bleu training had taught her to be fearful of experimentation. But the adventurous Brinkley helped her create desserts faithful to both her classical training and her own sense of what tasted good. At Michael's she came to realize that while there are certain parameters (eggs will curdle if you boil them; not enough sugar will make a cake dry) there also was, as Michael McCarty put it, "loads of room for creativity." Under Brinkley Nancy blossomed into a first-class pastry chef.

But Nancy felt she needed more grounding in the fundamentals. After working a while at Michael's she enrolled at the world-renowned Lenôtre pastry school in Paris. She then returned to Michael's for a year. Mark Peel, Michael's chef, jumped ship to join Wolfgang Puck in opening Spago and invited Nancy to be pastry chef there. Though they were only good friends then (husband and wife now), Nancy took the risk and moved into the limelight. There was limited space at Spago to make desserts, so she created them in the pizza station and the tiny back kitchen, turning out sweets that made even the most ardent lovers of Puck's pizza leave room for pie of a different sort.

After four years at Spago, Silverton and Peel moved to New York, hoping to open their own place. But they missed the fresh ingredients available in California. So after a year, they returned to the Golden State. They found a location in a building Charlie Chaplin once used as a studio, and in 1989 opened Campanile, named for the belltower atop the building. Today, it's one of Los Angeles's busiest restaurants, breakfast, lunch, and dinner. At the same time, Nancy's La Brea Bakery has become a success in its own right, providing bread for retail customers as well as for Campanile and a score of other restaurants.

Despite the bakery's demands, Silverton has focused intensively on the desserts at Campanile. Many would argue she's the finest pastry chef in America. And few would argue against that contention after tasting her warm huckleberry compote, ginger shortcake, rustic pear tart, black walnut-honey ice cream; milk chocolate mousse with white chocolate bark; or kumquat semifreddo. Her dessert philosophy is simple: "Desserts are comfort food. Crumbles and cobblers and shortcakes will always appeal. And if you're going to use a flavor, don't just hint. Make the flavor bold, or just don't use it. Use contrasts to make your dessert interesting: cold and hot; soft and crispy. And don't sacrifice freshness and flavor for architectural construction and complication.

"Use the best ingredients you can find, and keep your desserts seasonal. Don't make plum pie in winter. The plums grow so far away they have to be picked underripe to travel as far as they do. That's what I call bad technology. Instead, play with the seasons. When strawberries first come on the market, serve them sautéed. At the end of the season, make strawberry ice cream. In the middle? Strawberry shortcake!"

In this collection, Silverton has contributed kumquat semifreddo, huckleberry compote, and ginger shortcake.

JOACHIM SPLICHAL

Patina, Pinot Bistro

Los Angeles, Studio City, California

"DESSERTS," according to Joachim Splichal, "are as important as an appetizer or a main course. In fact, they are the finish of a symphony of taste which begins with the first bite you put in your mouth. So the dessert must be as balanced with the meal as the first note of a symphony is with the last."

It's not surprising that Splichal should use a classical music analogy to describe his cooking style. By the late seventies and early eighties Los Angeles had seen the demise of those classic Los Angeles restaurants, Perino's and Scandia. Eventually Michael's and Valentino replaced them, but by the nineties, and all the new restaurants seemed to be limited to fun, casual places. Then along came Joachim Splichal, who created Patina in the middle of Hollywood, and another classic was born.

It took Michael's and Valentino years to achieve veneration. How did Patina do it so quickly? Well, if you count the years training with Jacques Maximin and the years of experience at Seventh Street Bistro, Max au Triangle, the Regency Club, and worldwide consulting jobs, Joachim Splichal had lots of time to hone the skills that made his food so impressive at Patina right from night one.

With its understated tones of gray and brown, rich wood, and etched glass, Patina seems to have the kind of polish that only time can give, like Joachim's cooking. He confidently cooks serious dishes with a sense of humor (so that the results never seem silly or contrived) such as red berry crumble pie with vanilla milkshake sauce, and a macaroon filled with passion-fruit cream and sprinkled with fresh fruit "ratatouille."

Joachim Splichal's classic dessert, created in 1989, may well be his corn crème brûlée, which combines the crunch of corn kernels with the smoothness of rich custard. Some, however, might argue that the chocolate-croissant bread pudding included in this book is the classic dessert at Patina. Splichal's personal favorite is a tarte tatin. "It's simple, good, and old-fashioned," says the chef. "The way desserts should be."

If you like fruit desserts, pick your favorite from those Splichal has contributed to this collection: rhubarb and strawberry gratin, strawberry napoleon with strawberry sorbet, and strawberry rhubarb tart.

KEVIN TAYLOR

Zenith American Grill

Denver, Colorado

*I*N A CITY that is hardly a restaurant destination, Kevin Taylor's Zenith American Grill is a pleasant surprise. Taylor doesn't have the pedigree possessed by many of our better-known chefs, but then you can't eat years of experience. All you can really judge a chef by is the food he puts before you.

Taylor refers to himself as a cook, not a chef. The distinction, he believes, is that a cook concentrates on cooking while a chef concentrates on achieving star status. While I'm not sure I agree, having eaten some of my best meals at Spago, Chez Panisse, Citrus, and other restaurants where the chefs make a point of doing more than just cooking, Kevin Taylor is clearly one of America's finest cooks.

For Taylor, desserts are comfort food. "I won't create architectural desserts and I won't use bitter chocolate," says Taylor. "I'm not trying to challenge diners and risk alienating them by doing something cutting edge; I'm trying to soothe them. Since dessert is the last impression, it should be decadent and comforting, with earthy flavors—not a stylized creation with tons of garnish. For example, we have a chocolate cupcake on the menu made with flawless Belgian chocolate. But when you get right down to it, it's really the ultimate Ding Dong. That's what I mean by familiar and comforting."

Since Taylor cooks his savory courses without butter or cream, there's always room for dessert at Zenith. "I try to make desserts we remember from childhood. Nothing can replace those flavors, because the memories improve with age. But by making my rice pudding with raisins with real vanilla beans and serving it on a layer of caramel, I hope to approximate for the diner a sweet memory of youth."

If you can't make it to Denver to taste his Belgian-chocolate bread pudding, his butterscotch napoleon with bittersweet chocolate sauce, or his macadamia praline cheesecake with vanilla sauce, then enjoy the desserts he has wrought for this collection, such as *cajeta* ice cream, banana gratin with pecan custard, raspberry crème brûlée tart, and almond tuile with coconut orange sorbet.

JACQUES TORRES

Le Cirque

New York, New York

FROM HUMBLE BEGINNINGS, Jacques Torres has risen to star status in the pastry world. In the classic French tradition, he started as a pastry apprentice at the age of fifteen. At twenty-six he became the youngest chef to earn the prestigious title of Meilleur Ouvrier de France. So impressed with his talents was the legendary Jacques Maximin (who employed him at his Hotel Negresco in Nice for eight years) that he couldn't abide Torres's working for anyone else in France. When Torres felt it was time to move on, out of deference to his mentor he came to America (once again starting at the top), as corporate pastry chef for the Ritz Carlton chain.

It was there he came to the attention of Sirio Maccioni of Le Cirque, who in 1989 hired Torres as executive pastry chef. At Le Cirque, Torres fashions fabulous desserts for the star and the stargazer alike. Just as every chef who works for Maccioni must prepare pasta primavera, the restaurant's most famous savory course, Torres is obliged to make Le Cirque's signature dessert: crème brûlée. But seasoned critics who taste his velvety version with its smoky glazed-sugar crust concur that it's the best in the city. His raspberry napoleon; mango curls with mango ice cream; web of spun sugar with fresh figs and vanilla ice cream; and chocolate sorbet served in a porcelain egg are equally peerless.

"I have no philosophy about desserts," says Torres. "Except to say that you must insist on the best ingredients possible. Especially in the case of fresh fruit. The quality of your fruit must be the best or the end product will suffer. It's the flavor of the fruit in your dessert that will make it memorable. That's why I don't use too much sugar in my desserts. I want the flavors of the dessert to come through. And too much sugar hides the flavor. Desserts have to look good, but if they don't taste good, what's the point? You should never put appearance before flavor." You'll taste what the chef means when you prepare his chocolate banana soup, crêpes au chocolat, or pear in puff pastry with caramel sauce.

BARBARA TROPP

China Moon Cafe

San Francisco, California

ANYONE PLANNING SOMEDAY to open a restaurant serving Chinese, Eurasian, Pacific Rim, or another similar amalgam of cuisines couldn't do better than to apply for a job at Barbara Tropp's China Moon Cafe. But if you just love unique, witty, uplifting cuisine, go there whenever you can for such dishes as baked Buddha buns stuffed with curried vegetables, and pot-browned noodle pillows topped with assorted wok-fried vegetables. You'll find the noodle pillow dish in my first book, *Great Vegetables from the Great Chefs* (Chronicle Books, 1990).

Barbara Tropp earned her doctorate in Chinese poetry at Princeton and fell in love with authentic Chinese cooking while doing postgraduate work in Taiwan. Such food is simply not widely available in America, so Barbara started cooking and teaching all that she'd learned, and missed. Realizing she needed some real restaurant training, she took a food-prep job chopping vegetables at San Francisco's vegetarian Greens restaurant to learn the techniques and discipline she'd need to open China Moon Cafe.

From the understated, playful decor (hanging dragons, lovely porcelain), to her demand for the best raw materials (fresh water chestnuts, organic produce, no MSG or red food dye), to the obvious care Barbara Tropp takes with each customer and each employee at China Moon, it is readily apparent that she has created a unique atmosphere for exploring the many worlds of Chinese cuisine.

Having found desserts in China disappointing and unimaginative, I'm happy that Tropp has taken the best China has to offer for savory courses, but for the sweet serves French and Yankee desserts with Asian touches, such as ginger ice cream with bittersweet chocolate sauce; apricot, prune, and walnut tart; and chocolate-currant-almond cake with crème chantilly.

"I take the Oriental proclivity for combining tart and sweet and the Western desire for something buttery and rich and create China Moon desserts," says

Barbara. "The result is desserts that are not overly sweet and rich—desserts that complement the traditional Chinese food we serve here."

Such sweets include a vast array of tarts, such as crystallized lemon, Black Friar plum-frangipane, black fig streusel, and strawberry-orange cream. Tropp's light fruit ice creams, such as the ones presented in this collection, are made without a custard base and with half-and-half instead of cream, using fruits such as grapes, pomegranates, peaches, mangoes, and honeydews at summer's peak of flavor.

No meal at a Chinese restaurant would be complete without fortune cookies. Tropp's are called "cookies of good fortune," and they include walnut crisps, chocolate stars, hazelnut mounds, and crystallized ginger butter squares, among others. Don't look for typed fortunes baked inside. The medium is the message.

CHARLIE TROTTER

Charlie Trotter's

Chicago, Illinois

THEY SAID HE WAS TOO YOUNG. Untrained. Untested. The place was too ambitious. What was he doing spending as much time with the architects and building contractors as he did planning his menu and wine list? And yet, when the restaurant opened in the late eighties, it shot right to the top. Charlie Trotter was the young maverick who proved the critics wrong in Chicago by satisfying the only critics that count: the dining public.

Trotter has a clear and well-defined approach to cooking. "Our appetizers and main courses are vegetable-driven. What's fresh and in season is what gives our food its immediacy, its impact. Our food is prepared *à la minute,* so the flavors have to be fresh and real. In the same way, our desserts are fruit-driven. There are only one or two chocolate desserts on my menu. The fresh, sharp flavor of fruit in season makes desserts that have impact. Pastries can't do that. They've been prepared so far in advance that all you've got is sweetness and a nice presentation. That, in my book," says Trotter, "is not dessert."

What *is* dessert for Charlie Trotter? Two of my favorites are poached plums with plum sorbet and warm compote; and caramelized apple and Mascarpone in filo with red wine-black pepper sorbet. Another fine example of the chef's risk-taking is his "thinking man's rice pudding," made with quinoa instead of rice and served with carrot sorbet and gingered carrot coulis.

Charlie's career gives hope to anyone with the compulsion but not the training to be a chef. After graduating with a degree in political science from the University of Wisconsin in 1982, he embarked on a four-year period of work, study, and travel, including stints with Bradley Ogden, Norman Van Aken, and Gordon Sinclair. He lived in Chicago, San Francisco, Florida, and Europe, "reading every cookbook I could get my hands on and eating out incessantly." After doing some private catering, he decided to open Charlie Trotter's, which has risen to become one of only four restaurants in Chicago to be awarded a four-star rating by *Chicago* magazine.

The four-star desserts Trotter contributed to this collection are caramelized apple and Mascarpone in filo and crispy quinoa pudding.

JONATHAN WAXMAN

Napa, California

To the outsider, the road to chef-stardom might seem predictably straight. For Jonathan Waxman, it has been a roller coaster. After training at La Varenne in France, Waxman helped to set the tone for California cuisine in the late seventies and early eighties while cooking at Chez Panisse in Berkeley and at Michael's in Santa Monica. By 1983, Jonathan was ready to open his own place, and he felt New York was ready for some California cooking. So he opened Jams, where he quickly drew a loyal following of discriminating Gotham diners eager to taste lamb and greens flown in from Sonoma and Waxman's skill with the grill. He soon opened Hulot's, Bud's, and Sagebrush Cantina, all in New York, and even a London Jam's. Eventually it all became too much and, one by one, he shuttered the restaurants or disengaged from them.

But instead of moving to another stove immediately, he took a sabbatical. He traveled, ate, ran, and enjoyed life as few dedicated chefs ever have the time to do. I would see him searing something wonderful at Wolfgang Puck's Meals on Wheels Benefit each year during the late eighties, but he was not ready to get back in the kitchen full-time. After a consulting stint at Aspen's Caribou Club in 1992, he decided the time had come and opened Table 29 in Napa. There he did what he calls "middle-of-the-road-cooking." "I don't want to make my food too fancy or too plain. I just want to approach cooking as simply and wonderfully as possible."

At Table 29 he collaborated on desserts with pastry chef Toni Chiappetta, who had studied with the legendary Albert Kumin at the International Pastry Arts Center in New York before working at the Colony and Icarus in Boston, and at Sfuzzi in Philadelphia.

Before Waxman left Table 29, he and Chiappetta collaborated on desserts like chocolate-blackberry torte, coconut lace cookies, Russian tea cakes, banana caramel cream pie, sweet potato-pecan pie, and bread and butter pudding—all of which we present here.

JASPER WHITE

Jasper's
Boston, Massachusetts

WHETHER REFORMULATING CRÈME CARAMEL into Indian-pudding flan by using New England maple sugar, creating a frozen Mascarpone cream, a crème fraîche tartlet, or a refreshing mint tea sorbet, Jasper White is constantly dreaming up wonderful new desserts.

White had the requisite culinary education at the Culinary Institute of America and in restaurant kitchens in Seattle, San Francisco, and Boston, but the ability to discriminate between the satisfactory and the satisfying came much earlier. When he was a boy growing up in rural New Jersey, his Roman grandmother taught him a sense of taste, and his father, a restaurateur, taught him the importance of using the finest, freshest local ingredients.

Perhaps that is why when White opened Jasper's in Boston, he decided to draw so heavily on New England's bounty both from sea and land, instead of trying to re-create a New York restaurant serving "Continental" food in Boston.

After all, New England has some of the best seafood in the States, and some of the most dedicated farmers, many of whom grow organically (a passion for White) and specialize in foods unique to the region. One example is spring-dug parsnips, ready to harvest in the fall but left in the frozen ground until April to achieve a "spiciness" that most diners swear is a combination of ginger, nutmeg, and garlic.

When it comes to desserts, White wants us to rediscover the simple desserts of New England. "Cobblers, shortcakes, upside-down cakes, and vanilla ice cream are not only simple, they're classics," says White. "The fancy European pastries are not what I'm about. So I serve the desserts that have come down from the colonists. And while cakes are a part of that tradition, I don't favor cakes as a dessert after a meal. I do serve cake, but it can be too heavy after a hearty meal. I prefer to take my cake in the afternoon with tea or coffee, as used to be the tradition in New England."

At Jasper's you'll enjoy White's and restaurant baker Mark Cupolo's regional classics such as deep-dish Maine wild blueberry pie, cranberry-streusel tart, Indian-pudding custard, and maple-walnut ice cream. Yes, there are some wonderful cakes, such as cranberry-black walnut pound cake and pear upside-down spice cake, but you might take White's suggestion and save them for teatime. The chef's favorite is cookies. In this book you'll find Mark's butterscotch icebox cookies and sand tarts, among a host of other revisited (and in some cases, reinvented) New England desserts.

BARRY WINE

New York, New York

Wᴏᴇɴ Bᴀʀʀʏ Wɪɴᴇ ran the Quilted Giraffe in New York, he served the finest Japanese-influenced food in America, but his rich, homey Franco-American desserts bore no resemblance to the bizarre (it seems to many Westerners) offerings in Japanese dessert shops and restaurants. This kind of departure is typical for Wine, a former lawyer turned restaurateur who has never followed a well-worn path.

"We were living in New Paltz, New York, in the mid-seventies," says Barry, "and it wasn't that exciting a town, so I told my wife, Susan, 'Let's find something interesting to do on Saturday nights.'" The proximity of New Paltz to the Culinary Institute of America provided the Wines with a staff of technically trained kitchen help, so they opened the Quilted Giraffe. Truly self-taught ("I didn't even know you had to wash spinach"), Barry Wine set about becoming a success in the restaurant business the same way he had in the legal profession and in buying and restoring Victorian homes: by relying on his sense of what would work and ignoring the critics.

When he moved the Quilted Giraffe to Manhattan's Second Avenue, he was chastened for serving nouvelle cuisine when he lacked a French pedigree. When Wine overcame that round of criticism, he was assailed for charging astronomical prices. Then food writers trounced his mandatory service charge. But Wine weathered the critics as well as the early-nineties recession. His light, savory dishes, cooked *à la minute*, allowed the diner, whether opting for the multicourse *kaiseki* dinner or the a la carte selections, to enjoy desserts such as fruit crumples—pleated filo cases of apples and raisins or blueberries—with cinnamon ice cream. His pecan squares with ice cream and hot fudge sauce; chocolate soufflé with coffee ice cream; and hazelnut waffle with banana ice cream were equally satisfying. On those occasions when you actually *did* get full after ten small courses, you could still enjoy cranberry soup with fruit sorbets.

"We wanted desserts that weren't prepared earlier in the day, placed on the pastry cart, and rolled over to the table," states Wine. "Those are pastries, and pastries weren't special enough for what we were trying to do. Nor did we serve the constructed, architectural desserts that really anyone could assemble. In our kitchen we had two cooks whose only job was to prepare desserts to order for each customer. So your dessert was specially prepared just for you, fresh, right when you ordered it."

In 1992, Sony bought the building in which the Quilted Giraffe was located and made Barry Wine an offer he couldn't refuse. For now, his brand of innovative cooking is only available to those who reproduce his recipes in their own kitchens.

Wine was always pushing the limits of what New York restaurant-goers and critics alike thought was acceptable. And sometimes he crossed that line (as in the case of his mustard ice cream). But long after the controversies are forgotten, Barry Wine will be remembered for his unstinting demand for quality, for his daring, and for his enthusiasm.

Wine contributed chocolate desserts to this collection, such as white chocolate and raspberry cake, chocolate chip shortbread, walnut praline truffles, wild rice tuiles with marbleized chocolate mousse and hazelnut tarts with chocolate sauce. In addition we've included lighter desserts like rhubarb tapioca crisp, warm peaches and mangoes in a tamarind glaze, and cherry, almond, and champagne granita.

ALAN WONG

Le Soleil, The Mauna Lani Bay Hotel

Waikoloa, Hawaii

IF HAWAII IS A MACROCOSM of the harmonious blend of East and West, then Chef Alan Wong is the microcosm. Born in Japan to a Chinese-Hawaiian father and a Japanese mother, and raised in Hawaii, Alan Wong ladles ingredients from many pots in creating his cuisine. His restaurant is the logical choice for the annual Cuisines of the Sun Festival, which celebrates Eurasian cooking styles and features chefs from such places as the Oriental in Bangkok, the Peninsula in Hong Kong, and the Pan Pacific in Singapore, as well as chefs from Michelin-starred restaurants in Europe.

At Le Soleil in the Mauna Lani Bay Hotel on the big island of Hawaii, Wong employs classical French technique and the best local ingredients to create desserts like passion fruit big island goast cheese cake, frozen Kona coffee cappucino with mascarpone, and Kona chocolate pudding with Tahitian vanilla ice cream. On the light side, Wong prepares a gingered lychee sorbet. Banana lumpia, banana macadamia nut Kahlua crème brûlée, pomelo cheesecake, and macadamia fudge cake are other dessert offerings.

How does Wong approach desserts? "The same way I approach cooking in general. It has to appeal in terms of taste, color, texture, and appearance. The days of a one-dimensional chocolate mousse are over. You've got to build that dessert vertically, add a splash of color in the sauce, put some crunch into it, or it just won't appeal to today's diner. I take advantage of the local passion fruit, guava, bananas, and mangoes to make my desserts special."

Trained at a local community college and in the kitchens of the Greenbriar Resort and at Lutèce, Alan Wong is a star in Hawaii's rapidly growing pantheon of world-class chefs.

ROY YAMAGUCHI

Roy's

Oahu, Kauai, and Maui, Hawaii

*I*T SEEMS LIKE A LIFETIME AGO that I first met this shy, skinny kid with the killer looks and cooking skills. It was at Le Gourmet, a seventy-seat restaurant in Los Angeles, where Roy Yamaguchi got his first recognition. Then he hit Hawaii like a rogue wave, clearing from the minds of dedicated local diners all memory of the Polynesian tourist traps they were stuck with before Yamaguchi came on the scene. Now in addition to his bayview Roy's in the Hawaii Kai area of Oahu, there are restaurants in Maui, Tokyo, and Guam.

But in between were the dark "385" years, when the people who had helped put the financing together for Spago tapped Roy to cook at 385 North (ironically), a former Polynesian restaurant on L.A.'s Restaurant Row, La Cienega Boulevard. The place allowed Roy all the room he needed to experiment in "anything-goes" Hollywood, but it was too big (four times the size of Le Gourmet) to allow him to serve the high-quality food quality of which he was capable.

After five years he left for his native Hawaii to regroup. There, with some relatives and local investors, he opened Roy's in 1988, and he's never looked back. In the glass-walled restaurant with a view that goes on forever, locals (and tourists willing to venture from Waikiki) taste what Yamaguchi describes as "Euro-Asian" food (read 85 percent European, 15 percent Asian).

When it comes to desserts, make that 100 percent European, with local ingredients. Roy's desserts reflect his belief that basic French technique is where you begin. Couple that with exciting fresh local ingredients, and you come up with desserts such as those we've included here: tropical island tart, coconut-crusted Big Island goat-cheese cheesecake, and tropical fruit "ratatouille" *gyoza* with passion fruit cream and macadamia praline.

ROBERT ZIELINSKI

The Mansion on Turtle Creek

Dallas, Texas

WHEN I ASKED DEAN FEARING, the happy-go-lucky star chef of Dallas's Mansion on Turtle Creek, to participate in this book, he referred me to his talented pastry chef of four years, Robert Zielinski, saying: "He's the man that makes the sweets irresistible."

Zielinski, who collaborated with Fearing on the dessert sections of the *Mansion on Turtle Creek Cookbook* and *Dean Fearing's Southwest Cuisine*, is responsible for such restaurant favorites as blueberry-sour cream cake, Heath Bar cake, grapefruit tequila sorbet with flour tortilla cinnamon crisps, and the meal-in-itself dark chocolate "bag" filled with pastry cream, resting on a crunchy cookie crust. Those without Texas-sized appetites need not apply.

New England native Zielinski was a member of the first graduating class of the esteemed Johnson and Wales Culinary School in Providence, where he stayed on to teach after graduation. He credits the school's German master pastry chef, Hans Sohre, for his interest in and passion for the art of dessert making.

From Johnson and Wales, Zielinski went on to make pastries for hotels and restaurants in Boston and Louisville where, as executive pastry chef at the Seelbach Hotel, he met Fearing when the Mansion chef was visiting his home state. Dean knew he had found what he was looking for in Zielinski and brought him back to the Mansion, where he is as crucial to the continued success of one of America's finest restaurants as is his boss.

CREDITS

All recipes by John Downey copyright © 1992 by John Downey.

All recipes by Susan Feniger and Mary Sue Milliken copyright © 1990 by Susan Feniger and Mary Sue Milliken.

Banana Cream Pie with Banana Crust and Caramel Drizzles by Emeril Lagasse from *Emeril's New New Orleans Cooking* by Emeril Lagasse, copyright © 1993 by Emeril Lagasse. Reprinted by permission of William Morrow and Company.

All recipes by Michael McCarty from *Michael's Cookbook* by Michael McCarty, copyright © 1989 by Michael McCarty. Reprinted by permission of Macmillan Publishing Company.

All recipes by Jimmy Schmidt copyright © 1992 by Jimmy Schmidt.

All recipes by Barbara Tropp from *The China Moon Cookbook* by Barbara Tropp, copyright © 1992 by Barbara Tropp. Reprinted by permission of Workman Publishing Company.

All recipes by Jasper White from *Jasper White's Cooking from New England* by Jasper White, copyright © 1989 by Jasper White. Reprinted by permission of Harper and Row Publishing Company.

All recipes by Robert Zielinski from *Dean Fearing's Southwest Cuisine* by Dean Fearing, copyright © 1991 by Dean Fearing. Reprinted by permission of Grove/Weidenfeld Publishing Company.

INDEX

TABLE OF EQUIVALENTS

The exact equivalents in the following tables have been rounded for convenience.

US/UK

oz=ounce
lb=pound
in=inch
ft=foot
tbl=tablespoon
fl oz=fluid ounce
qt=quart

LENGTH MEASURES

⅛ in	3 mm
¼ in	6 mm
½ in	12 mm
1 in	2.5 cm
2 in	5 cm
3 in	7.5 cm
4 in	10 cm
5 in	13 cm
6 in	15 cm
7 in	18 cm
8 in	20 cm
9 in	23 cm
10 in	25 cm
11 in	28 cm
12 in/1 ft	30 cm

OVEN TEMPERATURES

Fahrenheit	Celsius	Gas
250	120	½
275	140	1
300	150	2
325	160	3
350	180	4
375	190	5
400	200	6
425	220	7
450	230	8
475	240	9
500	260	10

METRIC

g=gram
kg=kilogram
mm=millimeter
cm=centimeter
ml=milliliter
l=liter

WEIGHTS

US/UK	Metric
1 oz	30 g
2 oz	60 g
3 oz	90 g
4 oz (¼ lb)	125 g
5 oz (⅓ lb)	155 g
6 oz	185 g
7 oz	220 g
8 oz (½ lb)	250 g
10 oz	315 g
12 oz (¾ lb)	375 g
14 oz	440 g
16 oz (1 lb)	500 g
1½ lb	750 g
2 lb	1 kg
3 lb	1.5 kg

LIQUIDS

US	Metric	UK
2 tbl	30 ml	1 fl oz
¼ cup	60 ml	2 fl oz
⅓ cup	80 ml	3 fl oz
½ cup	125 ml	4 fl oz
⅔ cup	160 ml	5 fl oz
¾ cup	180 ml	6 fl oz
1 cup	250 ml	8 fl oz
1½ cups	375 ml	12 fl oz
2 cups	500 ml	16 fl oz
4 cups/1 qt	1 l	32 fl oz

Robert Del Grande ❦ Marcel Desaulniers ❦ Susan Feniger & Mary Sue Milliken ❦ Ken Frank ❦ Kevin Graham ❦ Jean Joho ❦ Emeril Lagasse ❦ Emily Luchetti ❦ Nick Malgieri ❦ Bruce Marder ❦ Michael McCarty ❦ Alfred Portale ❦ Seppi Renggli ❦ Anne Rosenzweig ❦ Jimmy Schmidt ❦ John Sedlar ❦ Piero Selvaggio ❦ Jackie Shen ❦ Nancy Silverton ❦ Joachim Splichal ❦ Jacques Torres ❦ Barbara Tropp ❦ Charlie Trotter ❦ Jonathan Waxman ❦ Jasper White ❦ Barry Wine ❦ Alan Wong ❦